From Reel To Real

An epic journey from addiction
To recovery and redemption

DWAYNE HIGGINS

EDITED BY
Douglas Ladron De Guevara
Greg Higgins

BOOK COVER
ILLUSTRATED AND PAINTED BY
Douglas Ladron De Guevara

Publisher: The Holy Spirit

Cataloguing data available from Library and Archives Canada
ISBN 978-0-9949193-0-4 (paperback)

Cover design by Connie Faulkner
Author photograph by Kevin McArthur
Text design by Peter Cocking
Painting on p. 185 is "Forgiven" by Thomas Blackshear

www.fromrealtoreal.com

This book is dedicated to

My Daughter Alyssa

Whom I Love as far as the East is to the West

And

My mother Pat Lawrence

Whose Love never left me, nor forsake me

————

Contents

Contents

Prologue

I N LIFE, WE go through many storms and trials, good times and
bad. Every step of the way we gain a little more knowledge and
life experience. There is pain and peace, suffering and growth,
sorrow and joy. God has blessed me in many ways, and along my path
I have gained some wisdom and knowledge. So, through this book, I
would like to share some of my life experiences with you. I'd like to
include you in the life I lead, to somehow help guide you in the right
direction. In some ways, it may help with your decision making and
possibly answer some questions.

The book is raw, real, and brutally honest. I hold nothing back, and
I will tell you exactly what it was like. It may open your eyes as to why
you are here, and to what your purpose in life is. To help you understand addiction, and about that *someone*. If any of my life experiences,
or the struggles and successes, and the real life stories covered in the
book can touch your heart. If I can help you get some answers, then it
would be a blessing, and an honor to have shared my story with you.

Alyssa's Story

A S I WAS about to begin writing the last Chapter of the book, I received a text from my *fourteen-year-old daughter* Alyssa, this is what the text read:

Hi dad, in English I have to write a narrative essay about something in our life, and I was wondering if it's ok with you if I can write briefly about what we've been through.

In its raw form, exactly the way she sent it to me here is:

Alyssa Higgins
Per. 4 English 10HP
Mr. Carrier
Narrative Essay
9/25/15

It all had started before I was born, when my mom and dad met on Venice Beach Boardwalk, roller blading. They immediately felt a connection and eventually a relationship was formed. They moved into a house together in Studio City. My dad was working with some of the top directors and celebrities in the film businesses, and my mom worked as an office manager for a dentist in Malibu. On September 8, 2000, my parents said, "A miracle was born" and they decided to name that miracle Alyssa. Once I was born, my mom told me she had never been happier. I was the love of her life, always by her side, and never cried because I never had a reason to.

Of course my father Dwayne, felt the same way, and still does because he tells me every day, but sadly that communication isn't real, or in person, but through technology. It all started when I was two years old. Driving on the other side of Malibu Canyon with my dad, we were trying to find somewhere to grab something to eat while my mom was at work in Malibu. In a little shopping center was one of my dad's favorite sushi restaurants, so that's where he took me. We went inside to eat, and after, all you could think of was a disaster.

Little did I know, due to the fact I was two years old, my dad had drank a lot during our lunch, so as he zoomed out of the parking lot, a couple minutes later, we heard the sound of sirens. We get pulled over, and he gets arrested, this was his third drunk driving charge. My dad had his two-year-old daughter (me) in the car, which added a child endangerment charge. After this specific event, my dad's life came crumbling to the ground, no house in Studio City, no more BMW, no money, no family, got deported back to Canada with nothing and as well as his life crumbling down little did I know once I grew up mine was too.

I was so little I didn't understand what happened, where my father went, what was happening in my life and my family, and most importantly, didn't know the condition my dad was in. He was addicted to pills, alcohol, drugs, and suffered the effects of separation, depression, and anxiety. After he had been deported to Canada, he kept consuming pills and drugs, which kept leading to bad decisions and bad outcomes.

My dad lost two of his closest friends, who were both struggling with their own demons, and addiction. He had to witness both outcomes of these deaths, one in L.A. and one while he was doing mission work in Mexico. Two years went by, and I had a huge lack of communication with my dad due to how young I was and in the view of the fact, my dad was still doing drugs and consuming alcohol . . . but!

When I was four years old my mom and stepdad Tom took me to go see my dad in Vancouver because my step-dad had a dental convention in the area. My dad Dwayne got to spend quality time with me and take me shopping, to Grandville Island, play land, and I'm sure a hand full more. But once again, bad things started happening, we were at dinner on our last night in Vancouver, my mom, stepdad, and I, would be leaving Vancouver the next morning, and all my dad's emotions built up and he started having a breakdown.

He was so high on pills, and it scared me, I don't remember when I was two, and my father got arrested, but I do remember spending time with my dad in Vancouver, and his break down. This memory may be so clear to me because after those last few hours of me being with my dad. I was four years old, and this would be the last time I would see my dad, I have not seen my dad in 11 years, because of his addiction.

He has never taken or picked me up from school, seen a dance show, taken me on vacation, never got to see his only child grow up and most importantly, hasn't gotten to say "I love you" to his daughter's face in eleven years...eleven long years without my dad in my life and I don't know how I'm doing it without him, but I am.

If I think this is terrible for me, I can't even imagine how he's feeling if he wrote in his book " 'To this day I fall apart when I see fathers with their kids walking in the park, seeing parents with their kids at the market or at a coffee shop. I see them playing and being together, and I am overwhelmed, my heart breaks and I tear up. I never did what I am watching them do, and that is being together. Kids smiling and laughing with their parents, it kills me, the brokenness and the loss of Alyssa and I see it day in and day out, parents being with their kids. I what to say that if you have kids, I pray you count your blessing, be oh so grateful that you have children in your life, you have the chance I never had. That chance is to be the parent God created you to be, you love your kids and treat them like gold because there are people like me who would give anything to just have ten minutes of what you have.' "

As I have matured and grown up, I slowly hear and find out all the stories about my dad throughout those eleven years over text, email, or call. The first seven or eight years were the most devastating stories a child could hear about their father. To start off the stories, my dad starting doing heroin which just led to worse and worse choices in his life.

He was found by a roommate, in pools of blood. He awoke in the hospital with 18 metal staples in his right wrist and 16 in his left. When he was under the influence, he jumped off a four-story building because of depression and the pain he was feeling inside, he ended up spending 6 months in the hospital. He had a third attempt and jumped two stories off another building, and much more.

My father was an addict. The past four years he has been working and working on fixing that problem in his life because it made him so destructive towards himself and made a much worse lifestyle than he had. Now he is now a very strong Christian, who is back on track. He went through eleven years of help and is finally ok. He is now writing a book, a memoir, about his journey, and the devastating effects of addiction. It is a book about loss and pain, love, hope and family, and in the end, salvation.

Although this was a very hard thing to go through not only for my dad but me as well, I am so proud. My father has proven to me that anything is possible. He is my inspiration. He has proved to me that you can overcome anything in the way of your life as long as you never give up and keep trying.

He went through eleven years of hell and now looking at him from my perspective is amazing, he's alive, no longer an addict, writing his own book, and he is involved with teaching bible studies to men coming out of addiction. My dad has done mission work in places like Mexico, Indonesia, and he just came back from serving at an orphanage in Africa for six months. He has overcome his fear, and the chains were broken, my dad has been set free from the bondage of addiction which has taught me always to be the best you can be. I love my father more than anything and couldn't be more grateful to have the ability to talk to him every day.

Shall we start at the beginning?

CHAPTER 1

The Journey Begins

I WANT TO IMPOSE upon you the vital importance of understanding the deadly nature of addiction; it is cunning, baffling, and powerful. Addiction wanted to kill me; it wanted to pretend it was my friend and lover. It wanted to numb me to the point where I would not hurt, or cry anymore. It buried the emotion, grief, and pain that I should have felt, but in the end, all addiction wished upon me was suffering, and death.

As my life unfolded, moving in and out of God's uniquely designed plan, I was running on my decisions, and my own free will, which lead me to be moving away from His plan. Following many years of falling, and getting back up again, I would ultimately realize the purpose for my life. I do hope that my story will provide a model for you to examine, as we learn together about our own personal purpose and destiny. The many deep, dark valleys and the amazing mountaintops I have experienced will hopefully provide a layout, a road map, for our journey in which we are about to partake in.

My goal is that through these experiences, you will be alerted to potential dangers, as well as being guided to find the right path to follow. My everyday life does reveal many important life lessons, as does each of your life journeys. The choices made along the way, intertwined with the destiny in which I was called for. We will, above all else, hopefully see through my mistakes and wrong choices; the eternal value of walking through life closely with the Lord.

Through the many twists and turns in my uneventful and at times very eventful life, was like looking through a wide-angle lens. Despite the many moment by moment poor choices, wrong motives, and consequential failures, I would be a success, and eventually find my way to the fulfillment of His purpose, and His ultimate destiny for my life.

I am honored that you have my book in your hands, staring into the pages, about to be a part of my life and my epic journey. This book is very personal; it is you and me, sitting here having a chat, a conversation. The first three chapters will guide you through my travels around the world, growing up as a military brat, and my high school days.

This is an autobiography, as well as a book about addiction, finding a solution, and finding that *someone*. We will twist and wind our way through my life, and soon enough we will be in L.A. I will explain the challenges of pursuing an acting career, and what it is like to work behind the scenes with the biggest celebrities and directors in the world. After we make it through the good times in L.A., be prepared to have your world turned upside down. It gets very bad; addiction shows up, and, well, we will get to that a little later. For now, let's go back to the beginning.

. . .

I was born in Ottawa, Canada. From the start, I was blessed with an exuberant amount of energy. This exhausted my poor mom; never sleeping more than twenty minutes at a time during the day. By the age of nine months, being so high strung, and full of energy, I was already up on both feet and walking.

At the tender age of one, it was time to make my first move. We were off to Germany; our family was stationed at an Air Force base in Baden, Baden. My father was a lieutenant in the Canadian Air Force. Growing up on military bases around the world would become a way of life; this also meant a military style upbringing.

My dad did not like living on base, in the little box houses as I call them. So we lived off base, in a house above an older German couple. Our house was situated on a dirt road; it was used by local farmers to get to the fields. I quickly learned, around the age of four, that I could run alongside the tractor, grabbing hold of the back, and with my little feet running as fast as they could, I would keep up. The farmer would grab me, and then hoist me up onto the huge fenders that covered the back wheels. I would sit there all day long, as the farmers plowed up and down their fields. At the end of a day, as they drove past our house, I would hop off the tractor, and head back home.

I really bonded with our downstairs landlords; they were a classic loving German couple. I loved German food, so for the entire time we spent in Baden I would have lunch every day with the both of them. This is where I learned to speak German, it did not take long for me to grasp the foreign language, and before I knew it, I was speaking German better than English.

A year before we would be transferred to another base, I was blessed with a little brother named Greg. He had the same personality as my father, very quiet, and shy. Greg could sit at home all day with a book, and be content. He would usually have one close friend while growing up. On the other hand, I had my mother's personality, outgoing, talkative, loud and vibrant. I was very athletic, and shy was not in my vocabulary. I knew everyone, everywhere, always on the go, not spending much time at home. This pattern would continue through the rest of my life.

One year on Mother's Day, I would touch my mother's heart with an amazing act of love. I had forgotten to give her a gift for mother's day. So, I left the house and walked out to the back fields. There I found a dead, old crinkled up Lilly, and also managed to find a half broken terracotta pot. Dirt and weeds were growing out of the sides of the aged pot, and I pushed the broken Lilly, with some soil into the pot. I was so proud walking back into the house with my little work of art. As I presented my masterpiece to her, tears began to roll down her face, and she started to cry. My mother was overwhelmed with so much joy and happiness because of my act of compassion and kindness. She said it was one of the most touching, and memorable moments of my childhood.

Normally, a military stationing is four years, but my parents loved living in Germany, so dad applied for a one-year extension; we would spend five years in Germany. So at the ripe age of six, it was time to make my second move; back to Canada, to the Province of Alberta. We were stationed way up north, in Cold Lake, another Air Force base, where they trained fighter pilots. We would spend four years in the arctic tundra, living in the PMQ's, the private married quarters. A nice way of saying, the little box houses.

This is where my passion began with sports. My mother was a very athletic lady and played every sport well. Being lucky enough to have her genes, playing sports came naturally to me. In the winter, we would shovel out the snow in the back yard, lay plastic down, and then fill it with water, making a skating rink. We played hockey every night after school, and one of my friends who lived around the corner from us was Billy Ranford.

If you don't know Billy, he went on to play in the N.H.L, for The Boston Bruins, and the Edmonton Oilers. In later years, Billy would go on to win every trophy a goalie could possibly win, playing professional hockey. You will hear more about Billy and me, and our amazing hockey experiences while playing in Europe a little later. Hockey, baseball, soccer, and football, you name it, I played it. I loved sports, and I excelled in every one.

My mother was Catholic, and my father was Protestant, quite a mix, but we were lead more towards the Catholic Church. We never prayed before meals, but I went to church with my mother every Sunday. It would take many years, and an incredible amount of suffering, devastation, and loss in my life before coming to Christ, and becoming a Christian.

When I was eight, I had my Confirmation and Communion at the church. At the time of Communion, I was walking up the aisle, and the front of my pants were soaked. I had peed my pants; and being the witty little man I was, I untucked my white dress shirt trying to hide it.

This may be a good time to confess that I had a serious problem with wetting the bed. I saw doctors and had procedures where they put wires up into me. I remember after one of the procedures while driving back from Calgary. We stopped, and I took the most painful pee I have ever experienced in my life. Shaking so bad, I could hardly stand; I was crying and screaming because the pain ripped through me as I was peeing. I wet the bed until the age of fourteen; this would have a major effect on me in later years.

At Christmas time, the kids would be able to have a glass of baby duck, a bubble alcoholic drink, like flavored champagne. I had my first experience with alcohol at the age of eight. Some kids drank half, and some did not like it. I drank my glass, and all I wanted was more, I would go around after dinner, and drink what was left in all the glasses on the table.

We would visit my Grandparents in Medicine Hat, Alberta. My Grandfather was a hardcore Irish alcoholic; he drank so much of the beer "Pilsner" that everyone nicknamed him pilsner. I would always go to my Grandpa, and he would give me drinks from his beer. The problem was I would take a drink, and another, then another, till he would have to grab the beer from my tiny little hands. Why did I want to drink? Was it because I liked the taste? Was it because I saw other people drinking, and having fun? Or at the age of eight, was it because I liked the effects of alcohol?

My father was an alcoholic, and drank every night; the one good thing about my father's drinking was that he was a quiet, calm, and a non-violent type of drinker. There was no violence or any type of abuse in my family. I was definitely blessed that way because many other kids had to endure a violent upbringing. Getting beaten, and tormented every night by an alcoholic military father.

The beautiful thing about my father was that he would be up at six in the morning to take me to hockey practice, no matter what. While driving to the early morning practice, we would pick up lots of other kids walking to the rink because their dads were in bed, hung over and unable to drive them. My dad was always there, taking me to all my sporting activities, no matter how much he drank, or how late he was up.

At the age of nine, I experienced something traumatic, and it would haunt me throughout my life. The girls name was Bev; she was such a sweet, innocent girl. One day a group of us were in her back yard, it was a beautiful day, the sun was shining, and spirits were high. The day would end in darkness; I had a golf club in my hands, and Bev with a few other kids were standing behind me. Unknowingly, taking a full swing back to drive a ball, the iron end of the club smashed into Bev's eye socket, shattering the bones, and crushing her eye.

Blood streamed from her face, pouring down her cheeks, and onto her clothes. The screams of pain tore throughout the neighborhood. Her parents came running out, yelling and panicking. I was standing there, with a blood stained golf club in my hand, in a state of shock. She was medevac in a helicopter to the children's hospital in Edmonton.

The guilt and shame overwhelmed me, and I was full of fear. I felt it was my fault, that I was to blame for causing such emotional damage, and anguish in her life. This amazing little girl would have to go through life with a glass eye because of my actions.

I buried it way back into my subconscious mind. The problem with doing this, especially in addiction, is we have not dealt with the problem. When we do not deal with the dark secrets of our lives, the deep rooted sin we bury way deep down will keep sprouting up. It will lead to destruction in our lives. We need to grab it by the roots and pull it out. I carried it around for most of my life, tucked away, and would not deal with it, or recall it again until my forties.

It was not too long after this horrific event that we would be up and moving again. Leaving all my friends, my school, and anything I was able to build upon behind. Knowing there would be no going back, and most likely never seeing any of the friends I made ever again. Military upbringing has its pros, and definitely its cons. I was only ten years old and was about to make my third move.

CHAPTER 2

Back to Germany

O N A PLANE again; I would get quite used to planes, and flying all over the world. It would become a way of life, but for now, it was back to Germany. This time, we were stationed in Lahr, the same region of Germany as Baden-Baden. As mentioned earlier, a military stationing is four years; and I also mentioned my parents loved Germany. Dad would get two, one-year extensions; and we would spend the next six years in Lahr Germany before heading out again. I arrived at the young age of ten, and would remain in Lahr until the age of sixteen, doing my Junior High school, as well as grade ten.

We traveled extensively all over Europe during our stay in Germany. I would like to share some of my experiences with you. Our trips did not include four-star hotels, but a trailer, hauled by a 1970's Grand Torino. We would pack up, and head out with another family or two. Remembering our travels on the autobahn, the super highway in Germany, there was no speed limit; big Mercedes sedans and BMW's would fly past us doing 200 km plus. Our trailer would sway back and forth as cars flew past us. This, in turn, would rock the car. My brother and I quite enjoyed this, but Dad was not so pleased.

One memorable trip was to *Barcelona, Spain*, with another couple. On our second day, we attended the Bull fights at a huge coliseum in downtown Barcelona. It was one of the best and worst experiences in all of our travels. The matador would put on this dazzling spectacle, and then he would proceed to puncture two Banderilla's into the bulls back, around the neck area. This was done to get the bull angry, not to kill it. A Banderilla is about three feet long, round like a spear, and decorated quite beautifully. The end has a sharp metal tip that would puncture and stick into the bull's neck.

After a bit more dancing around, the challenge comes; the matador would situate himself in a gladiator type stance. The bull would charge at him, and having his sword drawn he would then take the sharp double-edged sword, driving it into a specific spot on the bull's neck, thrusting it through, and down into the heart, killing the bull.

It was traumatizing, seeing the deep bloody wounds on such a beautiful animal. People are watching one of Gods creations die for sport, just to give them a thrill, for the simple pleasure of entertainment. I cheered for the bull, but in the end, the bull never won. How sad for the poor innocent bull.

We camped at an all-inclusive campground, water sports, campfires and lots of kids from all over Europe. Our camp site was situated just meters away from the Mediterranean Sea. I remember it as being quite dirty, it was by no means clear like the Adriatic Sea in Yugoslavia.

This may be a good point to Segway into our trip to *Yugoslavia*; it was not a communist country at the time we visited, thank God. On the way, my father, brother and I partook in a risky venture. We were near a border crossing into *Czechoslovakia*, and we decided to drive a few kilometers down the road, not far from a tall, aged, concrete guard tower. We pulled the car over onto the gravel shoulder, and parked alongside a rustic old wire fence, separating Yugoslavia from communist Czechoslovakia.

We exited the car and strolled right up to the fence, knowing the guard in the tower could see a freckle on our face if he looked through the scope of his rifle. We unzipped our pants, and all three of us took a pee through the wire fence into communist Czechoslovakia. Not meaning any disrespect for the country, but our bright idea was to pee into a communist country. I am glad we did not get shot; this may give you a bit of an idea about the insanity that runs through my family.

Our trip the next year was to *Italy*. How truly amazing and breathtaking it was to be standing at the foot of the *Roman Coliseum*, looking way up to the top of the mammoth colossus. It holds between 50,000 to 80,000 spectators. All one can think is how they built such a structure out of concrete and stone, so perfectly and eloquently back in the time of the Roman Empire.

Another place we went was the *Sistine Chapel*; the ceiling painted by *Michelangelo* is a cornerstone work of High renaissance art. On the large sanctuary wall, hung a *fresco- The Last Judgment,* which was also done by Michelangelo. One of the centerpieces of the ceiling decoration is nine scenes from the *Book of Genesis,* of which *The Creation of Adam* is the best known.

Then we were off for an exciting time at the *Vatican* for a day tour. It is a sprawling complex full of ornate statues, works of art, and tapestries from as far as the East is to the West. We spent one week in Rome, and another week traveling around Italy. All in all, Italy is an awe-inspiring country in which I would love to visit again someday.

England was calling. This time, we left the camper behind and boarded a plane to *London* for an exciting week of sightseeing. Our first stop was, of course, Buckingham Palace, the Queens official place of residence. We were blessed with seeing the changing of the guard, but I was not blessed with meeting the Queen. Just kidding, I am O.K. with not meeting the hierarchy of Europe. But later I would meet most of the hierarchy in Hollywood!

We did most of the touristy things, going to see Big Ben, The Tower of London (London Bridge), and The Palace of Westminster. I can go on and on about all the wonderful attractions London has to offer, but after the week, we boarded a train to Dublin, Ireland.

In *Ireland,* we had so many relatives to visit and meet. We were not blessed with staying in a beautiful hotel, but instead, we billeted at our Aunt's and Uncle's wonderful Dublin style homes. Once again we visited some of Dublin's finest tourist attractions, beginning with Kilmainham Gaol. This was once a prison built in 1796; internally the structure was cascading to the ceiling with huge iron bars. The cells where they kept the prisoners were tiny, 28 square meters, and they would fit up to 5 people in each cell.

One other simply unexplainable superstructure we visited was St Patrick's Cathedral; it is the largest church in Ireland, with an expansive lawn and garden. You could spend an entire day just touring the botanical gardens, the pathways, and the grounds.

We saved the last day for a tour of the Guinness factory, and the storehouse, where they make their famous beer. I was only twelve at the time, and I have to thank God for this. The tour might have had a different outcome if I had been a little older and in my addiction. Let's say in my prime, I could have ended up in Kilmainham Gaol for a few nights.

We needed to fly out of Dublin back to Germany, but we had a small problem. While on our tour of Ireland, I picked up a case of Chicken Pox. Knowing the Germans would not allow me back into the country, my mother came up with a way to hide my face while going through customs. We made it through, and onto our flight to Frankfurt. The love of a mother and her mischievous ways.

It was not too long after we would be in the comfort of our 1970's green Grand Torino, cruising through Europe, towing a trailer, on our way to *Switzerland*. Out of all the countries we toured, Switzerland is by far the most beautiful country I have ever visited.

Our first stop was Geneva and the Reformation Wall, which is located on the grounds of the University. It was built to commemorate the 400th anniversary of Calvin's Birth. The sculptures and memorials are breathtaking; the amount of work and the time it must have taken to achieve such creative design is staggering.

Later in the day, we went to the Jet d'eau, one of the city's most famous landmarks. It is one of the largest fountains in the world. 132 gallons of water per second are shot into the air, with the water leaving the nozzle at 124 mph, and then jetting 459 feet into the air. It completely blows away the fountains at the Bellagio hotel in Las Vegas.

Once we covered all the tourist sites Geneva had to offer, we would be packing up and on our way to Zurich. On our travels, we stopped at the town of Zermatt, which is situated at the foot of The Matterhorn Mountain. It straddles the border between Switzerland and Italy. It has one of the highest summits in Europe, with an elevation of 4,478 meters.

Let's cover one last trip, another incredibly beautiful European country, *Austria*, to the once Olympic city of Innsbruck. We toured the luge track, and the ski jumps that were used for the Olympics held there in 1964. During my time in Europe I was able to visit many Castles, one was The Ambras Castle. It is located in the hills above Innsbruck, built in the sixteenth century during the renaissance. It is hard to comprehend the size of the castles in Europe; it is staggering and incomprehensible as to how they could have built such intricate structures in their time.

We did a few more days of sightseeing and then made our way to Salzburg, the birthplace of Amadeus Mozart. One interesting fact about Salzburg is it was the location used to film the movie, *The Sound of Music*. Once again, we visited more castles, including the sumptuous baroquely decorated St. Peter's Abbey. It was founded in 696 by Saint Rupert, who is entombed next to an altar in the church. There also lays the tomb of Mozart's sister Maria Anna Mozart.

During our time spent living in Germany, we would have adventures sailing down the Rhine River, traveling all over the country, and visiting various cities. The most famous castle I had the pleasure of visiting was, King Ludwig's, *The Neuschwanstein*, located in the Bavarian region of Germany. Here is a little Hollywood for you. When you are watching any Disney movie, and you see the Disney logo with the castle at the beginning, the one where tinker bell flies around, wiggling her little wand, it is the Neuschwanstein castle.

I can go on and on, getting into much more detail about the sites, cities and countries we visited, telling you more about my journeys, and travels throughout Europe with my family. This would lead me to believe, that in my heart, it would probably entail me writing another book. By the age of sixteen, I had visited pretty much every country in Europe, excluding the Eastern bloc countries. So, let's move to my passion, Sports, and all the countries I was blessed enough to play in.

There is no better way to start another adventure than with Hockey. How Canadian of me; as mentioned earlier, my hockey career started in Cold Lake and continued with me to Lahr. I began playing in the Base league, on a team in the A-division. This is not a time to boast, but I was small, fast, and I could stick handle that puck from one end of the rink to the other, dropping it into the net.

I would like to continue sharing about another highlight in my life. I went on to win top scorer for two years in a row in the A- division. I remember walking up onto the stage at the awards ceremonies, getting my trophy, and being honored for my hockey excellence.

My father was always there, standing proud of his son. My dad never told me how good I did, or what an amazing accomplishment I had made. He would just stand there; giving me a smile, and a wave. My dad was a military man, and never gave any type of passionate love, a kiss, or a hug, and never a, "I love you son", or a, I am so proud of you son. I do know deep down in his heart he was proud and pleased with my achievements. Dad showed his love by being there, which he was, for all of my sporting activities.

It was off to the big leagues; a few coaches asked me to play for the Bad News Bears of hockey, in a European professional league. The team would consist of half Canadian players and half German players. We were all thrown together into the mix, and we would have to learn to play as a competitive team.

The city we played in and practiced at is called Freiburg, about 40 minutes down the autobahn from Lahr. After school, we would drive there and practice three nights a week. Our skates, sticks, and all our equipment, as well as our travels, food, and lodgings, were paid for. I want to make something clear; we the players were not paid, which was fine by us. All we wanted to do was play hockey.

We had an amazing team, and the good Lord blessed us with Billy Ranford as our goalie. I talked about playing hockey with Billy in my back yard in Cold Lake. Now here we were traveling all over Europe playing in a professional league. Billy would go on to play for the Edmonton Oilers, winning two Stanley Cups with Wayne Gretzky, Jari Kurri and the rest of the Oiler power team. The German players were such a talented group of guys, we all bonded together, and kicked butt all over Europe- our team rocked!

After school, we would travel, playing hockey in various countries, sometimes to France playing in Strasberg or Lyon. Sometimes going down to Switzerland, and playing the teams in Basil and Bern. We played all over Germany in Hamburg, Cologne, Munich, and Frankfurt. We visited and played in some other countries like Austria, Italy, and the Netherlands.

The crowning jewel was our trip to Caen, France for the European Nationals. Before arriving in Caen, we would visit Normandy; the entire team including myself walked the Beaches of Normandy, where the D-Day invasion happened on June 6, 1944. The feeling was very surreal and eerie; you could just try to picture, and imagine, what had happened on the beach that we were so privileged to walk.

It just gives me chills as I write this to you, trying somehow to put the experience into words. This is all so hard to try and absorb, and to put into consideration the events of June 6, 1944; and for me to manage a way to Segway back into an amazing, power packed, incredibly competitive hockey tournament.

There were young men from countries all around Europe, at peace, no war, no conflict, just an incredible conglomeration of nationalities, playing for the thrill of the game. We were in Caen, France, playing for the European Nationals. The Bad News Bears were unstoppable. (Well that was not our team name) but our half Canadian, half German team was dominating the tournament.

We played Finland, Austria, Norway and Poland, winning every game. It was time for the Championship game, between Sweden and us. The Swedish team was called the 66er's, and these men had grown up playing together for their entire young hockey careers. Playing together, year after year, knowing each other's moves, practicing as a team. Sweden had won the European Nationals for many consecutive years. Well, this was about to come to an end.

Team Freiburg was in the house. We were so fired up, and ready for the final game, ready to put an end to the Swedish domination. Billy was incredible in the net, and we played like we had been playing together for years, not the 6 months we had been together. In the end, we beat Sweden 17-1, winning the European Nationals and having the best team in Europe.

What an amazing accomplishment, considering the level of teams and players in the tournament. One last memory of this life experience happened while driving in the tour bus back to Germany from Caen. The military radio stations made the announcement across the airwaves that we had won the European Nationals. They played the song by *Queen*, *"We are the Champions"*. I can still remember sitting on the bus, levitating in my seat as they played that song while driving back home to Germany.

It's now time to hit the slopes of the European Alps, and get into my second favorite sport, skiing. Black runs in Italy, France, and glacier skiing in Germany. There is no better skiing in the world than in Europe. If I wasn't playing hockey, I would be on the side of a mountain somewhere in Europe, tearing it up, and endangering my life. The adrenaline rush of skiing down some of the steepest runs that the Alps had to offer was exhilarating.

Every year in school, we would take a two-week skiing trip. One of the places we went to was Italy, at *Mt Blanc*. It is the tallest mountain in the Alps, with the highest peak in Europe. I remember being at the top of the mountain. There was an old wooden sign with an arrow pointing one way, saying France. The other sign had an arrow pointing the other way, saying Italy. How cool was that, being on the top of the world, having to decide what country to ski into.

Another trip we took was local. We stayed in Germany; it has some of the best skiing in the world. We took a train to Garmisch-Parten-kirchen, one of Bavaria's most famous ski resorts. We spent a week in the Alps, skiing *The Zugspitze*, Germany's highest mountain.

The next two trips were familiar territory for me; one trip was back to Switzerland, to the picturesque village of Grindelwald. Need I tell you what the skiing was like there? Let's just say it has some of the steepest descents in Europe, and from a distance on a clear day, you are able to see the imposing north face of the Eiger Mountain.

The other familiar trip was to Austria, to the historic Tirolean town of Kitzbuhel. It is only 92 Km from Innsbruck. The greatest World Cup downhill ski race is held on the feared *Streif descent* on the celebrated *Hahnenkamm ski run*. It was a blessing to be able to ski all over Europe at such a young age. A little time to boast before moving on; by the age of fifteen I could have received my level 1 ski instructor's certificate. The only problem was I had to be over the age of sixteen.

O.K, winter is over, and it is now time for some summer sports. I was not just a winter athlete, but also a summer time jock. I played two main sports, one was soccer, and as you probably know, soccer is golden in Germany. I was playing on a Canadian Base team, and we would travel around the country, playing against teams in Dusseldorf, Frankfurt, Hamburg, Heidelberg and many more.

One day, a coach from one of the German National teams approached my dad and asked him if I would be interested in playing on their team. This was such an honor, being this kid from Canada, asked to play on a German National team. Of course, I accepted and began playing with them, traveling all around Europe. Some of the countries I was blessed enough to play in were France, Spain, Switzerland, Austria and Italy. What a privilege it was, to be able to play with such amazing German soccer players, in an incredibly demanding league.

The second summertime sport was baseball; I began playing T-Ball in Cold Lake, and then moved up the ranks, playing hardball. There was a league on the Air Force base with about eight teams; a lot of Air Force brats wanting to play baseball. My position was always back catcher or shortstop. Once again, there was a team put together using the best players from the league. I was one of the players picked, and we would go out, traveling all around Germany, playing against the American teams on military bases scattered around the country.

This is where I would like to bring up my small problem; being twelve, and thirteen years old, still wetting the bed. We would always billet at other kids homes on the American bases where we would be playing. I had such anxiety and fear of going to bed; sometimes I would carry that fear around all day, just thinking about what to do.

I would find a garbage bag in the billets house. Then, I would go to the bathroom, and cut the bag open. I would end up with a piece big enough to cover the area of the bed that I would be sleeping on. What a nightmare it was for me; I would have a change of clothes next to me. In the morning, I would grab the clothes, dart to the shower, clean up, change into unsoiled clothes, and begin my day.

So if someone you know is struggling with the same issues, please let them know that they are not alone. It is not talked about very often out in the open, but it is something prevalent in society, and *it is nothing to be ashamed of.*

Now that I have clean underwear on, it was off to Ramstein Air Force base, a huge American base in the South of Germany. We were the only Canadian team playing against seven American teams. Our little team was awesome, we had some really good ball players, and we made it to the finals.

What an amazing feat, to beat all the American teams, and make it to the final game. This was a big deal, because whoever won the game between the Americans and us would go on to play in the famous "Little league World Series," in Williamsport, Pennsylvania.

I would like to say the next thing you know, we were all on a plane, heading to Pennsylvania. But No, the Americans whipped us. We did not have a chance; in the end, we still went home with our heads held high, because making it to the finals was truly an amazing accomplishment.

Here we go; this book is also about addiction, alcohol & drugs. In Germany at the age of fourteen, I began an illustrious career in the field of addiction. I do want to make a clear point, not justifying anything, but I did not touch any drugs while in Germany. There was no marijuana, cocaine, pain pills; the only thing I was getting into was alcohol. There is no drinking age in Germany, so there was no problem getting booze.

Another thing, my weekend drinking never interfered with my athletic career, and there was never any drinking, or partying during the week. I went to school, and received good grades; I would usually get 60% to 70% in my classes. Every year my parents would hear the same thing; if Dwayne would only apply himself, and study harder, his grades would be in the 80's and 90's. I always did just enough to get by in school and pass my classes; my interest was playing sports.

While enjoying my youth in Germany, alcohol became a big part of my weekend adventures. There was a place called the CYC; The Canadian Youth Center was located off base. On Friday and Saturday nights, they would always hold dances. Most kids would attend the weekend extravaganza. Buses would travel to the small surrounding villages, picking up loads of military kids, and take them on their journey to the CYC. The bus made a few stops, but the one we were interested in was the downtown stop where most of us kids would get off the bus.

The bars were downtown, and with no drinking age, we would go and hit some of the local establishments. There were a few bars we would go to regularly on Friday or Saturday nights. The bartenders became good friends, so we would drink strong German beer, and have a good old time, dancing and listening to authentic German music. I drank the beer, but was never a fan of it; my drink was Sangria, a fruity red Spanish wine.

The problem was that at the age of fourteen, I had a favorite drink. I would get my bottle of Sangria every weekend while the other kids had their beer. Sometimes we would go way up into the Black Forest, behind the CYC. There would be a group of us, partying, drinking and fooling around with the girls. After a few hours of debauchery, we would make our way to the dance and have a great night. Then board the bus to take us home around eleven.

My parents were always in bed sleeping by the time I arrived home. There were times I got back in a drunken stupor, right out of it on my sangria. The amazing thing was I never got caught coming home drunk, guessing I was quiet. God knows, while out there partying, I would have been the loudest and most talkative person in the crowd.

I never did get myself into any trouble or committed crimes, and I never hurt anyone else. We were just kids being kids; we drank and had fun. In today's society, kids are drinking, partying, and having sex at such a young age. The problems with today's youth are the drugs and having sex at fourteen and fifteen years old. We did not have all the drugs that are as readily available as in this day and age. Kids are getting into the hard drugs at a very early age. I believe it has to do with bullying at school and the day to day pressures kids are facing at home; as well as social media.

This is the most self-destructive generation in civilized history, with suicide being the second leading cause of death among young people age 15-24. Teen violence has increased 180% in 10 years. It is the most aggressive, and violent generation, with alcohol-related deaths being the number one killer of youth. These statistics may cause some fear and anxiety for you, but as we proceed with the book, I will explain addiction. What makes our minds work, how we are wired different, and why we make the choices we make. It is about finding that *someone*, finding an answer to help us battle Satan's number one tool for destruction in our society today; addiction!

Kids are searching and reaching out for something. Could it be for acceptance, for someone just to hold them, someone to give them a hug, and a kiss on the cheek? I truly believe what our youth is looking for is to have someone say three simple words, *I love you*. I think it is dysfunctional families, and kids in abusive homes with no love. Single parents facing the incredible hardships of raising kids in today's society. It is the mother who is working having no time to bring up their kids properly in homes with affection, or love.

Why was I drinking, and going out partying on the weekends? I don't have a definitive answer, but I do have a few ideas. Was it because other kids were doing it? Peer pressure, trying to fit in, and be liked by everyone? It could be the military upbringing. By this age, I had already made three big moves. Was it dealing with making new friends in new schools all the time? Could it be adjusting to a new culture, or was it fear based? Knowing in the back of my mind, that I would be off and running again, leaving everything behind? The story of my life! I would soon be moving for the fourth time before the age of sixteen.

All of us Military kids had to endure the same trials and tribulations life had to throw at us. For my friends and myself, moving seemed to be part of life, it was normal for us. But, there was cause and effect.

Maybe that's why we all went out on the weekends and drank? Or, was it because I liked the taste and effects alcohol had? From the baby duck at Christmas time, to drinking Grandpa Pilsners beer, I had an addictive personality. Did I wake up one day, and pray to the Lord, asking if I could go through life being an addict or alcoholic? I think not.

Why is it that people go out for dinner, order a glass of wine, and then drink only half; then get up and leave? When someone like me drinks my glass, drink the half they left, and my mind and body screams for another glass, and another?

If drinking is hereditary, then why does my brother not drink at all, with the exception of Christmas, or maybe at some fun outing? My father is an alcoholic, My Grandparents on both sides of the family, alcoholics; is it generational? The other part of this is my brother has never touched a drug in his life. The question is, why does he have a totally non-addictive personality? Me, well I am a garbage can when it comes to drugs and alcohol. In my addiction, there is no drug I have not tried. When it came time to use, I did a lot. I will have the answers to these questions, and much more for you later in the book. For now, let's keep pushing forward on our journey into the world of addiction, hope, and transformation.

Let's call it a God Shot; I swear to you, with total honesty, something happened yesterday. I was just finishing off writing about my drinking career beginning in Germany, at the age of fourteen. Then my cell phone sitting next to me rings, it is Jenell, the mother of my now fourteen-year-old daughter Alyssa.

I have not seen, held, or given Alyssa a kiss on the cheek in eleven years. The reason is my addiction, but I also have to put into consideration my bad choices. Emotionally, this causes me the most shame, and guilt. It has been the hardest issue in my life to deal with, always struggling, to somehow find some closure. Like everything else from my past, I buried it with drugs and alcohol.

Jenell starts talking about all the problems she is having in her nightmare divorce, with her millionaire dentist husband from Malibu. A lot of money involved, which means very, very expensive lawyers. The conversation eventually turns to our daughter, and how at fourteen she is drinking, and partying on the weekends with her friends, sound familiar? Alyssa got very drunk one weekend after drinking vodka and tequila with her friends and blacked out. This is not a good thing, and to top it off, Jenell found a bag of marijuana in a drawer in her room.

What is a father to do from a thousand miles away? I send Alyssa a text, saying that we needed to talk; she responded that she was on her way back from school, and she would call me when she arrived home. When the call came, I knew in my heart that I would be loving, kind, and caring, I would be the Christian I am.

The first thing I told my amazing daughter was that I loved her with all my heart, and nothing she did, or would do, could ever change my love for her. I asked her to be completely honest with me, and she was. I asked her about the drinking and partying. She told me that all the kids at Malibu High were drinking, that all her girlfriends drank on the weekends and smoked weed.

My smart, witty daughter then said. "Didn't you start drinking, and partying at the age of fourteen?" She had me, and I truly believe my talk was not going to change what she and her friends were doing. I told her about the consequences of drinking, telling her not to drink vodka or tequila because it makes you crazy. I did say, if you are going to drink, then make it beer or wine. "Really," she is going to do it any-way, and hearing her dad go on and on would not change what she was doing. I asked if she only smoked weed on the weekends, and she said yes, that she never drank or smoked weed during the week. I commended her on that.

I told her there is no love with boys; all boys just want to have sex. "Let's be honest here." What all fourteen-year-old girls want, and what all women want, is to be loved by someone. Everyone is seeking love, to be held softly, to be heard, and to be shown that someone really cares for them. It devastates me, and the heartbreaking thing is that I cannot be there for my daughter. I cannot comfort her, or hold her in my arms, and tell her how much I love her.

I feel so distant; I made choices in my addiction that tore my fam-ily apart. Addiction took away the only two people I actually loved. Because of my bad choices in life, I am not able to be with my daughter. The person she is seeking, and reaching out to for love, is not there. The father she is seeking out is not there because of my addiction; it is cunning, baffling and powerful. This crushes my heart and soul. I have tears running down my cheeks as I write this, my daughter has no dad to be there for her.

I despise and hate addiction more than you can imagine. I cannot put it into words; it has taken everything from me, including my daughter. It is evil, it is progressive, and it is a lifelong disease. There is no getting rid of it, and there is no cure. The only thing one can do is maintain a *Spiritual program of recovery*. All I can do while being so far from her is continue with our phone calls and texts, trying through a phone, to somehow show her that I love her with all my heart and soul. It causes me such emotional pain and distress. I can't be there for her. All I can do is console her, and somehow by the grace of God, she may turn her life in a different direction.

I warn her and tell her that something bad will probably happen to her or her friends soon. The effects of the drugs and alcohol will cause grave emotional damage. Someone could die in a car accident; one of her friends may commit suicide because they are using drugs and alcohol, trying to mask their depression. Someone may have a drug overdose, or maybe, someone will get their drink spiked with (Molly) GHB, and rape will occur. This is real; these are real possibilities. I am sorry to say, it is inevitable. The way our culture and society is today, there is not much one can do. As parents, how can you control what happens outside the house? "Really," there is not a lot we can do; you can't keep your kids locked up at home. You can show your kids how much you love them, and *tell them* because it's what they need to hear.

All right, here we are nearing the end of my six-year tour in Lahr, Germany. Something is weighing on my heart, and I want to share with you about two horrific places we visited. The first place is located in *Dachau, Germany*, the first of the Nazi concentration camps opened in 1933.

The death camps, as they were called, are located on the grounds of an abandoned munitions factory about 16km from Munich. I remember walking up the dirt road to the front gates of Dachau where millions of Jews took the same walk; it was horrifying. A feeling overtook my entire body, trembling with anxiety, and fear, thinking about what went on inside those gates.

At the entrance to Dachau stood an old rustic metal sign for all to see, the sign reads "Arbeit Macht Frei," translated means "Work means freedom." There was no freedom once the people entered through those gates into the pits of hell. I believe if there was a place on earth that could be as close to hell as one could imagine, it would have been the Nazi death camps. There is good and evil in the world, and you cannot have good, without evil. These unspeakable acts of human nature take one to another world; evil won over in the killing fields, evil played the trump card.

There was a shooting range on the grounds, or, should I say, an execution gallery. The SS used the cynical term "special treatment" for these criminal executions. They would line up the prisoners and shoot them. There were thousands upon thousands of innocent people lined up and slaughtered on that site. They would then bulldoze the piles of bodies into pits, and burn them. The smell must have been atrocious, the odor of burning flesh filling the air, and floated over the neighboring villages. The people claimed to have smelled nothing; I find this disconcerting. People living in constant fear, I cannot imagine what they went through; trying to live day to day, starving with no food, and disease running rampant throughout the barracks.

Being there in person was something I will never forget. Seeing the crematoria where they would cremate body after body. Standing in front of the ovens, a flood of emotions overtook my body, and I could not move. You could walk through, seeing the ovens that were used to discard of any human remains. This reflects the Nazi propaganda, and the absolute insanity of one man, Hitler. It was an endless cycle of death.

One of the most disturbing buildings was the KZ Dachau, where the Nazis did their medical experiments. Headed by Heinrich Himmler, hundreds of prisoners suffered or were executed, at the hands of the Nazis. They would expose the prisoners to vats of ice water, and then strip them naked in freezing temperatures. Victims would shutter and shake, writhing in pain, foaming at the mouth, and lose consciousness. Attempts at reviving the subjects included scalding hot baths. Most of the medical records were destroyed by the Third Reich to conceal the atrocities.

Walking through Dachau was quite traumatizing. I was only sixteen at the time, but that was old enough to feel deep sorrow and sympathy. I had such care and concern for the innocent lives that were destroyed, seeing the mass graves that concealed thousands of victims. This should have never happened, but we live in an evil fallen world.

Auschwitz-Birkenau, The German Nazi Concentration and extermination camp was in contemporary Poland and operated from

1940-1945. Standing on the long straight rail line leading towards the stone cold structure, was another moment I will never forget. Thinking of how many rail cars full of Jewish people went through and under the arched entrance to Satan's playground.

Pure evil was the ominous feeling, a stench that filled the air; it was chilling- and to be honest, quite sickening. It was as though an evil spirit was running up my spine, and through my body. Auschwitz was the major site of the Nazi "Final solution" to the "Jewish question." Just writing this makes me sick. How can any human actually do the things they did to another human being?

Rail cars would come into the camp and deliver the Jews to the infamous gas chambers where the Nazis used Zyklon B to exterminate the prisoners. The Nazis would then take the piles of bodies out to the fields where they would exhume and incinerate them.The trip to Auschwitz was much more irritating and disturbing than Dachau. I felt such a heavy weight in my heart; it was horrific. There was something about the whole site that just reeked of evil. It just boggled my mind, (speaking of having a boggled mind). There were approximately 1.1 Million people that went through Auschwitz. I am not going to call them prisoners because they were human beings.

They were all killed, or exterminated at Auschwitz, with 90% of that total being Jewish people. Approximately 1 in 6 Jews killed in the Holocaust died at the camp. If they were not killed in the gas chambers, then they died of forced labor, medical experiments, infectious disease, starvation, and from individual execution. Sometimes you have to ask the question- why? How can something this wrong happen? Some things we will not know, or understand, this side of Heaven.

One other thing I find hard to understand is Suicide; I attempted suicide three times while in my addiction. My last attempt was a four-story dive off my mother's balcony while coming off heroin and prescription pain pills. We will get to that a little later, but for now, I would like to tell you about two suicides that happened in my family while we were still stationed in Lahr.

I have one thing to say about addiction; it is pure evil. There is nothing good about addiction, and in the end, all it wants to do is kill you. It has no other purpose, but to slowly take everything from you, family, friends, career, and material possessions. It wants to completely destroy you, and take everything you love, or care about, away from you. Finally, all you have left is absolute fear, loneliness, and a complete loss of hope; without hope we have nothing.

This is exactly where addiction took my Grandpa- not my Grandpa Pilsner- but my father's dad. Only meeting him once in my life, and being very young, I do not remember him. All I know is that he was an alcoholic, who never showed love to his children. He never told them he loved them, never picked them up, or gave them a hug.

How can I be upset, discouraged, or have any resentment towards my dad? When this was all he learned growing up, my dad did the best he could; only knowing the way he was raised, the way his father brought him up. My dad was always there for me, no matter what; he showed his love by physically being with me. He was involved in all my sports, travels, and personal outings, and he was never violent or abusive. I know in my heart my dad truly did love me, even though he never said it.

Addiction took my grandfather to the lowest depths of the human spirit; addiction told him he had no hope, no love, and nothing in his life worth living for. His only option in his mind was to end it all and to drive his car out to a field in the middle of nowhere. All alone, and being at the lowest place you could possibly imagine, he took a hose and hooked it to the muffler of his car. My grandfather then ran the hose from the muffler into the driver's window. With the car running, and the exhaust slowly flowing through the hose into the hollow shell of a grave, my Grandfather gasped his last breath; *addiction killed my grandfather*.

The second suicide had to do with my Uncle Ed, who was an amazing man. I was fortunate enough to have met him on numerous occasions. My fondest memories of him were his humor, his charm, and his loving, caring heart. People loved him; he just had that kind of personality. The dark side was he suffered from mental illness. He kept it well hidden, a sort of silent mental illness.

Ed was too proud ever to have it diagnosed. In those days, there was by no means the medication, or the amount of understanding that we have today. The amount of research done pertaining to mental illness has progressed leaps and bounds. I personally believe, there is still, and always will be, a gray area when it comes to treating mental illness.

We believe he may have had Borderline Personality Disorder (B.P.D), which is a pervasive pattern of instability of interpersonal relationships, self-image, and emotions. People with borderline personality disorder are also usually very impulsive, oftentimes demonstrating self-injurious behaviors (risky sexual behaviors, cutting, and suicide attempts).

B.P.D. occurs mostly in early childhood, and there were two things that had a major effect on him in his childhood. At the age of nineteen, he impregnated a girlfriend, and he wanted to have the baby more than anything in the world. The problem was, the mother of the impregnated girl was going to have none of it and talked her daughter into aborting the baby. After talking to my mother, my uncle Ed's sister, she told me it had a major effect on him. He did not take the abortion, or the loss of his child very well, and she said it had a long-term damaging effect on him.

Another thing was his father, my Grandpa Pilsner, being an alcoholic, caused Ed grave emotional distress. With Ed having B.P.D, I am sure the effect was much worse for him than it would have been for a normal child being raised with an alcoholic father. Ed had mentioned in the past that he did not want to incorporate any of the traits his father possessed; he did not want to be like him, in any way shape or form.

Another thing about my uncle was he was never violent or abusive to his three children. He was always gentle and kind, and he was a very good father and husband to his wife. My uncle never drank, he was not an alcoholic. He may have had a glass of wine at thanksgiving or a beer at Christmas. Ed's father was my Grandpa Pilsner, whom as you know was a hardcore Irish alcoholic. An amazing statement Ed once made was that he did not drink because *he did not want to end up like his father*. Ed's only addiction was to Coca-Cola, and he would drink two-2 liter bottles of coke a day.

It all happened on Easter, at a festive fun-filled family event, with kids, Easter egg hunts, and a turkey dinner with all the trimmings. I am so true to this book that I want to relate to you and share the experience's I am sharing in an honest and personal way. So, I spoke with Corinna, my amazing cousin, Uncle Ed's daughter, to give you the story from a front line perspective. Corinna was only nineteen at the time of this horrific event. She and my two cousins have had to live with this experience to this day.

It all started out innocently enough. Ed was out in the back yard playing with his Granddaughter, Corina's one-year-old child, Brendan.

The two of them were having a fun time when they were called to come in for dinner. This is where the untold turn of events began to happen. First off, for some reason, Ed was seated at the kids table, and not with the adult's, I believe Ed was not too pleased with the seating arrangements.

The next event takes us into the unknown world of mental illness. Ed only liked the white meat of the turkey. Well, by the time the turkey was dished out, all the white meat was gone. Ed received his plate with only dark meat on it. He flew into a rage, stormed out of the dining room, and into the living room. He was swearing and yelling. Corinna said that her dad never swore, but he seemed to be overwhelmed, falling into some sort of explosive disorder.

There were kids toys scattered around on the couch. He began grabbing the toys, throwing them off the couch, screaming *"get these toys off the f-ing couch, they don't belong here."* Ed then went into the kitchen; grabbed a bottle of rye out of the fridge, and a glass from the cabinet. He then proceeded to pour a tall glass of straight Rye. He then stormed to another part of the house and grabbed a metal first aid kit. When he was walking past Corina toward the bedroom, he spoke his last words to her. The last words my sweet, young innocent cousin heard were very disturbing. Ed said *I will show you what a drunk will do.* She then realized that the metal first aid kit was where he kept his bullets.

He went into the bedroom, slammed the door, and proceeded to call my Uncle Mike, Uncle Tom, Auntie Kerri, and my mom, his brothers, and sisters. He told them that he was going to kill himself. My mom said he was calm. They all tried to talk some reasoning, and understanding into him, but it was to no avail. After talking to Ed, my mom called the local police.

My Uncle Mike then called the house, and Corinna answered the phone. Mike asked what was happening. She said Ed was in the bedroom, and she could hear him going through the closet. Mike immediately told Corinna to grab the kids and get everyone out of the house. As they were exiting, police sirens could be heard in the distance. The next noise was the sound of a 12 gauge shotgun. Ed put the shotgun to his head and pulled the trigger. Blood was splattered everywhere, and pieces of his skull were embedded into the wall. *Mental illness killed my Uncle.*

As I mentioned in the prologue, the book would be honest, real, and to the point. In my journey, there is pain and peace, suffering and growth, sorrow and joy. Believe me, this is just the beginning of our journey.

We have covered all the sports and the exciting times as we traveled through Europe together. How at the age of fourteen, I began my drinking career, the atrocities in the concentration camps, and two suicides in my family due to mental illness and addiction. Here we go again, the story of my life; it was time to pack up and go. This would be the last move I would make with my family. We boarded the plane, back to Canada, to another military base, in Red Deer, Alberta.

CHAPTER 3

High School

HERE WE ARE again, a new Country, new City, and new friends to make. It was time to fit in, time to throw on a few of the masks that were tucked away for such an occasion. I had an Olympic-size swimming pool filled with masks. Who was the real Dwayne? Who is the guy wearing all those fake masks? It was never the real Dwayne; it was a guy who could fit in anywhere, with anyone. It was going to take a lot of time until I would not need to head to the pool and pull out a mask to fit in.

At the age of sixteen, upon entering High School, I was only about 5'1"; let's say I was short. I truly believe it played a huge factor with wearing masks and having to fit in.

This never bothered me; I was O.K. being short, and I felt confident. It was about my personality, not my height. God blessed me with an outgoing personality and a tongue. God forbid someone teased me, or tried to make fun of me. I was like a baby wolverine; I could, and would, verbally assault you if you tried any type of abuse or a put-down. This was something I had perfected over the years, probably as a defense mechanism.

I would only spend three years in Red Deer before making another move. We were stationed at an Air Force Base in Penhold, about twenty minutes from Red Deer. This time, unfortunately, we were living in a little box house on the base. I only lived at home till the age of sixteen, and then moved to Red Deer. I had a job at London Drugs, as a stock boy; keeping the job for two years, working my way through High School.

The reason for the move was to be closer to school and work. So many people I know in addiction have left their homes at a very young age. I have come to discover three reasons; the father or mothers are struggling with addiction or violence. The third is divorce or separation in the family. It leaves the child thinking it was their fault. In a lot of cases, dealing with the tough and trying times, and the circumstances; it can lead to addiction.

A lot were abused sexually by parents, relatives, or babysitters. The statistics for addicts who have had to endure sexual abuse and violence in the home is staggering. I was in an anger management class last year, with twenty men. Sixteen of the men in the group were abused sexually, and most of them, by more than one person. There was no parental influence, no one to care for them, and no one to show them, love. All they knew was to escape, to run, and with nowhere to go; it was the streets.

Most, being so young, needed a way out. The only way out was to use drugs or alcohol to bury the pain, to somehow mask their emotions. The hell they had to endure, and the baggage they have had to carry through life because the filthy acts of sexual abuse. A lot were molested by a parent, but in most cases it was a close relative or the babysitter. Can you imagine living in fear every day, knowing you were going to come home and get abused sexually, or get a beating from your father? How can anyone live like that?

So is it human nature, or the addict that lives in us, telling us to go and get drugs or alcohol to hide and mask the incredible amount of suffering coming from an abusive home? I want to be straight up with you; this is happening at homes in your community; by your neighbor, and by people you have met at the local supermarket. Everything seems to be crumbling down all around us, and you wonder why addiction runs so rampant in society today; this is a sick and evil fallen world we live in.

By the grace of God none of this happened to me in my upbringing. My heart goes out to the massive amounts of people who are suffering and dealing with such devastation in their lives. I know many of these people personally, who go through life overflowing with guilt, shame, and anger that reaches deep down into their souls.

They did nothing wrong; they were the victims. The most amazing thing is that there is *hope*, and with hope, we can endure. There is an answer; there is *someone* who can take away the pain, and show you, unending love. In life, we need to understand forgiveness, mercy, and grace.

When we came back from Germany, I tried out for the Red Deer Rustlers, a Junior A hockey team. It was pretty much one level below the NHL- this may have changed over the years. It was a time of sorrow in my life; I was too short to make the team; if only a few inches taller, and a little heavier, I would have made the team. It was not my speed or the lack of stick handling skills; it was my height. Quick note; Billy Ranford went on to play for the Rustlers; then he was drafted into the NHL.

My skiing career continued. I raced giant slalom and downhill on the provincial ski team. We raced all over Alberta; in Banff at Lake Louise, Heavenly, and Sunshine Mountain; we also went up North, and skied in Jasper. There is some amazing skiing in the Canadian Rockies, with some of the best powder runs in the world. It doesn't compare with the European Alps, but the Rockies have been rated with some of the best skiing in North America. I loved skiing more than anything; there is nothing like being on top of a mountain, with miles of fresh powder to ski down.

I attended school at Lindsay Thurber High, with about fifteen hundred students, a fairly big school. It did not take me long to get to know everyone. I would walk the hallways of the school and as I passed the jocks, the nerds, and the heads (Guys doing drugs); I knew them all. Walking past this group, or that group, whatever group it may have been, I knew them all. Of course, I was never close to any of them, and I did not have a best friend; I would not allow that. My relationships were all superficial, never getting very intimate with anyone.

I was always popular in school, probably because of sports, and my grades were always just enough to get by. That was good enough for me; my attention was more focused on sports, and not on school or drugs. I thank God for my ability to play any sport and play them well. This helped keep me from the world of addiction; for the time being.

The best way to fit in was to be on the high school football team; and of course, I made the team. I was the kicker because of my soccer career in Germany; I could put the ball through the posts from forty plus yards out. They also made me the running back, for a little guy with short legs; I could run like a gazelle. Football really helped me to fit in. I was friends with all the players, all the popular guys, and most girls in the school. The games were on Friday nights, and the whole school would turn out.

The bonus was the parties after the games, house wreckers as we used to call them. It was not good; we did unthinkable things, like throwing microwaves down the stairs into the basement. We would fill the washer with laundry soap, turn it on, and fill the place with bubbles. There would always be fights, furniture would get broken, and there would always be holes in the walls. At the time it was fun, we were out of control, I mean really, thinking back; how stupid. It was so wrong to go into some kids home for a party with the intention of wrecking the place. It happened often, but we were the guys on the football team, the popular guys, so everyone thought it was funny, or, that it was cool to destroy someone's home.

One night, I had my mom's new mustang out on the street, in front of a house we were going to for a party. My friend Brad had a truck, with massive tires on it; you almost needed a step ladder to get up into it. Well, another friend exited the passenger side of the car and left the door wide open. Yes, Brad was backing up his truck, and he snapped the door clean off the car. I drove home later that night and parked the car in our driveway. In the morning, when mom and dad went outside and saw the door jammed into the back seat of her new mustang, things did not go well for me.

Girlfriends, I had plenty of them in High school. I had a heart of gold, and always treated women the way I would want to be treated. I did not have sex until the age of seventeen. At that time, and definitely in our society today, they would have called me a "late bloomer."

The first girl I had sex with did not go so well; I did not know what I was doing. After my first attempt at making love, the wonderful experience turned into a nightmare. The condom had broken half way through. So, on my first venture into the world of sex, I impregnated my partner at the age of seventeen; not such a good beginning. We were very young, and she did get an abortion. I don't want to delve into the right and wrong of abortion, or have a debate, but we did abort the baby, and our relationship ended not long after.

We were Canadians, and in Canada we would go out to farmer's fields and party, summer or winter, it did not matter. Wow, going back I see a pattern here; farmers' fields seem to be popping up in my story quite a bit. We would bring wood pallets, loaded into the back of trucks out to the fields. They would be stacked up high, and we would have huge bonfires, at times there would be 100-150 people drinking beer and rye partying in the middle of a field. It could be the middle of summer, or during the winter, partying in -20-degree weather. Fields, fires, and parties were a regular weekend thing for us. We did this more than having house parties; the good thing is there was nothing to destroy in a farmer's field.

One other place we partied a lot was at my friend's father's hot tub store, PTA pools. The company installed pools, and hot tubs, and had a store with a showroom, with functioning hot tubs. We would go there late in the evening, with booze and girls, hot tubing and partying all night. I don't want to get any more descriptive as to the events that followed; I will leave that up to your imagination.

Our High school prom was quite a celebration; it was an exciting time in my life, a sense of accomplishment. I graduated high school in 1984, and was blessed by taking one of the best-looking girls in the school to the prom; her name was Tracy. She was incredibly beautiful, but she was just a friend; unfortunately we never dated. It would have been wonderful to have it the other way.

The after party was arranged by the school so there would be no drunken driving accidents. Our parents dropped us off at the high school parking lot, and then they bused us to an outdoor location where the party took place. We drank and celebrated all night. After the evening wound down, we were bused back to be picked up at the school.

A very unfortunate incident occurred that morning. A good friend of mine, who will remain nameless, was an amazing hockey player. He had a good chance of making the NHL, but something happened. He went out to the garage of his house after coming home from the prom, took a gun, put it to his head, and pulled the trigger, killing himself. This remains a mystery as to why such a talented individual would commit suicide the morning after the prom.

My high school partying was more of a weekend warrior approach; there was never drinking during the week. I went to school, passed my classes, and played sports. There were no hard drugs involved in my youth, the only thing we did was smoke hash. There was no cocaine, heroin, pain pills, crack, or weed, none of that was involved in my high school years. We would drink, and hot knife hash—let me explain.

Before heading out for a night of partying, we would go to my friend Brads welding shop. He was the one who backed up his truck and snapped the door of my mom's car. We would have checker tournaments; that's what we called them. Taking a chunk of hash, we would break off little pieces, and roll them into little balls. Next, lay them out in rows on the workbench, hence little checkers. A propane torch would be lit, for a blue tipped flame to blast out, providing the heat needed to get the knives hot. Yes, regular kitchen knives, we would hold the tips of two knives in the flame till they were red hot. Then we touched the tip of one knife to the ball of hash. We would then pull the knife with the piece of hash up towards our mouth, not touching our lips. We took the other hot knife, and touched them together, squeezing the little ball of hash between the two hot tips of the knives. A blast of smoke would ignite into the air, and we inhaled the blast of smoke into our lungs; we did this a lot.

Drinking Vodka, not a good thing; I call it the blackout drink. You have one, and you feel fine, then another, and another, still not feeling anything. Then it hits you like a ton of bricks and lays you out; hence the blackout drink. I am telling you this because I have a little story to tell you about drinking vodka, and then driving home.

I was sixteen at the time and was in Red Deer at a girl's house. She was having a party; we were drinking vodka, having a good time, laughing and getting silly. Then, I had the bright idea to drive home. It was about a ½ hour drive from her house to my house. I made it through the streets of Red Deer, and to the two-lane road leaving the city, heading towards the base. It is a long straight desolate road, with nothing on either side. It was like driving out to the country, with fields as far as you could see.

It was around the halfway mark that the vodka began to do its thing. I was getting pretty messed up. Being stupid and sixteen, I made a wrong choice and kept driving. There was one small problem; running down the stretch of road stood one lonely tree, a big one. It was on the opposite side of the road, about a hundred or two hundred feet out in the field. The crazy thing is there were no other trees between Red Deer and the base, just this one.

While driving back in a drunken stupor, I crossed over into the oncoming lane. I was doing about 80km an hour; when the car sailed off the road. I flew about forty feet; the car was airborne. My little brown Pinto came crashing down, plowing through the field, and running head-on into the tree.

The front of the car was v-shaped because it hit the tree head on. I was so drunk I flopped around like a fish. The spare tire from the back flew through the inside of the car and was now embedded in the front window on the passenger's side. The steering wheel was warped and twisted beyond belief from my chest and ribs crashing into it. My head had smashed into the windshield and shattered the driver side of the window. There was smoke streaming from the engine into the air. The car was totaled; it was literally wrapped around this tree. "I should have died that night."

Here is the insanity of it all. I came out of the crash without a broken bone, and I staggered away with nothing wrong with me. Still being in a black out, my memory was fragmented; someone picked me up at the scene of the car crash. The unknown savior dropped me off at the gates of the base. To this day, I do not know who the mystery person was.

I made my way from the gates to my home. When I walked into the house my dad asked where my car was; I responded that I did not know. My dad slapped me because I was so drunk, and not making any sense. Through my entire upbringing, this was the one and only time my father ever hit me.

I had to work the next morning at London drugs; as to my car's whereabouts, this was still a mystery, so my dad drove me to work. On the way, my dad and I had an eye-opening experience; we saw the car wrapped around the tree. My dad lost it, he freaked out after seeing the wreckage, seeing the car mangled, and twisted around the tree. My father started to drive erratically to the hospital; he wanted to get me to the emergency after seeing the wreckage. He thought I had broken my ribs or had internal bleeding. He said I needed to get to the hospital because something had to be wrong. I went in; the doctors looked me over and did a few tests. They found nothing wrong with me. I came out of the accident unscathed; *this was the first time I realized God had his hands on me.*

My afternoon class for the last semester of High School was at CKRD, a radio and television station. I was training to become a radio announcer at the age of eighteen. It was sort of an on the job training, with credits for school. I would spend my afternoons learning the ropes. I was trained to do voice overs for commercials. I learned how to splice the voice overs together, and make commercials to run on the air. I was also trained to use the mixing board in the main booth.

I did not need much training when it came time to speak, or to read the news on air. As I said, God gifted me with a tongue, and I knew how to use it. After completing my training, they hired me on as a radio announcer. At the age of eighteen, I was working on the air, playing music, doing the news, and having fun.

I really enjoyed the job, until I was bitten by the acting bug. My thoughts were on Hollywood, and pursuing an acting career. After six months of working at CKRD, I decided to pursue my dreams. I was about to make the biggest move of my life. Not that moving was challenging after my upbringing, but this would be a leap of faith.

I want to mention my first brush with celebrity while working at CKRD. A young man was hired on as the sportscaster for the T.V. division of the station. I had many conversations with this particular man, and we became friends. Moving ahead a bit, after seventeen years in L.A., I came back to Canada. As I was watching T.V. during the Olympics in Beijing, I see this mysterious man hosting the Olympics for Canada. Also, while watching a hockey game, I see the same man as Don Cherry's sidekick; the mystery man is Ron Mclean.

The same young man from CKRD back in the day was now Canada's broadcaster. I would have many more run-ins with celebrities in the coming years. It was time to take my leap of faith. With three thousand dollars in my pocket and a Suzuki GSXR 750 motorbike between my legs, I made the move. I had never been there before, and not knowing a single person in L.A., I still decided to follow my heart, and my dreams. I was off to Los Angeles, California. Hollywood was calling, and I was on my way.

CHAPTER 4

L.A.—The Acting

AT THE AGE of nineteen, I was heading to one of the biggest cities in the states, Los Angeles. The journey took me three days, driving around ten hours a day. My motorcycle was a rice rocket, a slang name for a Japanese racing bike. It was by no means a nice big touring bike; it was a crotch rocket- not the ideal one to be used for a long distance road trip. I left Canada and made my way into Montana, then through Idaho.

After the first day of driving, I pulled into a motel on the side of the highway in Idaho. I could not pull the bike up onto the center stand. My neck was so tweaked from being in a racing position for ten hours. There were another two days of this to go before entering Los Angeles, the concrete jungle. The next morning I was up and ready to make my move at around 7:00 am. I had a bite to eat, and was off and running, hitting Nevada by early afternoon. Almost making it to Las Vegas, I had to make an early stop, around 2:00 p.m., and check into another roadside hotel.

After having a very restless sleep, I was up around 9:00 pm. My bike was air cooled, which meant driving through the desert, and Las Vegas during the day would not be good for the bike. I made the last leg of my journey at night when it was cooler.

All was good, my energy was high, and L.A. was only 8 hours away. I grabbed a bite to eat at a local choke and puke. This is what I call the restaurants that are scattered along our transcontinental highways,

40

where you can get the best clubhouse sandwiches, with french fries and gravy.

Making my night time journey through the desert, and into the city of Neon lights, Las Vegas; was quite an amazing sight. My first time seeing Vegas at night all lit up was awesome. There was no stopping; I just kept traveling through, continuing on the last part of my grueling road trip, arriving in L.A. around 10:00 am.

Entering into "The City of Angels", I drove through the Cahuenga pass, seeing a city sprawling out as far as the eye could see. In the distance was the skyline of downtown L.A. It was awe-inspiring, breathtaking, and scary at the same time. There was no end to it, the expansion of homes, buildings and high rises; it just kept going and going. Here I was, this young kid from Canada, all alone in a city like L.A., pursuing one of the hardest careers to break into, acting.

Thank God for my military upbringing, and all the travels around the world. It helped me to adjust and accept where I was. My past travels gave me the courage and strength to keep pushing forward. Mentally, I knew *someone* had a plan and a purpose for my life. In my heart, I believed it had to do with the journey and the challenge which was set before me.

Here is an idea of just how big L.A. is. If you were in Calabasas, the first suburb coming into L.A. from Santa Barbara, and drove all the way through, Tarzana, Sherman oaks, then make your way through Hollywood and into downtown, you would be about half way. Now keep heading out towards West Covina and into Pomona and finally out to San Bernadino. This takes you to the other end of the city. It is about one hundred miles across, with eleven million people. I felt like a small speck of dust, but an energetic and charismatic, driven speck of dust.

I found myself in a dungy little motel in the heart of Hollywood. After checking in I went to Carl's Jr, a fast food restaurant down on Sunset Blvd, about 3 blocks from the Motel. After indulged into a few greasy burgers and a strawberry milkshake, I took a cruise down the infamous Sunset Strip, all the way to The Pacific Coast Highway. It is about a forty minute ride from Hollywood to PCH, where Sunset Blvd meets the ocean. There was no helmet law in California, so of course, being the rebel kid from Canada, it was off with the helmet. The journey began with me wearing a pair of shorts and a tee-shirt, on a racing bike. This would not be considered smart or safe, but I was living the

California dream. The problem was I did not have a hot California blonde on the back of my bike, (come on now, give me a break). This was my first day in L.A.

With the wind in my hair, and the sun shining on my face, I began my tour down Sunset Blvd. It begins by winding itself through Hollywood. Then I hit Beverly Hills; where I continued to make my way down into Westwood, and Brentwood, ending in Pacific Palisades. As Sunset Blvd meets PCH, there stands the famous restaurant *Gladstone's*, a perfect place for drinks and food. They also have a large outdoor patio overlooking the jewel of the West Coast, The Pacific Ocean.

I parked my bike, walked onto the sand, and went for a swim in the Pacific Ocean. It was such a wonderful experience. I had made my three-day journey and was now enjoying the California sun, and swimming in the ocean. The next day while driving around L.A. checking out the city, I would find myself back on PCH. Something told me to take the coast highway up to Santa Barbara. I followed my intuition and headed up the coast.

There was a reason for this; it would turn out to be a major turning point in my life. Santa Barbara is an amazing town located about an hour and a half up the coast from L.A.; it is compared at times to the American Riviera. As I entered into Santa Barbara, seeing a huge beach on my left, I parked my bike and walked out onto East Beach. It is a very popular beach with volleyball nets strewn all up and down the sandy oasis. Walking down the beach, I ran into five or six college guys sitting around smoking a couple of joints.

I introduced myself and sat down to partake in the weed fest. We talked and smoked weed for about an hour; then they invited me to *The Jungle House.* This was their home and party house. They were famous for their insanely wild annual Halloween Parties. During my stay there I attended one of their extravagantly, well-organized, Halloween events. It was not located on campus, and it was not an alpha beta pi fraternity. It was a house on the south side of S.B, with seven college guys living there. The guys were all mainly from the San Francisco Bay area, living together, going to college, and having huge parties at the Jungle House.

On my very first night in Santa Barbara, I was invited to go with the guys to a party up in the hills, near Montecito, a very wealthy part of the city. It was amazing being surrounded by so many beautiful College girls. We had the ocean breeze, a view of the coastline, and a lot of weed and booze was being consumed. I was lead into a room, where on the table laid a pile of a white powdery substance.

Everyone was indulging in the festivities. It was cocaine, and I had never tried it before. So on my second night in California, I did my first line of coke. I don't think my mom would have been very proud of her son. I would like to say that I just did the one line, but, that's not what happens when you do coke. The way it works, you do it until there is *nothing* left. All you want is *more*, and we did more, line after line until it was all gone; you devour it, all, and when it is all gone; you want more.

Then the wretched feelings of coming down off it, I had been up all night, the sun is rising, and there is no more coke left. I was sweating; anxiety took over my body, and I felt like warmed over death. All I wanted to do was die. It was a horrible experience coming down off cocaine, after a night of debauchery, partying, and women. I will say in the end; it was not worth it. Having a hangover from booze is one thing; dealing with a come down off coke is a whole different world.

I did a lot of partying while in Santa Barbara. The parties continued, I was living in California with a bunch of college guys, I was only nineteen, coming up on twenty, what do you expect? We drank, did drugs and went to a lot of clubs. My motto was work hard, play hard. I maintained my addiction at the time and was able to continue pursuing my dream of an acting career.

I would end up spending the first six months of my California experience living at the jungle house and enjoying the college lifestyle, even though I was not going to college. I was in pursuit of an acting career. I found a modeling agency called *LaBelle Models* in Santa Barbara; I signed with them and began putting my portfolio together. My involvement with them included doing some modeling, photo shoots, and gathering head shots for a portfolio.

I had the challenge of putting together a resume to be used when entering into the acting field in L.A. I did not have much to put on the resume, so I did what everyone else did; making up a few choice items to add to the resume. There were a few plays and acting classes added to beef it up a bit. Not very honest, and not recommended if you happen to get into this field.

One model who was teaching classes, and modeling at *LaBelle,* was *Kathy Ireland*. I had met with Kathy a few times and had a few conversations with her at the agency. Kathy was more of an acquaintance than a friend. She went on to become one of the top supermodels in the 80's and 90's. She was also in thirteen consecutive sport illustrated swimsuit issues. It was nice to have spent some time with Kathy. She was very polite, insightful, and a pleasure to be with. It was an awesome, productive six months in S.B. Signing with a modeling agency, getting headshots and putting a resume and portfolio together.

I want to share with you something of vital importance. In the upcoming chapters, there will be a lot of mention about celebrities. Celebrities I met and partied with, top models and actors I worked with. As I mentioned in the prologue, this is an honest book. I will never say a celebrity was my friend if they were not. If I worked with a celebrity or became acquaintances on the film set, then that's what you will read. If I was at a party and was introduced to a celebrity, that is what you will read. If a celebrity became a close friend or someone I dated, or who shared a part of my life, that is what you will read.

There is something else you should know. Through my experiences in L.A., meeting and getting to know many celebrities; they are normal people like you and me. Just because they make movies, and have their pictures on billboards and magazine covers; just because they are rock stars, and perform on stages around the world does not mean they don't have to suffer the consequences of life.

They deal with and go through the same life issues you and I go through. Money and fame do not take away from the trials and storms life has to offer them. They have marital and relationship problems, they go through divorces and suffer health issues. They have kids to raise, have arguments and fights, and battle with addiction and mental illness. Either personally, or their kids are involved with drugs and alcohol, and they go to treatment. They have car accidents and deal with court issues. Celebrities are not immune from life; they go through and suffer the same things as you and me.

For some reason, the world puts them on a pedestal, believing they live this amazing, worry-free, stress-free, glamorous life, not true. I have met enough of them and have gotten to know many celebrities in my fifteen years of working in the industry. In the next few chapters I will mention many celebrities; so as you read, try to keep this in the back of your mind.

Let's not forget about all the partying. We would go out to UCSB, the University of California Santa Barbara, where nonstop parties were going on. UCSB is one of the biggest party campus's in the states. Most of the frat houses are located on top of a ridge overlooking the Pacific Ocean. It was quite beautiful, and the sunsets were out of a picture book. I just had to look past seeing all the offshore oil rigs in the distance. Overall, it must have been an amazing place for these students to have gone to college.

I did not get drawn into the craziness for the most part; I partied, and had fun, not really getting into the drugs. There were times we would party, do cocaine, or ecstasy, but it was not very often. For me, it was drinking. I maintained my drinking, having fun, meeting girls, and really enjoyed life in Santa Barbara. I came to California for a reason. I had a plan, I was driven, and I knew I had a mission set before me. My heart said to pursue my dream, and begin an acting career; the drugs and alcohol did not interfere.

One night out on the town, I found my first love. State Street is the main street that runs from the beach, all the way up through Santa Barbara. There are many nightclubs located along the strip. One club was called *Zelos*, and this is where I fell in love. A few of the guys from the jungle house and I decided to go out to *Zelos* for a night of partying. The crazy thing is I did not want to go out that night. The boys persisted, so I decided to go.

Thank God for intervening. If I had not gone, I would not have met Rhonda, and my journey would have taken a different path. My friends and I walked into the club and found a table. As we were enjoying the evening, my friends knew a few girls sitting at another table, so we went over to hang out with them. It was love at first sight. I'd never experienced this before, but there she was, a glowing, blonde, petite, incredibly beautiful nineteen-year-old gift from God.

Her name was Rhonda, and we hit it off from the beginning. We were talking, laughing and enjoying each other's company. I asked her if she would like a drink. She responded with a yes, so off I went to get us a few drinks. There was a problem. The money was gone; I had spent my small twenty dollar fortune already. But there was hope.

At the bar, a young college guy standing in front of me had ordered two champagnes. After ordering, he decided to leave. I don't know anyone who orders two drinks and dashes off to the washroom before picking up their drinks. So in front of me were two glasses of champagne, waiting for the taking. Looking to my left, and then to the right, I grabbed the French beverage from the bar and made my way back to our table.

I approached Rhonda with two stolen champagnes in my hand and shared my spoils with her. Of course in her eyes, I had gone to the bar and bought the drinks. She did not know I was broke, and could not afford a postage stamp. But hey, the opportunities arose, and I jumped on it. I shared the truth with her a few months later, and we both laughed.

After a wonderful night of dancing and drinking, we went back to the jungle house and hung out. Rhonda was wearing a mini skirt, and I had my rice rocket motorbike. So when it was time to take her home; Rhonda being the champ that she is hopped onto the back of my bike. Mini skirt and all, we rode off into the night, with her arms wrapped around my waist. We tore through town, making the twenty minute ride out to *Goleta* where she lived. I walked her to the front door, gave her a kiss like a gentleman. The rest was history. (P.S—I had my California blonde on the back of my bike).

Rhonda and I partied quite a bit in *Ventura*, a city about half hour up the coast from Santa Barbara. She had a few friends living there, so we frequented the coastal city often. Her friends enjoyed doing cocaine, so we had many nights of drinking, partying, and snorting coke in Ventura. The partying was not a big part of our lifestyle. My days were productive, working with the *Labelle Agency*, and Rhonda had her job as a dental assistant.

I had done some modeling, put together a portfolio, and had a resume adequate enough to begin pursuing the incredibly challenging career of becoming an actor. So, after three months of dating, we made the move. We were off to Hollywood. Initially, we went out to West Covina, a suburb of L.A., where her parents lived. We stayed with them for a month until we found a place of our own to live. Our first place of residency, *The Princess Grace Apartments,* located in the heart of Hollywood in a grungy area, about two blocks up from Hollywood Boulevard.

Rhonda found herself a job just off Wilshire Blvd, in West L.A. working as a receptionist for a computer firm. I did what actors do best, found a job as a waiter. When I was starting out, there were a few other guys who were pursuing their dream, and they guided me to the *Samuel French Bookstore* on Sunset Blvd. It was there I picked up the

Bible for actors, *The Agency Book*. It contains all the Acting Agencies in L.A., with addresses to send your B&W 8 x 10 head shots, with your resume attached to the back.

The process of finding an agent is putting together a package of headshots and resumes, and sending them out to about thirty or forty agencies. If you get a response from two or three, you were doing well. It took a while, but, in the end, I did get a few responses, and auditioned for a few agencies. My first agent was *The Dale Garrick Agency*. His claim to fame and biggest client was *Tina Yothers,* who was starring on the hit T.V. show *Family Ties*.

Michael J. Fox was also starring on the show. He was my inspiration; and the reason for pursuing my dream of becoming an actor. Michael was Canadian, his father was in the Canadian military, and he was short like me. So with all these qualifications, I thought if Michael could do it, so could I. He was by far my greatest reason for heading to L.A., and getting into the acting business. This would be a good place to mention my meeting with *Michael J. Fox*.

Years later, when I was doing props and SP/FX, (special effects), we were filming a *Doritos* commercial on the Paramount back lot. I thought it would be a good idea on our lunch break to walk through the maze of stages, and pop into the set where they filmed *Family Ties*. I walked in and sat in the bleachers where the studio audience would be sitting. I watched them run a few scenes. When they finished, I walked down onto the floor and introduced myself to Michael J. Fox.

It was wonderful to chat with him for a while, since we were both Canadian, (and short), we hit it off. We exchanged a few words and glorified Vancouver, Canada, where he was from. After having a fifteen-minute conversation with the mega star, I headed out and made my way back to work on the Doritos Commercial a few stages away.

O.K, back to the love of my life, Rhonda. After six months of dating, we decided to get married. She had her job, and me, well I was a waiter, so we did not have much money. I was blessed to get a job at the infamous *Brown Derby Restaurant* located at Hollywood and Vine. It was said that *Clark Gable* proposed to *Carole Lombard* there, and it was frequented by *Hedda Hopper, Lucille Ball, William Holden* and many other celebrities.

The Derby is famous for *The Cobb Salad*. I waited tables there for about a year and did all right making tips. Rhonda had her receptionist job, where she did OK financially. Between the two of us, and with the prices in L.A. being so high, it was as a struggle to make ends meet. We did not have much money, which meant our apartment was a bit barren. But we made due, and we were in love.

It was off to Las Vegas, for a Valentine's Day wedding. When we arrived in Vegas, we went to City Hall for a marriage license. You can't imagine how many other people had the same idea. When we arrived at City Hall, there were hundreds of couples lined up; it was a big party. Rhonda and I spent hours waiting, but we had so much fun with all these couples waiting to tie the knot. People from all over the states, lined up, drinking, laughing, and having an amazing time.

I believe it was the only time in my life where I had to wait in a line and had the best experience one could imagine. I have a pet peeve about standing in lines anywhere, for anything. After hours of fun, we made it to the front and received our marriage certificate. With a few friends, we were off to *Cupids Wedding Chapel*. This was far from a classy place; it was a bit cheesy and was one of the many wedding chapels located along the strip.

We made our way into the Chapel of love and registered to get married. No, we did not have an Elvis impersonator marry us. There was one couple in front of us, and they were alone. So, we joined in as witnesses and watched them get married. The big event arrived, and we were next. I was twenty, Rhonda was nineteen. We were very young, but we were in love, a young puppy love so to speak. There were no wedding bells, or rice being thrown, just a simple marriage, Vegas style.

After the wedding ceremony, the two of us, along with the other couple, and a few of our friends went to the casinos. We did a lot of drinking and played a little roulette. My family knew nothing about my getting married. From a pay phone in the lobby of Caesars Casino, I made the call to my amazing mother. She answered the phone and after saying hello, I mentioned that I was in Vegas. The next thing I said was; I just married an amazing California girl named Rhonda.

I took the receiver and handed it to my wife so she could say hello to her mother- in- law. My mom was a bit shocked. She was getting a phone call from the lobby of a casino in Las Vegas from her son, telling her that he was married. The good thing is that Mom was very happy for us, and she gave us her blessings.

After the marriage, we moved to the Valley, to another apartment, on Vineland Ave in *Studio City*. This place was a two level, U-shaped building, and was open air. When you walk out your front door, you are standing outside, not in a hallway. We had a pool in the middle. Most apartment complexes in L.A. usually come with a pool. Rhonda quit her job at the computer firm, and found another job, as a waitress on the Sunset strip at a club called *Carlos and Charlie's*. She made very good money working there.

I continued trying to pursue an acting career. It is a very demanding business to break into, with the competition for parts being out of this world. It was next to impossible to book anything. I went out on many auditions; for commercials, T.V. roles, and movies. The competition to break into the acting business is furious. Sometimes there are a hundred to two hundred and fifty guys vying for the same part. I don't want to deter anyone from pursuing their dream of being an actor, but I need to be brutally honest with you.

The chances of making it as an actor are about the same as winning the lottery. In the five years I spent pursuing my dream, out of the hundreds of guys I met; only one made it. His name was *Glenn Quinn*, and he would later become my best friend.

Glenn would later go onto T.V. fame, playing the part of *Mark,* on the hit T.V. show *Rosanne*. After Rosanne, he played *Doyle* alongside *David Boreanaz*, and *Charisma Carpenter* on the T.V. show *Angel*. This was a spin-off from the show *Buffy the Vampire Slayer*. David went on to get his own T.V. series called *Bones*.

David became a frequent acquaintance through my relationship with Glenn. There were a lot of nights spent with David, at Glenn's house, partying and doing things I cannot mention. I have so much more to share with you later in the book about my insane and crazy relationship with Glenn.

One amazing thing about him is he made it into the business without having family or friends involved in the film industry. He auditioned, and booked the part, the old fashioned way. The way most successful actors make it into the film industry is having some sort of a relationship with someone already involved in the business. Their fathers or mothers are Producers or Directors; they have an uncle or aunt working in the business. For example, *Nicolas Cage's* uncle is *Francis Ford Coppola*. Not wanting to take anything from Nicolas Cage, because I really do enjoy his acting. But really, how do you think he received his first role in the film *Valley Girl*? Do you think it could have anything to do with who his uncle was?

This is just one example, of the many actors who are successful because a family member or relative is involved in the film business. The industry, as they call it, is definitely a "who knows who" business. The more people you know, and the closer you get with the right people, is about the only real way to make it and have any level of success.

I had some mild success in my pursuit of an acting career. In the beginning, we would crash auditions, mainly commercials. Glenn and I would exchange information, along with a few other actor friends. If someone had an audition, we would tell each other. This way, instead of having one or two auditions a week through our agents, we would have eight or ten meetings, crashing each other's auditions.

The casting process for a commercial goes like this. Let's say, for example, it's a *Fast food* commercial. There is the initial audition, where they see about a hundred fifty guys for the part; this would be the first audition. Then, they will have what is called, a *callback*, which means they have narrowed it down to somewhere around sixty guys. After the callback, they will have a *second call back*. Now it's down to twenty guys. The first audition is just you in front of the camera. The callback is also done in front of the camera with no one present. The second call back usually means the Director, Producer, and sometimes people from the Ad Agency will be present.

In the end, they will narrow it down to one out of the twenty, casting the right person for the part. There is always the possibility of a third call back, to narrow it down a little more. In commercials, they are definitely looking for a specific look to cast each part. It is a grueling, stressful, competitive process. Always doing it over and over again, commercial after commercial, and not booking anything. I had to be prepared in the art of dealing with rejection. It is real, and a big part of the business, it is something I didn't get used to. Maybe that is why there are so many needy and insecure actors out there.

Over the years, I booked a few commercials, one of which was a *Pepsi Commercial* with a very famous director named *Leslie Dektor*. This job was a big break for me because it allowed me to get into *S.A.G.*, *The Screen Actors Guild*. It is a catch 22 getting into the union. First you cannot work on a union job if you are non- union. Second, you cannot get into the union unless you are on a non-union job that goes union. A bit confusing, but what isn't in Hollywood.

There is one, and only one other way to get into the union, called a *Taft-Hartley*. This is where the law allows a signatory producer, or director, to hire a non-union performer if that non-union performer possesses a quality, or skill essential to the role. This is how I was blessed enough to get into S.A.G. Mr. Dektor saw some quality in me that the other 200 guys trying for the part did not have. (Thank you Leslie). By my going union, I was then able to join *A.F.T.R.A.*, the other smaller acting union, *The American Federation of Television and Radio Arts*.

I was now part of both unions. This is a big deal for anyone pursuing an acting career. Getting into S.A.G. and A.F.T.R.A. is an imperative part of the process if you want to move further ahead. The funny thing is- I played a hockey player! Imagine that, and my big line in the commercial was in a dressing room scene. I took the drink and said *This is Pepsi*, followed by a big smile for the camera. I knew I made it to the big leagues when I received a call from my Aunt Kerri. She was in London for a visit and had seen my Pepsi commercial running on air. I also did a *Mountain Dew* commercial, where I played a high school football player, and played a marketer, in an *AT&T* commercial.

I have added a few attachments in the next couple of pages; one is my Hollywood acting resume. The second is a newspaper clipping, from the days of pursuing my dream. Believe me, I wish the resume was full of more credits from T.V. shows and Movies, but this was not part of Gods plan for me. It was definitely a stepping stone for what was to come next.

DWAYNE HIGGINS

* CANADIAN CITIZEN
U.S. WORK VISA

SAG-AFTRA

Toni Kelman/Arletta
7813 Sunset Blvd, Los Angeles, California 90046
Talent Agent   (213) 851-8822

HEIGHT: 5' 7"
WEIGHT: 150 lbs
HAIR: BROWN
EYES: BLUE

FEATURE FILM

PERSISTANCE OF VISION	GREG	ECLECTIC FILMS
BATTLEGROUND	SOLDIER BOY	ACTION INT'L PICTURES

TELEVISION

LUST FOR LOVE "PILOT"	PARKER	CHRIS BEARDE TELEVISION
DAYS OF OUR LIVES	RECURRING	COLUMBIA PICTURES

COMMERCIALS

LIST UPON REQUEST

STAGE

HOUSE OF BLUE LEAVES	RONNIE
LONE STAR	RAY
DOES A TIGER WEAR A NECK TIE	BICKHAM

TRAINING

RICHARD BRANDER	CURRENTLY
MARK TILLMAN	TAKE ONE STUDIOS
JACK HAMMOND	SCENE STUDY
KEN GILBERT	COLD READING/IMPROV
UNIVERSITY OF CALGARY	DRAMA MAJOR

SKILLS

VARIOUS DIALECTS (SCOTTISH, BRITISH, FRENCH)
ALBERTA PROVINTIAL SKI TEAM, SPEED SKATING, WRESTLING, FOOTBALL, WATERSKI
AND LACROSS.
WEST GERMAN NATIONAL HOCKEY TEAM, MOTORCYCLE RIDING, DUNE BUGGY AND
SNOWMOBILE.
HANDBALL, TENNIS, BADMINTON, SWIMMING, BASEBALL, SOCCER, RACQUETBALL,
VOLLEYBALL AND HORSEBACK RIDING.

4B   THE ADVOCATE, Thursday, October 1, 1987

Entertainment

Dwayne Higgins happy in Hollywood

By BOB WEBER
of The Advocate

When Dwayne Higgins of Red Deer roared off on his motorcycle bound for Hollywood, almost everyone thought he'd be roaring right back.

Even his mother, Pat Higgins, thought he'd be back in a week.

That was last July. Dwayne Higgins, 20, is still in Hollywood. He's already got one movie under his belt and a second one coming up.

"I'm clicking at a really good pace," he says.

Accelerating to this pace was hard work. At first, he found the "go go go fast fast fast" life of Los Angeles exhausting. He moved to smaller Santa Barbara. It was, he says, a kind of halfway house between Red Deer and Hollywood "to get used to the fast lane."

He was accepted into a modelling agency in Santa Barbara, and began to work and develop a portfolio.

About seven months ago, Mr. Higgins moved back to Hollywood. He signed up for drama classes — his only previous acting training had come from Lindsay Thurber High School.

He found a good agent, which wasn't easy. Mr. Higgins sent out 27 resumes to resumes and pictures on people's desks.

He waits days to find out if he's on the short list. Then, he auditions again. Some productions have as many as four short lists before the part is awarded. "It gets worse and worse the more callbacks you have to wait for," he says.

Finally, things started to go his way. He married his wife Rhonda, who he met in L.A., last Valentine's day. In August, he got a small part in Battleground, a low-budget film not released in North America.

And last week he got the nod for Persistence of Vision, a feature film being produced and directed by Michael Vanhoff. The part is a big step forward for Mr. Higgins. It may get him into the Screen Actor's Guild, which would make it much easier for him to get other parts. Persistence of Vision should be out by next summer.

Mr. Higgins says it takes determination and self-confidence to earn a place on the screen. And he knows there's a lot more work ahead yet. This isn't a story about local boy makes good, he says. "This is about local boy makes so far so good."

But he's pleased with the progress he's made. "Things are going super-good for me right now."

DWAYNE HIGGINS SMILING THESE DAYS
... "things are going super-good," he says

various agencies, and got one reply. "Down here, that's considered good," he says.

He began hustling for work. His agent sent him out to a couple auditions every week. If nothing was lined up, Mr. Higgins would lie his way past security guards and sneak into auditions. He'd dress up and breeze into major casting offices as if he belonged and leave his

As for T.V. and movies, my career only went so far. I auditioned for many parts and had some success. I did two low-budget movies; one was called *Battle Ground,* where I played a soldier. The other was a bigger budget movie called *Persistence of Vision.* I played a character named Greg; how ironic that my brother's name is Greg. The character was nothing like my brother so I could not use him as a character reference.

I took some acting classes while pursuing my dream. One acting coach I worked with was *Richard Brander.* He is an amazing acting coach. Richard had trained quite a few celebrities in his time. Some of the actors were *Kevin Costner, Milla Jovovich,* and *Farrah Fawcett.* He also trained *Diana Ross* for her role in *Lady Sings the Blues.*

One actress in my class was *Jennie Garth*; she went on to play *Kelly Taylor* on the T.V. show *Beverly Hills 90210.* I became pretty good friends with Jennie, going over scripts together, and doing a lot of acting scenes with her in class.

Mentioning *Kevin Costner* reminds me of a brief encounter with him. This happened years after Rhonda and I were together. I was working on a commercial, and we were shooting at Universal Studios. I had finished filming for the day and was driving off the backlot when I saw Mr. Costner sitting in front of his trailer. At the time, I lived about six blocks from the back gates of Universal, in Studio City. I was living with Jenell and my one-year-old daughter Alyssa at the time.

Jenell was a big fan, so I told Jenell to grab Alyssa, hop in the car, and I would take them to meet him. We drove back onto the lot, and went over to Costner's trailer; this all took about ten minutes. We walked up to him and began to have a great conversation. We also took a few photographs with him holding Alyssa, and Jenell was at his side. He was very polite, and always had a smile on his face. He signed an autograph for my little Alyssa, and for Jenell. He was working on the film *Dragon Fly* at the time.

Taking Richard's acting classes helped me tremendously. I had learned a lot from his training and went on to book a small part on the *Soap Opera, Days of Our Lives.* It is filmed at the *Sunset Gower Studios* in *Hollywood*. It was quite an experience being on a Soap opera, always a lot of lines to memorize. In soaps, they do all the blocking, lighting, and filming for an entire episode in one day.

Another T.V. show I managed to land a part in was called *Lust for Love*, a pilot for NBC, a reality show, about a family that lived in The

San Fernando Valley. I played the teenage son, even though I was twenty-three. The Valley is a section of L.A. that lies on the other side of a stretch of mountains separating greater Los Angeles from the Valley.

A *pilot* is an idea, a single episode of a show that in hopes will get picked up by the networks. Each year there is a time they call *Pilot Season*, in which the networks will do about twenty pilots each. They will go through a huge casting process, hiring actors to fill all the roles in each pilot. There are so many auditions around this time of year with all the pilots being filmed.

After filming the shows *a.k.a Pilots*, they will run them in front of test audiences. In the end, the network will pick one or two shows out of the twenty they made and put them on the network schedule. I am sorry that *Lust for love* did not get picked up. It did not turn out to be a *Seinfeld* or *Friends*, but it was an amazing feat to have even made it that far. The competition in the industry is very cut throat. Just to get cast for the role, and to film the pilot, was still a major accomplishment for me.

. . .

Another milestone in my career was with the hit T.V. show *Twenty-one Jump Street*, starring *Johnny Depp*. It was the show that turned Depp into a teen idol back in the late 80's. Near the last few seasons of the show, Johnny Depp left to pursue his film career. They needed to find another actor to replace him for the role. I auditioned and made it all the way to *Network*.

When I say network; it means they have narrowed it down from the hundreds of actors to around four or five. Going to the network could be ABC, NBC or, in this case, FOX, and I auditioned for the network producers, and director. There were about twelve to fifteen producers from the studio in the room while I was doing the scene. They make the final decisions after the audition process. I am proud to say, that I was one of the four actors who made it. There was just a few of us competing to replace *Johnny Depp*, trying to slip into his role on the show.

The news was not good; I did not get the part it went to another fairly popular actor at the time named, *Richard Grieco*. He was a model for *Calvin Klein, Armani,* and *Chanel* before he booked *Jump Street*. So really, what were my chances? It was one in four, and that's not bad considering the hundreds that were auditioned. Only four of us made it to the network. But hey, for a young kid, an air force brat from Canada, making it that far was still something to write home about.

There was one other T.V. series that I almost landed a part on, a show called *Saved by the Bell* for the role of *Zack Morris*. The part was for the lead character, and it was a series that followed a group of teenage friends. A lighthearted comedy, that touched on social issues pertaining to teens growing up in the early nineties. I went on four auditions before making it to *Network*.

I remember the day, driving to *NBC* for the final reading; it was between me, and two other actors. There must have been between twelve to sixteen producers and executives from the network there for the audition. It was a bit nerve-racking, with that many eyes on me, watching my every move. The read went well, but the problem was I looked a bit too old for the high school character they were searching for. I was around twenty-four or twenty-five at the time. So, again, I did not get the part; it went to *Mark-Paul Gosselaar*.

The thing with pursuing a career in acting is you had better be prepared for a life of *rejection*. Over and over again you will get close, and sometimes real close. But in the end, most of us will never get the dream role. Acting/ modeling and music have to be some of the hardest careers ever to achieve any form of success in. The competition is fierce, and the amount of people trying to break into these careers is phenomenal. Without knowing the right people, chances are far and few between of making a living doing any of these three careers. Remember, this is my opinion from actually living it, pursuing it, and personally knowing hundreds who have tried. I also want to encourage you, if you have a dream, I insist that you follow that dream, follow your heart, and push towards your goals. You will never know until you try.

Before closing, let's talk about another T.V. show, *The Newly Wed Game*. O.K, I did take part in a game show during my stay in L.A. Even for game shows, there is an audition process. They don't just walk out onto the street, and pick some people to throw onto the show. Rhonda loved the show, and they were having auditions. She sent in some photos of us, filled out the forms, and the next thing you know, we were called in for an audition.

Rhonda is so cute, and bubbly; there was no way we were not going to get picked as one of the married couples. We were chosen, and we appeared on the show in 1989. At the time Rhonda and I were on the show, it was being hosted by *Paul Rodriguez*. He replaced *Bob Eubanks*, who had been the host for an eternity.

At the beginning of the show it was close; then the other couples answered a few questions correctly. We had stumbled on a question or two, but we would not give up. The end of the show came upon us, and we were sitting in last place. But, there was the bonus question, the last question, worth the big points. The other couples fell apart, Rhonda and I answered correctly, and we came out on top. We had won that episode of the Newly Wed Game.

The sad news is our marriage came to an end after three years. We were very young, and I was pursuing an almost unattainable dream of becoming an actor. The only reason she left Santa Barbara was to be with me. I had loved Rhonda very much. There had been many tough times, and she always stood by me. Our break up was amicable; we both came to the conclusion that we were young, and out of love.

I helped her move, packing up all her belongings, and I drove her back to Santa Barbara to pursue her own life. We remain friends. Rhonda is remarried to a wonderful guy named Steve. They have two amazing children and live a Christian life.

It was a very proud time in my life, booking a couple of commercials, and doing a stint on a Soap opera. Working on a few films, and almost landing parts on two highly successful T.V. shows. I decided to slowly stop pursuing a career in the acting field. Not to say the next few chapters are not full of celebrities, and an amazing career doing Props & SP/FX. This would be the stepping stone, leading to a career Art Directing with some of Hollywood's biggest actors, and directors.

CHAPTER 5

L.A.—Behind the Scenes

IT WAS TIME to make another move. By the age of twenty-one, I had made *ten* moves. During my Seventeen years in L.A., I would make another *eleven* moves, which brings us up to *twenty-one* by the age of Thirty Three. Later in the book, after I get back to Canada, we will continue our count.

This time, it was up to the Hollywood Hills, to a complex called *The Whitley Terrace Apartments*. Once again, it was a U-shaped building, with a pool. When I looked up to my left, I could see the Hollywood Sign, and to the right was the Griffith Park Observatory. Looking out over the pool was a crystal clear view of Downtown L.A.; it was breathtaking unless of course the smog was distorting the view.

I need to try to put this into words. What happens next in our story would change the direction of my life for the next fourteen years. I had been in L.A. for three years, pursuing an acting career. But really; I was mostly waiting tables and doing catering jobs with various companies trying to make ends meet. One day I received a phone call from my very good friend Mike. He asked if I wanted to be a P.A. on a Snuggles commercial.

Remember I mentioned that getting into the film business was about who you know. This applies to acting as well as getting work behind the camera. Whether it is being a producer, grip, an electrician, art directing or doing wardrobe; whatever it may be, it is about knowing someone who can get you in the door. I believe God used Mike to open that door. God will use people, places and things in our lives. We just need to be intuitive and aware when doors are opening, and when doors are closing.

Wow; did the door ever open for me! Let me begin by explaining what a Production Assistant is. A P.A. is someone who, while working on the film set, can have various tasks, such as "Set PA", "Truck PA", "Locations PA", "Office PA", "Set Runner" and "Extra PA. A production assistant is a position where you do pretty much anything the producer needs. Not putting down any P.A's, but it is the lowest position in the behind the scenes hierarchy.

I took the job. It was my first day on the set, and the producer tells me to go help the art department. This is the life changer I was talking about. I was assigned to Jim, the set decorator. The art department is responsible for arranging the overall *look* of the film, or commercial (i.e. modern/high-tech, rustic, Victorian, etc.) as desired by the film director, or the commercial agency.

Individual positions within the department include production designer, art director, assistant art director, storyboard artist, concept artist, set decorator, set dresser, property master, property assistant, lead man, and swing gang. The art department is a big crew of people. I ended up working with Jim for the whole week helping out with the sets and props.

When I mentioned the door swung open, it did! This was my first and the last job as a P.A. I ended up working with Jim for the next three years. I did not have to work for a year or two as a P.A, making contacts and working my way up the ladder. It happened on my first job behind the scenes. This was a big break and a career changer for me. I would end up working behind the camera, in the art department, for the next fourteen years of my life.

I would dabble and continue with acting for a bit, but it faded out. I eventually stopped the acting dream and started a more prosperous and adventurous career working behind the scenes. What a blessing this turned out to be! I started out at the bottom of the art department in the swing gang. The swing guy's job is to drive around during the day in a 5-ton truck, picking up props and set dressing from various prop houses and F/X shops scattered around L.A. After returning to the sound stages or the location; we would unload the set dressing from the truck. Then, working with the set decorator and art director, everything would be put in place.

Example, let's say the job was a *Snickers* commercial, and it entailed a high-end law office, an upscale living room, and a kitchen. The sets would be built on a sound stage, and we would dress in the conference table, chairs, artwork and anything else for the law office. The living room would be dressed with a couch, love seat, coffee table, rugs, and plants. You get the idea; we made the set look the way it must look for the particular scene being shot.

One of my first jobs was a commercial for *Nike*, with *Mark McGwire*, who was playing for the St. Louis Cardinals. He held the best at-bats run ratio in baseball history. Babe Ruth was second. The segment with *Mark McGwire* was filmed on location out in *Long Beach* at the *Queen Mary*. We filmed for two days, shooting on the upper decks and in the cabin rooms situated in the underbelly of the ship.

The other sports celebrity in the commercial was *Marion Jones*, who won 3 Olympic gold medals at the Sydney Summer Olympics. The bad news is, years later she would be stripped of her titles after admitting to steroid use. This segment was shot on location as well, at *Venice Beach*; we used a steady cam for most of the commercial. We spent three days following Marion running through the neighborhood and dashing in and out between the vendors along the boardwalk.

A steady cam is a type of camera that is harnessed to the camera man. It floats on a jib arm so he can control the camera, being able to swing it in all directions as he runs behind the actor. I am sure you have seen it in movies and commercials where someone is being chased with the camera following their every move; this is done with a steady cam.

You can *YouTube Marion Jones, Nike* and watch the spot. It became a very famous commercial because it has three or four different endings, which you are only able to see on the internet. Check it out when you have some time.

Since we are on a run talking about Athletes, I would like to mention a trip to Arizona one year. It was during the Major League Baseball training camp season to do a *K-Mart* commercial with *Sammy Sosa*. It was pretty cool being at the training camp with all the players from various teams in M.L.B, practicing and playing ball.

There was one scene where they had Sammy throwing baseballs. It took the better part of the afternoon. I was the prop master on the job, (will explain in a bit). I was side by side with Sammy all day handing him baseballs. We were told before the commercial by the producers not to ask for autographs from him. Well, since I was talking with him all day, and getting acquainted, I went undercover and secretly had him sign a ball. It was not for me, but for my Uncle Mike. He was a big fan, and he had asked me beforehand if I could get an autographed ball. I aim to please. He was ecstatic; you may remember him from the story about my Uncle Ed's suicide.

One last Athlete I would like to mention is *Oscar De La Hoya, "The Golden Boy,"* I was doing an Insurance commercial with him. A friend and I were hanging out off camera near the craft service table (where all the food is), and Oscar walked up to us. We all started talking and spending some time together. Then he decided to go get his *Gold metal belt* from the *Barcelona Olympic Games* to show us. We actually had fun joking around with Oscar. My friend was quite a card, so we laughed a lot, and had a good time. We took some pictures with Oscar and the Gold Metal Belt. Then it was back to the set and back to work.

We sidetracked a bit with the athletes. Let's continue on with my journey in the art department. I did swing work for about a year and then progressed to the leadman position. I was the person who is in charge of all the swing guys. I worked with the set decorator and art director, going over what needed to be done. Also organizing the day for the swing guys as to when and where they needed to go for all their pickups. The job also entailed doing all the paperwork; mileage forms, P.O. logs, petty cash receipts, rental and deposit checks, and time cards for when the commercial wraps up.

Remember, during all this time I was working with Jim learning the ropes. I would work with him for three years, climbing the ladder, working every position in the art department. I eventually worked my way up to doing Props and SP/FX (Special Effects). I would end up doing this for most of my career. Years later I also stepped into the position of art director, designing sets for a lot of music videos and commercials. I really loved doing props and FX, because in commercials the prop master does all the FX. This includes making rain with huge rain towers; snow F/X's, creating wind using massive Ritter fans and all the product shots for the commercial.

The Product Shot is what you see at the very end of any commercial. Everything I am about to explain to you is the job of the prop master. Let me take you onto the set of a Product Shot and tell you what it takes to shoot a bowl of cereal. Let's use *Kellogg's Corn Flakes* as our example. The first thing is the prep. I would go to *Crate and Barrel*, *Pier One Imports* and *Bed Bath and Beyond* to do some shopping.

It began with me picking six to eight various sets of bowls, milk &orange juice glass's, placemats and silverware. The ad agency and director would then go through my choices, hand picking the right placemat to go with the right bowl. Then, picking out just the right milk& orange juice glass's to complete the set. Finally, they would go through the selection of spoons because the spoon will be sitting on the perfect placemat next to the perfect bowl for the shot.

I would take the box of corn flakes sent to me by the ad agency to an F/X shop and have it color corrected. There are no bar codes or ingredients labels on the box. It is not like a regular box you find in the store; it is made especially for filming the product shot. The corn flakes you see in the bowl did not come straight from the box. They have been shaken through a 3x3 box made from one by two pieces of wood with a chicken wire bottom. I would pour all the flakes in and proceed to shake them for a minute or two. After the process is finished all the small and broken up pieces would fall through the bottom; leaving the big beautiful flakes.

The berries sitting on top of the flakes have been perfectly placed. The camera is in position with the lens about a foot or two from the table set up. The director is looking through the lens, telling me to move berry x, camera right a 1/2 inch. So, with a pair of tweezers I would move berry x camera right, and then we would move onto another berry and do the same routine until all the berries are in a perfect position.

Now the finisher, I would put out the *Hero* cereal box. The word hero means perfect in the commercial world. I would set it in just the right position, at just the right angle on the table. I would take the agency picked placemat, and set it in place. Then I take the hero bowl and place it on the perfect placemat in just the right position. Then I put the perfect flakes into the bowl at just the right level, then placing the berries perfectly in place.

The orange juice and milk glasses needed to be filled, using a funnel to pour the liquid through so it goes straight into the glasses. There cannot be any milk or orange juice splashed on the sides, and they must be filled to a specific level. I would then place the glasses to the upper left of the bowl, in just the right position, and set the spoon in place, perfectly, next to the perfectly place bowl. Now everything is in place.

The perfect flakes are in the bowl, the berries are perfectly placed, glasses are full, and the cereal box is in its perfect position. The camera is ready. Just before we roll film, the milk must be added to the bowl of cereal, just to the right level, leaving only a small ring of milk showing above the perfectly placed flakes. You don't want soggy flakes in the product shot. This is just the tip of the iceberg for what goes into a product shot. Let's not forget the four to five hours it takes to light the set and the massive film crew it takes to get this one shot. Only in Hollywood!

After working with Jim and learning the ins and outs of the art department, I would eventually go my own way. Soon I would be working with some of Hollywood's biggest directors. As we continue along, I will explain how things are done in the film biz. My job after leaving Jim was prop master. Doing all the SP/FX and product shots made the job very exciting and creative.

One of the Art directors I worked with was a lady named Lynda. You want to get in with the right people, so you work all the time. Lynda had been art directing for a long time and was locked in with some very big directors, and production companies. This, in turn, kept me busy all the time.

One production company Lynda was in with was *Harmony Pictures.* They had a contract with *Hallmark,* so we did three to four commercials a year. They were huge jobs! We built the entire store on a sound stage. If you went to the mall and walked into a *Hallmark Store*, there would be two card aisles running the length of the store. All the side walls are lined with cards, ornaments, and books. The front of store displays would show whatever they are promoting at the time; seasonal displays i.e. Christmas, Easter or Halloween.

We had a warehouse full of the display cases, side walls that went together in four-foot sections and the card aisles. We had all the racks, plus enough merchandise to fill an actual store. It took three, five-ton truck loads to get everything to the stage. In the end, with a crew of twelve to fifteen people, it took three days to put together an entire store. Our set would look exactly the same as the interior of any hallmark store in a mall.

Then we would shoot for three or four days. It is built on a sound stage for freedom of movement. They could take a section of wall out, or move card aisles because we had them on coasters to roll. This is all done for lighting purposes, and to be able to get the camera in various positions. None of this would be possible if we went to a real store to film.

A typical commercial may take a week to film. This would include a prep day, a pick-up day, with two days of filming and a wrap day. I was making money for the first time. Please allow me to let you in on the insane amount of money you make working on commercials.

First off, commercials pay way more than a movie or T.V. series because a commercial will normally take around a week, maybe two weeks if it is a bigger job. A T.V. series will go for seven or eight months, possibly a bit longer. If it is a movie, it could go for a year or more. This means you are working longer, so the pay rate is much lower.

You want to do at least two commercials a month. So you need to be locked in with the right directors and producers. Over the fourteen years of working art department, I mainly did commercials. That was my bread and butter.

There were a few movies, and lots of music videos. The problem with music videos is that you normally have fourteen to sixteen hour days, and the pay is not good. I tried to stay away from working on them. To give you an idea, here are some salary rates for the commercial Art Department that will blow your mind. Remember these rates are not today's rates, the rates mentioned below are what we were making in the early and late 90's; twenty-five years ago.

- Swingman: $275
- Set Decorator: $400
- Prop Master: $450–$550
- Art Director: $650–$800
- Production Designer: $950–$1100

These rates are based on a ten hour day. After ten, you go to time and a half, and anything after twelve hours is double time. These are American dollars; there are ridiculous amounts of money to be made working on commercials.

I remember propping and doing F/X on a *Gatorade* Commercial with *Michael Jordan* at Raleigh Studios. We had big plexiglass water tanks made for dropping the Gatorade bottles into. An air compressor rig was attached to the bottom of one tank, and it ran up through a hole we drilled to make huge bubbles. There was a perpetual waterfall we made with water running down a glass face so that we could shoot through it. Various watercolors were added to smaller tanks for visual effects and for the product shots.

As I mentioned with the Corn Flakes, every commercial ends with the product shot. Whatever the product may be; it will be sitting there looking perfect. For Gatorade, we had the color corrected plastic Gatorade bottle, made perfect for filming. I would set it on a little turntable, with a Verica to control the speed of the turn, to rotate the bottle.

Now, the crushed ice you always see on the sides of a bottled product in any commercial is done using a product called *Poly Sorb*. It is a powdered substance, that when water is added and mixed, it looks like crushed ice. You stir it up, and then apply it to the sides of the bottle, so it looks cold and frothy. The beauty is that it does not melt under the hot lights. Crushed ice would only last a few seconds before melting and running down the bottle.

The tricky part, you mix water with glycerin and put it into an eye dropper. Then, on cue, the bottle turns very slowly, with the Verica controlling the turn speed. The poly sorb (fake crushed ice) has already been perfectly applied to the bottle. Then you squeeze the eye dropper, so a bead of watered down glycerin runs down the side of the bottle at just the right time.

Everything is controlled, and done perfectly; the time it took to light and set up the product shots for the Gatorade commercial took an entire day. We had a sixteen hour shoot day on Gatorade; I made around $1100.00 in one day after all the over time.

I call the commercial world, *the perfect world* because the sets and products must look perfect to make the sales. Just look at a *Big Mac* or a *Whopper*, or even the bowl of *Corn Flakes*. They all look perfect, ready for the consumer to want to go out and buy. That is what you will notice the next time you watch a Pepsi, coke, or any beer commercial; it looks cold, wet and ready for you to consume. You will always see that little stream of water running down through the fake crushed ice on the side of the product, right on cue.

Making this kind of money, and doing the creative and exciting job of props and F/X; I saw my acting career start to fade away. If we were filming or doing prep work, I would not be able to go out on auditions.

I became comfortable with this, working behind the camera, being busy all the time, and making money. So in the end, I switched from the dream of an acting career, and began a new one, working in the art department doing T.V. commercials.

I want to mention someone who had a huge influence on my life and career. She is an amazing, wonderful, and an incredibly talented woman. I would pretty much spend three years of my life working exclusively with her. You may not know her name, but I can 100% guarantee that you have seen her work many times. Her name is *Peggy Sirota*. She is one of the biggest *Fashion Photographers* and one of the most sought after *Celebrity Photographers* in the world.

Peggy has photographed some of the most famous personalities in the world, including *Steven Spielberg, Madonna, Jack Nicholson, Brad Pitt, Julia Roberts, Harrison Ford, Cameron Diaz, President George W. Bush, Nicole Kidman, George Clooney, Jennifer Aniston, and Tom Cruise.* As well as athletes, *including Michael Jordan, Tom Brady, Tiger Woods, John McEnroe, Sugar Ray Leonard, Dale Earnhardt Jr., Andre Agassi, and Kobe Bryant.* Her portraits have graced the covers, and pages of *GQ, Vanity Fair, Rolling Stone, Esquire, Interview, French Vogue, Italian Vogue, Vogue Bambini* and many others.

Peggy is also one of the most sought after commercial film directors in L.A.; and that was my in. I had been propping for years in the commercial world, and my resume had a few big name Directors on it. I had an appointment set up to meet with Peggy at *H.S.I. productions*, one of the production companies that she frequently worked with. During the meeting, we got along famously. I understood Peggy's vision, and what the look and feel she wanted to attain was.

I ended up working on every commercial Peggy did, and a lot of her photo shoots for three years. I was her favorite Prop and FX man. I was locked in with this incredible talent; working with her would turn out to be an amazing stepping stone for my career. This is a list of some of the commercials and photo shoots I did with Peggy, *Burberry, Gap, Nautica, Barney's, Oscar De La Renta, Banana Republic, Nike, Lucky Brand Jeans, Adidas, Levis, and Neiman Marcus.* Some of the fragrance campaigns include *Clinique, Dove, Lancôme, Maybelline, Revlon, Clairol, L'Oréal,* and *Oil of Olay.* Other advertising clients include *American Express, Kraft, AT&T, Sony Pictures, Apple, Disney,* and automotive clients include *Acura, Mercedes, BMW, GM, Toyota, Buick, Infinity and Chevrolet.*

This is just a small list of the commercials that I did with Peggy. There were many more; she became a very good friend, someone whom I grew very close to. This did not happen very often in my life, but with her it was different.

While working with her, I ended up doing every kind of FX's for filming that you can imagine. She is a fashion photographer at heart, so most commercials we did had that Peggy feel. This means there was pollen, bubbles, smoke, or flower petals always flying through the air. Shooting through different kinds of glass, beveled glass, frosted glass, all for visual FX.

We had rain towers, with rain falling, wind blowing, and plexiglass with water running down, like a perpetual waterfall. There were snow machines with snow falling. Ritter fans are blowing leaves through the air. Speaking of fans, I became the master of working the Re-Fan. It is a very powerful little fan; about two feet round, light, made of plastic, and has a control device on the back so you can vary the speed of the blades.

When you are watching commercials, you will always see the actress, or models hair lightly blowing. Again, this is perfectly planned. Watch for this next time you see a commercial for any fashion product. I did photo and commercial shoots with every top model in the industry. I was the guy in charge of getting their hair to blow just right, running around the model, or actress, and always staying clear of the camera. I would be dancing around with the fan in both hands, blowing their hair, so it flowed ever so nicely.

To be honest, it was a tough job. Peggy would want it to flow a certain way; it could not blow too little, or too much. Plus, the talent was always moving around, so staying out of the shot was at times challenging. In the end, with Peggy at the helm, and me with a Re-Fan, I was able to meet a lot of the top supermodels and actresses on both sides of the industry.

It was always a very creative and exciting job doing props for Peggy. She would come up with ideas on a whim. I would have to figure out a way of doing the effect sometimes on the spot. The biggest commercial I ever did was a car commercial for *Infinity* with Peggy. It took us all over the States.

The filming began in *L.A.* Shooting for three days out on location; we had water trucks, and hoses being used all day, every day. The road in any car commercial will always be wet; yes, a trick of the trade. The road always looks better wet because it highlights the car. The next time you see a car commercial, watch for the road. I guarantee it will have been watered down, and look wet.

One other prop used in all car commercials are fake license plates. You will never see a car commercial with the plates being from a State or Province. My Prop kit, which was extensive, had four huge rolling kit boxes, all on Pneumatic wheels so they could be rolled over all the cables that were strewn across a sound stage floor. There was an onset cart, and two other kit carts; enough to fill a 15ft cube truck. I had an extensive selection of License plates in my kit. I would have them made at an F/X shop, where they could make any type of generic plate I needed.

Some were black with white numbers and letters, and some white with blue numbers and letters. It always depended on the director and agencies decision on what type of plate to put on the car. On this job, with so many cars and locations, we had to use a large variety of plates. Take a look next time you see a car commercial. There will be no expiry tags or identifying States or Provinces on the plate; it will be clean.

After L.A., we made our way to *Las Vegas, Nevada;* we filmed out at the *Hoover Dam.* This was cool because we were filming down at the bottom of the dam. We had access to go into and through the under-belly of the dam while filming. We were the film crew, so we were able to go to places that the tour would never allow others to go.

We then boarded a plane for *New Orleans, Louisiana.* We shot around the French Quarter, and in the downtown core. It happened to be *Mardi gras* when we were there, so we indulged in some of the nighttime debaucheries. After four days of shooting we were back onto another flight, off to *Miami, Florida.* The next day we drove out to the *Keys* and filmed at *Seven Mile Bridge.* Then it was deep into the *bayous,* filming for three days.

The finisher was *Hawaii.* We flew to the *Big Island* and filmed for three days in *Hilo and Kona.* While we were there, one of the locals we hired knew of an inlet where we could go and swim with the dolphins. Being in the ocean after filming all over the states, surrounded by dolphins was an incredible way to end the job. What an experience! It was the job of a lifetime, and I love Peggy.

Alright; so far I have managed to keep the book in somewhat of a chronological order. We have worked our way through my life up till now. In the rest of this chapter and the following three chapters, there will be a lot of jumping around. Remember, I am taking seventeen years living in L.A., and cramming it into six chapters. To be totally honest with you, I could write a book just about my life in L.A.

It will be intriguing, and very interesting, trust me. There will be a mention about some of the celebrities and directors I was blessed enough to have work with. I will continue to include specific things that we did and how they are done. Basically, I will keep letting you in on some of the tricks of the trade.

Let's go big, starting with *Madonna*. I worked with her for two weeks. We were shooting a music video for the *James Bond film, Die another Day*. She was very nice and personable; I spend a lot of time with her on the set. We provided swords and various props for her throughout the shoot.

There was a scene where her stomach gets slashed, and blood comes out. I was applying fake blood to her hands, shirt, and stomach. Madonna was very patient and was even cracking jokes as I applied it. Whenever you see blood in a movie, it will be *Karo syrup*. When it is mixed right, and you add the red coloring, it has the same consistency of blood.

There was also a huge sword fighting scene in the video. We had somewhere around twenty display cases, all made with breakaway glass, or candy glass as it is called, so there was no way Madonna or her stunt double could get cut, or harmed while filming. In the scene, both of them had to fight their way through the museum set. In the shot, they smashed and crashed into the cases, breaking them to pieces. We had double and triplicate cases standing by. After each take, we would clean up all the mess, dress back in new cases, redress the set, and do another take.

The crazy thing is the items in the front display cases, the ones that did not get smashed to pieces, contained props from all the old James Bond movies. We had a shipment sent from *London, England* containing some pretty cool *James Bond gadgets*. Here is a list of some of the original props that I was blessed with handling and being in charge of.

- The Original Golden Gun—The Man with the Golden Gun
- The Bowler Hat—Goldfinger
- Attaché case, Silver Halliburton—Goldfinger

- Pen Gun—Never Say Never Again
- Rolex wrist watch—Never Say never Again
- Fake Faberge Egg—Octopussy
- Spear Gun—Thunderball

What a rush it was, having all these original James Bond props at my disposal. I cannot count the number of crew members that had their pictures taken, holding and standing next to all these James Bond gadgets.

We had a scene where smoke was used for a special shot. Madonna was going to be tortured in an electric chair. In this scene, we needed a stream of smoke that fades away leaving a symbol imprint on the chair. The product we used for the smoke effect is called *A/B smoke*. A symbol was applied to the back of the chair, looking like a tattoo Madonna had on her arm. When the camera is ready, we spray/apply the A part of the liquid to the symbol on the back of the chair where they wanted the smoke to be streaming from. Then on cue, we sprayed the B liquid to the A liquid already on the chair. The reaction of the A/B liquids combined together makes a stream of smoke, eventually dissipating, leaving behind the imprinted symbol; only in Hollywood!

Lastly, there was a huge tank we designed and had built. It contained water for a scene where Madonna is dunked in it, as torture. Inside it, we had huge blocks of ice that were fake. I had the ice made at an F/X house. The blocks were square and smoothed; made from acrylic. When Madonna was dunked into the tank, she would not be cut or harmed by doing the scene. It also prevented the water from getting too cold, so when she was pushed into the water, it was room temperature. If you want to see the music video for *Die Another Day* with *Madonna,* it is on *YouTube.* But wait till you finish this chapter before heading off to watch the video.

Two other celebrities that I worked fairly close with were *Cindy Crawford* and *Jennifer Aniston.* When I say close, I do not mean close friends, but close because I had to load them each up with props for an entire day. First I was doing a *Blockbuster commercial* with *Cindy Crawford.* The scene was her walking up and down the aisles of the store, with a stack of about eight video cases in her arms.

I had three set ups of perfectly stacked videos, all matching exactly the same. I had them stacked and applied together using *Zap a gap,* and *Zip kicker*. Zap a gap is a glue type substance. You apply it, in this instance, to the video case. Then you spray the zip kicker to the zap a gap glue. You can see it crystallize, and harden before your eyes; it will pretty much make anything stick together; another neat little trick. I spent the day chatting with Cindy between takes, putting my stacks of videos into her arms. She was very down to earth, polite and a wonderful lady to work with.

Another job I did was a deodorant commercial to air in Europe. It was for a product called *Lynx* starring *Jennifer Aniston*. I believe it won some award for best commercial in Europe that year. The director's name, *David Kellogg,* and the production company was *Propaganda films*. One scene was in a bedroom set, and Jennifer was ironing clothes on an ironing board. She was made to look like this smoking hot housewife, wearing these little tight white shorts and a dressy blue short top.

I needed to have a perfectly arranged stack of clothes, about two feet high, sitting on the end of the ironing board. They also wanted to have steam coming out from the iron, so the trick used for the steam is *Calcium turnings*. They are jagged silver pellets, and they come in various sizes. I drilled a small hole in the top of the iron, with an opening in a place you could not see. The trick is I dropped some of the pellets into the opening. Then I added hot water; it begins to sizzle, and then steam comes billowing out. The number of pellets determines the amount of steam, so more pellets, more steam, fewer pellets, well you know, less steam.

I spent the day stacking clothes, making irons steam, and hanging around with Miss Aniston, talking between takes. Doing props also means having fake logos and book covers designed. In this case, at the end of the commercial, Jennifer is sitting in bed with a Prop book I designed and had made, that says, *How to keep your man.* The job of prop master includes such a large variety of tasks and skills; doing rigs and special F/X and the infamous Product shots. Once again, you can *YouTube* the *Lynx commercial* with *Jennifer Aniston* and watch it.

Two of the nicest celebrities who I was blessed enough to have worked with in L.A. were *Olivia Newton-John* and *Celine Dion.* It was during this time of my career where I was doing a lot of music videos. One of the music videos was with *Olivia Newton-John*, and the song was called *Falling.*

We had one elaborate set, with huge eight-foot high bay windows. There were long white sheers and curtains flowing from all the openings. We had no glass in any of the windows because we needed to blast air through so the sheers would be blowing in the wind. In videos and commercials glass in windows is rarely used. The main reason is reflections, and secondly in most cases, you would never use glass; plexiglass is easier to install, and it will not break as easily as glass.

We used Ritter fans to keep the wind blowing. They are big fans built on platforms, with four pneumatic tires. On the front extends a long bar, with a handle so you can pull it to the desired location on the set. They have four-foot blades and a control so you can adjust the wind speed to whatever is asked. At top speed, they can do some damage, causing a wind storm if needed. We filmed for two days, and I really had a wonderful time getting to know Olivia. She was an amazing lady. Very personal and she was so pleasant to talk to, and be around. I have attached a picture of myself with her when I was twenty-six.

The other lady who was so nice and polite is *Celine Dion*. How ironic that she is Canadian as well. The video was for her Vegas show

Called *A New Day;* it was to premiere at *Caesars Palace* in *Las Vegas.* This was another elaborate set, with laser lights everywhere; I had smoke and steam coming out from various parts of the set. The steam machines were rented from F/X houses. I would hook a line to it with a water hose, and inside a huge tank heats the water. Then I ran the lines out from the machine to the location I wanted the steam to be coming from. There are four to six outlets for different lines to be run. There is a control valve so I could regulate how much steam I wanted wafting out of each line for the scene.

Steam and smoke are used a lot in music videos and movies. You can always see it streaming out from a manhole cover, or in an alley scene. There is always smoke and steam when you see anything that has to do with New York. Another F/X machine we used for Celine's video is called a *DF50*, a diffusion machine for an atmospheric smoke effect. It is not steam, or smoke, but more of a light haze for ambiance. It is controlled with a remote control. The *DF50* is a black metal rectangular machine about three feet long by two feet high. There is a one by three inch opening at the front of the machine where the haze of smoke streams out from. On top is a 2-inch pin to hook a Re-Fan, as I mentioned earlier, it helps blow the fusion smoke around until there is a light layer of haze filling the set.

You see this light haze of smoke in most Beer commercials when they are filming bar scenes. In pretty much every music video made you will notice the effect. Just watch for it next time you see a music video. We filmed for a week with Celine. There were a variety of props that she had to handle throughout the shoot. I spent a lot of time with her, and we talked quite often on the set between takes.

You will notice that I have talked to many celebrities between takes. That's because doing props; you are always closely involved with the actors. So while you are standing around between takes, and set ups, there is lots of time to have a conversation, and to get acquainted. She was so humble, and down to earth. It was a delight working with Celine, and to have the chance to hear some of her stories. At the end of each shoot day, Celine would go out of her way, walking through the set, thanking individual crew members. This is unheard of! In all my years of working, there was no celebrity who would walk around the set during the wrap and thank crew members personally. She had to be Canadian!

The twins, *Dylan and Cole Sprouse,* had their big breakthrough in the film *Big Daddy* with *Adam Sandler.* The poster for the movie was Adam and Dylan standing together, taking a pee up against a door. Dylan and Cole went on to do the Disney T.V. series called *The Suite Life of Zack and Cody.* This show skyrocketed the boys to superstardom.

I am talking about the twins because before the Disney series; they did a movie called *Just for Kicks.* It was a soccer movie that I prop mastered. My good friend Mike, whom I mentioned earlier, the friend who asked me to be a P.A. on the Snuggles commercial, was the Art Director. It was a fun shoot, and during the two months of filming, I became very close with the boys and their mother/manager Melanie.

When we were getting close to the end of filming the movie, Melanie approached me and asked if I wanted to move to New York and work with the boys on a new series they were about to begin filming. I felt so blessed and honored that she would ask me to go to New York to work with boys. At that time in my life, I had a house with Jenell, and we were expecting a baby. I declined the invitation, but if it were not for Jenell and Alyssa, I would have been on a plane and off to New York.

NBC Promos; I was fortunate enough in the 90's, to do the promos for the NBC fall lineup. The best way to explain it is when you are watching T.V., and you see the cast of a T.V. show standing their kind of doing that T.V. pose. Then, at the end it says *Tonight on NBC,* ending with the name of the show. Well, that is what the promos are.

We filmed for three days at the *Howard Hughes Hangars* in *Playa Vista,* which is located next to *Marina Del Rey.* The hangars are huge; you need a golf cart to get from one end to the other. Or it is a real long walk. The hangars were originally used to build *The H-4 Hercules,* also known as *The Spruce Goose.* It is now used to shoot commercials, T.V. shows, and a lot of movies. The movie *Men in Black* was filmed at the hangars, along with many others.

We had a large number of sets built, or vignettes for each show that would come through over the three day period. There were etched glass acrylic signs, with the NBC logo embedded on them. As well as projected, superimposed, kind of subliminal messages projecting the NBC logo onto set walls or onto the various backdrops we used. We would have each vignette ready to film the cast when they showed up. Let me explain how it worked.

The cast of *Friends* would show up, and we would film them in front of a set that was designed for that particular show. Then we would film the cast of *Just Shoot Me, Seinfeld, E.R, Law and Order* and *3rd Rock*. I could continue on and on with the whole NBC lineup for that season, but I am sure you get the idea. All the cast members, of all the shows on NBC, came by the stages for three days. So, I was able to meet briefly with all the cast members, of every show on NBC at the Howard Hughes Hangars in L.A.

I have been covering a lot of my career working behind the scenes, doing props, and SP/FX. On the next three pages, I have attached my Property Master Bio, a Resume, along with a newspaper clipping. On the resume, there are only the pertinent Directors and Commercials that I worked on. If I were to put all the commercials I have done, it would take pages to list them all.

DWAYNE HIGGINS

PROPERTY MASTER

BIOGRAPHY

DWAYNE HIGGINS is a Canadian citizen; he has worked in the entertainment industry in Los Angeles for 15 years. While he has worked on feature films, and TV shows, the wealth of his experience is in the commercial industry.

Dwayne has worked with some of the biggest Directors in Hollywood, which include, David Lynch (at Asymmetrical Productions) Tony Scott (at RSA Productions) Dominic Sena, (Gone in 60 Seconds) Michael Bay (Transformers), David Fincher (Fight Club). He has also worked with Madonna on her video "Die Another Day" for the James Bond film and with Celine Dion on the video for her Las Vegas show.

DWAYNE HIGGINS

ART DIRECTOR · PROP MASTER · SP/FX

COMMERCIALS	PRODUCTION COMPANY	DIRECTORS
Pepsi	Radical Media	Anthony Hoffman
MCI	Radical Media	Anthony Hoffman
AT&T	Propaganda Films	Dominic Sena
Olympus	Propaganda Films	Dominic Sena
Mercedes Benz	HSI Productions	Peggy Sirota
Coca Cola	HSI Productions	Peggy Sirota
Gatorade	HSI Productions	Peggy Sirota
Snickers	A&R Group	Steve Purcell
McDonalds	A&R Group	Steve Purcell
Saturn	A&R Group	Steve Purcell
Blue Cross	Tony Kay Films	Tony Kay
Budweiser	Tony Kay Films	Tony Kay
Dow Chemical	Incognito	Barry Young
Healthy Choice	Incognito	Barry Young
Saturday Night Live	NBC 2000 Promo	Mark Bennett
K-Mart "Sammy Sosa"	Phoenix Pictures	Alex Herron
Sony Playstation	Phoenix Pictures	Alex Herron
Olivia Newton-John Video "Falling"	Universal Music Enterprises	Alan Metter
Blink 182 Video	HSI Productions	Sam Bayer

COMMERCIALS	PRODUCTION COMPANY	DIRECTORS
Clear Blue Easy	Asymmetrical Productions	David Lynch
Sci-Fi Networks	Asymmetrical Productions	David Lynch
Madonna Video "Die Another Day"	Maverick Records	Gerry Rose
Celine Dion Video "Vegas Show"	Cesar's Corporation	Arthur Pen
Lynx "Jennifer Aniston"	Propaganda Films	David Kellog
Duracell campaign	Propaganda Films	David Kellog
Fosters Berr	Propaganda Films	David Kellog
Levi's "Elevator"	Anonymous Content	Michael Bay
Lexus "Skid"	Anonymous Content	Michael Bay
Nike "Marion Jones," "Mark McGuire"	HSI Productions	Johan Renick
Coca Cola	Propaganda Films	David Fincher
Coors Lite	HSI Productions	Sam Bayer
Travel Association of America	HSI Productions	Sam Bayer
Saturn	Palomar Pictures	Neil Abramson
North West Airlines	Palomar Pictures	Neil Abramson
Snapple	Headquarters	Joe Public
KIA	Headquarters	Joe Public
AT&T	Red Dog Films	Marc Chiat
TWA	Red Dog Films	Marc Chiat
Magnavox	Giraldi/Suarez	Bob Giraldi

BEHIND THE SCENES

Ex-Red Deer man a props master for some of Hollywood's biggest stars

By PENNY CASTER
Advocate staff

When you see Madonna's next video, check out the blood on her hands and shoulders.

The fake blood was mixed and applied by former Red Deer resident Dwayne Higgins, who headed for the bright lights in search of fame and fortune at the age of 18.

He's now a props master, and the fake blood thing he did for the video Madonna made to go along with the latest James Bond release is probably among the simplest things he does in his job.

When Hollywood directors need smoke, steam, explosions, gore, or you name it, Higgins can supply it.

Now 36, he headed for the bright lights soon after graduating from Lindsay Thurber Comprehensive High School.

He'd done some radio work in Red Deer before leaving and hoped to make it to the silver screen as an actor.

Five years later, after stints in various commercials, three months on Days of Our Lives and a couple of low-budget movies, a friend asked if he wanted to be a production assistant.

That's about the lowest job in the whole Hollywood hierarchy, says Higgins during an animated phone call from his Los Angeles home.

"You are a slave."

But a paid slave, and it was work, so he did it, beginning with a Snuggles fabric softener commercial.

One day he was told to help the art

department — in movies or commercials, that's the department that creates a 1950s kitchen, or whatever the director dreams of.

He spent the next four years working for that particular art director.

Then, gradually, he moved up the ladder doing the many behind-the-scenes tasks that are transparent to the viewer of the finished product yet vital to its success.

Eventually, Higgins branched off to become a props master.

Sometimes he works alone, sometimes he calls in others and directs his own team.

No matter what he's asked to do, the golden rule is never say "No, it can't be done."

"Say, 'Sure,'" says Higgins. "Even if you think there's no way it can be done. Then you walk away and think, OK, how are we going to do this."

A V-8 Juice commercial he worked on created a tricky problem. He had already orchestrated a huge vat of swirling V-8 juice, but the director decided he wanted the camera to zero in on a bottle of the stuff, have it tip, then film the bottle neck, then cut to the swirling vat.

But it didn't work thanks to camera shake.

So Higgins suggested bringing the V-8 Juice to the camera. A doweling rail was built.

Then Higgins and an assistant pushed another piece of dowel through two holes drilled in the bottom of the jar, and working in tandem, pushed it towards the camera, and at just the right moment, tipped it.

Dwayne Higgins with his daughter Alyssa: tries to avoid the star scene

Photo contributed

Thanks to the magic of green screen technique, the "contents" were added later.

Green screen, like blue screen, means items are filmed with a blank background, then things can be added. It was used extensively in Forrest Gump.

Companies whose products Higgins has helped make commercials for include Banana Republic, Mercedes Benz, Chevrolet and Nike.

Many big-name movie directors also make commercials, says Higgins. "Because they make $10,000 to $15,000 a day."

He's worked with several major di-

rectors, including David Lynch.

Among the celebrities he's brushed shoulders with at work are Crystal Gayle and Olivia Newton-John.

His most recent encounter was with Madonna.

He had to apply, clean off, and reapply the blood-like concoction on the star several times as scenes were shot and reshot.

One day she turned up on the set with both her children and a trio of nannies.

But this is Hollywood and there is a downside to the glamour.

Please see SCENES on Page A2

I could continue writing for days, page after page, listing celebrities I have done commercials and music videos with. But, I want to move on to some of the directors I was fortunate enough to have worked with. I would like to begin with an incredible director, *David Lynch*; he is a genius and a multi-talented man.

David was nominated for three Academy Awards; he is recognized, and famous for directing such movies as *The Elephant Man, Dune,* and *Blue Velvet*. He also directed the T.V. series *Twin Peaks,* and *Mulholland Drive*. As I mentioned before, most big directors also do commercials, and most have their own production companies. David's Company was *Asymmetrical productions*.

I was introduced to David and he hired me on to do a *Clear Blue Easy* commercial with him. It was a three-day shoot, with some intricate props and F/X involved. David did not like having meetings at the production company; instead, he preferred meeting at his home on *Nicholas Canyon Road* in the *Hollywood Hills*.

In the mornings, I would drive up to David's house to have coffee and meet with him. He walked me through his amazing art studio where he created some very dark pieces of work. He also had a sculpting studio and a huge workshop. We would go over all the details of the job, talk for a while about life and art; then I would be off to prep and find what David requested for the job.

When the commercial was coming to the end of filming, David asked if I would continue working with him, to do a special for the Sci-Fi Network. Of course, I said yes, very enthusiastically. I mean this was David Lynch asking me to do another job with him. This time, we had to have a huge meeting with all the executives from the Sci-Fi Network. It was fairly funny; I will explain. The meeting was at their head office on *Sunset Blvd*.

There must have been fifteen people from the network, all honoring, and almost worshipping David, because he decided to direct this special for them. Here I was with David, representing his production company at this huge meeting. David was so nonchalant about the whole thing, sitting there smoking his cigarettes, and ashing them out onto his finished plate of cold cuts and fruit. I know he knew the whole concept, and how he would do the project already in his head. Really, there was no need for the meeting. I believe he decided to go to appease the network. It was quite an experience.

We filmed for almost two weeks on a sound stage in Hollywood. It was a very intense job; David always had an idea and a way he wanted things to be done. In the commercial world, there is never a No, or I can't do it; it is a Yes. You better figure out how to do the rig, or F/X just the way the director wants it; when they want it.

It was a challenge, and challenge is good. I just loved working with David. The D.P. or Cinematographer he used was *Peter Deming*. He is known for his work on the *Austin Powers* movies. We became pretty good buddies over the weeks I spent working with him and David. When we were finishing up the Sci-Fi special, Peter came up to me and said he had talked with David. They wanted me to go to New York the following month to work on another project they were doing. I was honored.

I mean really, how awesome was that! The bad news is I was already booked to go to *Shreveport, Louisiana* the next month to Art Direct a music video for *Kenny Wayne Sheppard*. He is a famous blues/rock musician, so I had to decline the offer to go to New York. Once again N.Y. was calling, and once again, I could not make it. I would eventually make it to N. Y. three times, but it was never for work.

Tony Scott was another incredibly famous director who I worked with. If you don't know his name, these are a few movies he has directed; *Top Gun, Days of Thunder*, both with *Tom Cruise, Beverly Hills Cop II and Enemy of the State*, with *Will Smith*. Tony's brother is *Ridley Scott*; he directed *Gladiator, Alien, Thelma & Louise* and most recently *Prometheus*. Their production company is called *R.S.A. Productions*; Ridley originally started the company to film Commercials.

I did three jobs with Tony Scott. One was a *Miller Beer* commercial, which we shot out in Death Valley. We were in the middle of the desert, and it was very hot filming in 100 plus degree temperatures. I also did a *Marlboro* commercial with Tony that was shot in Utah; and a commercial for *Coca-Cola*.

Tony was an amazing man, with an Einstein touch about him. He wore the same outfit every day; a pair of white tennis shoes, a faded reddish pair of shorts, white Tee shirt and a Kaki colored camera vest. He was by far the most adventurous directors whom I worked with. The sad news is on the 19th of August 2012 he committed suicide. Tony jumped off *The Vincent Thomas Bridge* in *San Pedro*, in the port district of Los Angeles. It was later mentioned in an interview with his brother Ridley that Tony had been fighting a lengthy battle with cancer.

The directors I have been mentioning are all big time Hollywood directors, doing commercials in their off time from filming movies. I want to end with two other directors whom I did some commercials with.

First is *Dominic Sena;* he directed *Swordfish,* starring *John Travolta* and *Halle Berry,* and he also did *Gone in 60 Seconds,* starring *Angelina Jolie* and *Nicolas Cage.* I did three commercials with Dominic. The first was a *Budweiser Beer* commercial that we shot up in Santa Cruz, Northern California. The other two were a *Pepsi* commercial and a *Saturn Car* commercial.

Many years later, when I was living in Vancouver, I sent out resumes looking for work. Within days, I was getting calls. The job I took was for a *Marie Calendars* commercial. The Producer told me that he hired me because I had Dominic's name on my resume. He said if you have worked with Dominic, then you are definitely skilled enough to work for me.

The other director is *Tony Kaye,* best known for *American History X* starring *Edward Norton.* He also won a Grammy Award for the music video *Runaway train* by *Soul Asylum;* Tony is a *six-time Grammy nominated* music video director.

I did two commercials with Tony; a *Blue Cross* Commercial, which we filmed in Malibu the day after the fires ravaged the city. We were filming at different locations where the fires were burning the night before. There was still smoldering ashes covering the ground. This was as real as it could get; especially for a Blue Cross commercial.

The second commercial I did with him was for *Lexus.* We filmed Downtown L.A.; and yes the streets were watered down, and the generic license plates were put on. I just want to add that out of all the directors I worked with, Tony would have been, well, let's say, Unique. He was definitely someone who was in their own world, and a bit out there, in a very artistic way. There is only one *Tony Kaye.*

I would like to finish off with a *Cinematographer/ D.P.* named *Janus Kaminski.* He was a person whom I had grown close to and someone who became a very good friend of mine. Janus is one of the best Cinematographers in the world. He is *Steven Spielberg's* D.P. and has won an *Academy Award* for both *Schindler's list* and *Saving Private Ryan.* He has also been nominated another four times, for other Spielberg movies he has done.

I met Janus while I was working on a *Duracell* commercial with *Propaganda Films*, and *David Kellogg* was the *Director*. I had previously worked with David on the *Lynx* commercial with *Jennifer Aniston*. Janus worked with David all the time. If he was not working on a Spielberg movie, he was doing commercials with David. He is another one of the top Commercial directors in L.A.; I worked with him for about two years. It was a learning experience; we did some big budget commercials over the years.

We also did all the *Duracell* commercials over that two-year period for the *Robot family Campaign*; I believe we did six spots. I don't know if you remember the commercials? There is the Mom, Dad, the young boy, and girl. They would be in makeup for six hours to achieve the robotic look for the commercial.

We were filming in Malibu on a job, and everyone had to get into Zodiacs to get out to the barge we were filming on. They loaded up the Robot family onto one of the zodiacs, and after their six hours in make-up, you will never guess what happened? A huge wave came in, and it tipped the boat over. They all fell into the ocean.

This was not good. The crew was on the barge ready to shoot, Janus had the lighting perfect, and the camera was in place. There was nothing we could do till they went back into make-up. It was a very long shoot day. The hair and clothes were made of some high-tech NASA plastic that was attached to their bodies. When people see the commercials, they don't see they are real people. Go to *youtube,* enter *(Duracell Robot Commercial)* and you will see what I am trying to explain.

I must have done twenty plus commercials with Janus, and we became very good friends over the years. He was married to the actress *Holly Hunter*. She would come by the set to visit all the time. Holly is another very bubbly, down to earth person. Unfortunately, they are a rare breed in the business; too much ego and pride with most of the famous people I have met; but Holly was a little angel.

Through my relationship with Janus, I was able to meet a couple of other celebrities you may know. I was doing an *M&M* commercial on the sound stages at *20th Century Fox*. Janus was working on another stage filming the movie *Jerry Maguire*. I was done shooting that day; so I stopped by the set to visit.

While they were on a break from filming, Janus introduced me to *Tom Cruise*. I was able to spend about fifteen minutes talking with Tom. It was pretty cool, hanging out, chatting, and spending a little time with another mega-star. He is not as tall as you may think!

One other time, ironically on the back lot of *20th Century Fox*, Janus was working on *Jurassic Park*. The scene was where a truck is hanging over a cliff. In actuality, they had a huge crane holding the truck, using the side of a three-story parking structure as the cliff. They had long green vines dangling all down the side of the structure. Then using *Green Screen* they would superimpose the side of the cliff they were trying to replicate.

I was working on a commercial, and once again, after I was done for the day I strolled over to their elaborate set for a visit and to say Hi to Janus. This time, I had the chance to meet *Steven Spielberg* and his executive producer *Kathleen Kennedy*. There I was, in the midst of Hollywood royalty, on the set of Jurassic Park!

At the time, it was pretty cool. As I think back, they are just people. People like you and me, making a living, surviving here on God's green earth. This goes for everyone I have mentioned in the last two chapters. Yes, it is Hollywood, and the celebrities and directors I have mentioned are put on a pedestal by society, as though they live this amazing, perfect life; No. They live a life just like you and me. It was an amazing experience. It was part of my life, and it was a life that many people will never live. Working with the top directors and celebrities in Hollywood was just part of my job.

What it boils down to; no matter who I worked with, or how famous a person was, to me I was just working on another movie set, doing my job. At the end of the day, I went home, just like the rest of the crew and the celebrities who I was working with. The time has come, let's get into the party mode because that is the next part of my life.

CHAPTER 6

L.A.—Stories

THIS CHAPTER WILL cover the partying, celebrities I partied with, and places I traveled to while living in L.A., I believe the only way to begin is with my one and only best friend, *Glenn Quinn*. He was the boyfriend on the T.V. show *Rosanne* and played *Doyle* on the T.V. show, *Angel*. He was the only person out of every "want to be actor" that I knew whoever made it. Before we get going, you can *Google Glenn Quinn*, and click on images; you may know him?

A lot of this chapter has to do with Glenn since he was on the top rated T.V. show in the late 80's early 90's. He was invited to attend many Hollywood events. Glenn and I were best friends, so he would always invite me along with him to all the parties. I knew him long before he ever made it as an actor. I remember back when he was waiting tables at a restaurant called *Jerry's Deli* in the valley. He would come home with 5-10 steaks, all hidden and jammed into his pants; stolen from Jerry's. I lived with Glenn on two occasions, once in a house in the Valley, with four other struggling actors. The second time was after he had made it and was working on Rosanne. We lived in a nice place just off Sunset Blvd, across the street from The Guitar Center.

I need to restate it again, he was the only best friend I had, or would ever have. You know my upbringing, so you understand why I never allowed myself to get attached to anyone. After Glenn, until today, I have not had anyone remotely as close to me as he was. The reason is simple; my best friend died in my apartment many years later. I don't want to feel that hurt, pain and emotional distress ever again. I had to endure all of those emotions and feelings after Glenn's passing. I will get to that part of the story in the next chapter. It breaks my heart as I write this, but for now, we need to keep pushing forward. Let's re- live all the fond memories I had with my best friend.

We went to New York twice, both times it was during the Christmas holidays, and each trip was a bit of a blur. We had a lot of fun, went to the top night clubs in New York, and did a lot of cocaine. One year we stayed at an older hotel, just off Columbus Circle. Glenn loved the movie *Goodfellas*, and they had filmed a few scenes of the movie at the hotel, so he wanted to stay there.

One night, we arrived back around 2:00 am and the bar in the lobby of the hotel was deserted. It was open, but no one was working. I had the bright idea that we should go pour ourselves a few drinks. So we went to the bar, Glenn sat down, and I bartended. The next thing you know, *Brian Setzer* walked in and decided to join us. He was the lead singer from the band *The Stray Cats*, a very popular rockabilly band in the 80's. You may remember the song *Stray Cat Strut*? He now has a band called *The Brian Setzer Orchestra*. He sat with us for an hour or two, drinking and having a good ole time. No one from the hotel ever showed up, so after a fun filled night with Brian Setzer, we headed to our room, it was off to bed.

On our second trip to New York, we went to the village one night, up to *Sarah Gilbert's* apartment. Sarah played one of the daughters on *Rosanne*. There were a bunch of people there, but one guy in particular that Glenn and I hung out with was *David Blaine*. He is a very famous *magician/illusionist*. I am sure you saw him when he stood on top of a 100 ft. pole in the middle of New York, or possibly when he was suspended in a plexiglass box above the Hudson River?

We all ended up going to a night club in Manhattan, and later that evening, someone whom we will call anonymous, gave Glenn and I some very strong Morphine pills. I had never done them before, nor had Glenn. It would be a little later in life when we would dive into the world of opiates. But for now, we were let's say inexperienced. So we took the pills, and I want to say we had a great time with everyone, dancing, and enjoying what New York had to offer. No; this was not the case.

We ended up going back to our hotel room. The both of us were so sick that we puked up yellow phlegm all night long. We vomited for hours, one after another; Glenn would run into the bathroom, and pray to the porcelain god. Then I would run in, and do the same, this went on for what felt like an eternity. It was one of the worst nights of my life as far as I can remember.

The suffering and the physical pain caused because of those morphine pills; it was not worth it, and I wished we had never touched the stuff. It was a life lesson, but being an addict, it would not be long until I would forget our gruesome night in New York. We would return to what I want to call, Satan's poison, or Opiates. I am an addict, and my brain does not want to remember evenings like that one.

My brain wants to experiment; my addiction wants to do whatever it can to numb the pain; and suffer the consequences later. In the life of an addict, we act on impulse, not understanding our choices. We don't look that far ahead; it is always about the here and now. It would take a lot of time until I came to the understanding that in the end, the opiates or whatever drug it may be, will ruin you, or kill you. This is real, as you will soon see.

At the time, back in L.A., I was living with an amazingly intelligent supermodel named Gina. It was a platonic relationship. I lived with her for two years, first in Hollywood, and then we moved to Santa Monica. One beautiful sunny day, Gina, Glenn, and I were all on the roof of our apartment in Hollywood, hanging out at the pool. This was one of the biggest days in Glenn's life.

He received a page from his agent because there were no cell phones back then. Everyone had pagers in those days. So Glenn made his way downstairs to return the call. When he came back up to the roof, he had the biggest smile on his face. He yelled out with great joy that he had just booked *Rosanne*. Of course we did what we did best, we all went out and partied into the wee hours, celebrating my best friends amazing achievement. Glenn had landed a recurring role, on one of the top T.V. shows running at the time.

Since I am on the topic of Gina and partying, I need to bring my friend Mike back into the picture. He was the one that introduced me to her, and he hooked me up on that Snuggles commercial, which opened the door into the film business for me. The three of us were inseparable for many years; we did everything together. We went shopping on *Melrose Ave*, went to clubs, and we went to *Lake Tahoe*, twice. Each trip was during the Christmas/New Year's holiday season, staying at Gina's parent's condo. It was like the old T.V. show, *Threes Company*. We were always together, going to the beach, BBQ's every Sunday night with a group of friends at our place. They were some of the best times I had during my stay in L.A.

I need to mention the *1989 MTV Video Music Awards* that were held in L.A. that year. Mike just happened to be dating one of the top executives at MTV during the time the awards show rolled into town. We called it *MTV Week*. The three of us and Mikes girlfriend went to all the events and functions that were held all over the city promoting the Awards.

The big bonus was that we went to the *MTV Awards*, which happened to fall on my birthday. What a B-day present, to go to the Awards. Since Mike was dating (Anonymous), we were able to VIP our way into all the parties. One night we went to a gathering of around a hundred and fifty people, a pre-awards party held at a small club on Sunset Blvd. This is a small list of the celebrities whom we were rubbing shoulder with all night, *Arsenio Hall*, who hosted the awards that year, *Guns N' Roses, Aerosmith, Paula Abdul, Metallica, George Michaels, Lenny Kravitz* and *Jon Bon Jovi*.

I can go on, listing some other bands, and celebrities, but, once again, I am sure you get the idea. It was a small club, with a limited number of guests, so everyone was hanging out, drinking and socializing. It was through Mike's girlfriend, who knew all these people; that we were able to attend the event and meet pretty much all of the above names listed. Yes, this was definitely a night in my life where I was, let's say, *living the Hollywood Dream*.

As I write about certain events in the book, it will sometimes trigger other events where I spent some time with a celebrity. This time, it was the mentioning of *Jon Bon Jovi*, from the MTV party. Everyone knows who Jon Bon Jovi is, so I believe there is no need to explain. One year there was a birthday party for one of the top music video directors at the time, and the production company was called *The Company*.

They produced music videos for most of the top performers in L.A. It was a small party, and my friend Larry was a producer at The Company. He invited me to attend, and there were around sixty people, drinking and celebrating. They had the director sit in a chair in the middle of the room. It was time for the grand event, the surprise; a 300 lb stripper came out, and started her show, dancing around the poor director stuck sitting there.

I was a bit revolted by it all, so I decided to take a walk over to the empty bar and get a drink. There I was, hiding out in the bar until the show was over. Well someone else felt the same way I did. He walked up beside me, and we both started talking about how wrong the whole thing was. This person was none other than *Jon Bon Jovi*. The Company had done a music video for him, and he was friends with the director.

We must have stood there, out of sight from the main event, talking for around ten minutes. We talked about not really wanting to see any of the performance by our dearly beloved stripper. None the less, there I was, hanging out for a bit with Jon Bon Jovi. It was just another night in Hollywood.

After Glenn was on Rosanne for a while, I would go to the set and visit; sometimes we would meet for lunch. There were a lot of times I would go to the Thursday night tapings. Most sitcoms are filmed before a live studio audience. They rehearse for the week, and then on a specific night, they tape the show with an audience.

I was able to meet *Rosanne* and *Tom Arnold* on numerous occasions. The first time I walked onto the set, I remember Rosanne yelling, "who are you, and why are you on my set." Thank God Glenn was close by and said I was a friend of his coming by for a visit. When she heard the news, she calmed down and came up to me introducing her, and Tom. Let's just say they were an interesting couple, and we will leave it at that.

I would sometimes go watch the live taping, and then after the show was done, we would go hang out with *John Goodman* in his dressing room. At times, there were other cast members, and friends, partying into the wee hours. Over the years, because of Glenn, I was able to get to know John fairly well. He was polite and very fun to be around. John played Rosanne's husband on the show, and he has been in many movies that you may have seen. Sometimes after the taping of the show, the entire cast and crew would go out to a local bar, not too far from the studios and party.

One night at one of these events (wrap parties) I was introduced to the assistant director of the show. She was a wonderful and very attractive woman. We spent a lot of time together. After the wrap party, we all went to *Johnnie Galecki's* apartment. I knew him very well through Glenn. *Johnnie* is now on the *Big Bang Theory*, and he played *Sarah Gilberts* boyfriend on Rosanne.

I was a little drunk at his place, and Johnnie and I got into a bit of a tiff. The reason is something I do not want to get into detail about. It did not end up so well. We had an argument, and I walked down his hallway and punched a hole through the wall. Johnnie was very upset, and he kicked me out of his place. A few weeks later, I saw him again after a taping, and we ironed everything out. Forgiveness is a beautiful thing, and we continued to remain friends.

Another lady I became very good friends with from the show was *Sarah Chalke*. She took over *Becky's* role on the show and was basically called the *New Becky*. You may know Sarah from the T.V. show *Scrubs;* she played *Dr. Elliot Reid*. One night I was taking her to go see *Cirque Du Soleil*, in Santa Monica. Earlier that day, I brought my new Black Supra to Circuit City, to have a stereo put in.

Cirque Du Soleil was performing *Algeria* that night. We attended the performance, and after watching an amazing show, we strolled out to my car to drive home. When we opened the doors, we were hit with the wretched fumes of gasoline. The whole inside of the car reeked with the odor of it. I mean real bad. When the stereo was being installed; they accidentally drilled into the gas tank puncturing it. The drive home was all about windows being rolled down, and heads hanging out the open windows. We laughed about it later, but at the time it was rough. Sarah was always in good spirits, a very down to earth Canadian girl, from Vancouver. We were just friends; we hung out but never dated.

More adventures with Glenn. One year he was racing in the celebrity part of the Long Beach Grand Prix. Each year before the Grand Prix, they have a race, with 8-10 various celebrities. A week before, they go to the track and practice every day. I went with Glenn one day to hang out and watch them practice.

When we arrived and were pulling into the parking lot, there stood *Cameron Diaz*, standing in front of her new Mercedes crying. You may know her from the *Charlie's Angel's* movies. At the time, she was just beginning her career. She was starring with *Jim Carrey*, filming *The Mask*. We walked up to Cameron, and consoled her, speaking words of wisdom, trying to comfort her. I cannot let you know why she was crying; that's beside the point. In the end, we were all laughing, and smiling; it was a beautiful day.

When the day of practice came to an end, Glenn and I, along with two other celebrities, went to a club in Long Beach. The two men were *Vince Neil* from the band *Motley Crew,* and *Matt Leblanc* from the T.V. show *Friends*. We were all in this club drinking and having a blast. There were women all around us. I am sitting with Vince Neil talking, when all of a sudden, the music starts to play, and it's Motley Crews hit song *Girls, Girls, Girls*. There I am with Vince Neil, surrounded by a throng of women, and they are playing his song. Let's just end with, it was a good night and we all had a lot of fun. (Allow your imagination to run wild).

During the height of Glenn's career, he was dating *Christina Applegate* from the hit T.V. show *Married with Children*. I meet her on numerous occasions. We would go out to bars and parties, and sometimes Glenn and I would meet her and her friends for lunch. I was also invited to go to her sixteenth birthday party at a very popular hotel on the Sunset strip. There were about fifty people, many who were starring and working on various T.V. shows and movies.

I am leaving them anonymous because later that night cocaine became a big part of the event. It was quite a night, a fun and crazy night. But I do want to be clear that Christina did not do any coke. She and some of her friends just had their drinks and enjoyed the evening without using. Christina was a super nice girl; she had no ego or pride and was a very polite down to earth woman.

Glenn was working on the movie *Shout,* at *Universal studios,* a movie about troubled youth in a boy's home. Again, as always, I went to visit him one day on the set, and there he was my spitting image. You see, when I was waiting tables people always asked me if I was this guy's younger brother. In my acting headshots, I looked like a young John Travolta.

John Travolta was the star of the movie, and when I showed up that day, Mr. Travolta walked up to me, gave me a hug and said I was his brother. Boy did we laugh; I told him that people always told me I was a spitting image of him when he was younger. I stayed for most the day and had lunch with John. We really bonded, and had some good discussions. He said if he was ever doing a movie where they needed to cast a younger version of him, he wanted me to play the role. What an honor, for John Travolta to say he wanted me to play a younger version of himself if a part ever arose in the future.

Heather Graham was the female lead in *Shout*. You may know Heather from the Movie *Boggie Nights*; she played Roller Girl. She also was the female lead in *Austin Powers The spy who Shagged Me*. More recently, Heather was little baby Carlos's mom in *The Hangover* movies. Heather has been in many movies. She also became an acquaintance through my relationship with Glenn.

Another girl Glenn was later dating while we were living together off Sunset Blvd was Aimee. She was the love of his life, and he always had a spot in his heart for her. Aimee is Heather's sister, and Glenn met her while filming *Shout* with Heather. Since I am talking about Heather, it has triggered my memory about two other events that occurred a little later in life.

One event took place while Glenn and I were at one of our regular local watering holes, *The Coach and Horse*. It is a bit of a grungy bar on Sunset Blvd. We were drinking our day away, sitting at our regular booth, and Heather walked in with her then-boyfriend, *James Woods*. You may know James from the movie *John Q* starring *Denzel Washington,* and more recently *White House* starring *Jamie Foxx*.

James Woods has been in tons of movies, and there he was with Heather. They sat with us for the afternoon. Glenn and I drank all day while Heather and James were much more moderate drinkers. It was very interesting, listening to all the Hollywood stories Mr. Woods was sharing with us; another good day in L.A.

Once again my memory kicks in. The mentioning of the movie, *Boogie Nights* reminds me of a Porno star that I was dating. Yes, don't freak out, but I was dating a porn star for a few months. First name *Tianna,* that's all you get. Her big night came, and she was going to the Porno awards at the *Sheraton Universal,* located next to *Universal studios*.

She had been nominated for a few awards, (don't ask me what). I really did not get that involved. Now really, awards show for Porn, how insane is that, what will they think of next? She had her table booked with her other nominated friends for the show, and she wanted me to go with her. Now I know many guys who would give their left arm to go to such an event, but even back then, in my crazy party days, I declined the invitation.

I chose to go downtown L.A., to a club called *Truth*, with a bunch of friends, instead of being Tianna's date for the awards show. Truth is four stories high, and will fit around 2000 people. It was such a cool nightclub because each level had a different theme. The first floor is all Jazz music, with some blues, a dance floor, and a huge round bar. The second level is an empty theater, like a movie theater. It still had all the seats, and the stage, huge red velvet curtains hanging, with balcony seats. It was a place to hang out when you needed a break from the other three floors. It was also the place to sneak away to do your drugs; there were a lot of people doing ecstasy, mushrooms, and of course, cocaine.

The third level was Disco; mirror balls hanging, 70's disco music, and a huge plexiglass dance floor, with lights shining up in all kinds of colors. People all dressed up like John Travolta in Saturday Night fever. It was actually very entertaining and fun. The last floor, the fourth one, was Techno- trance music, and laser lights; it was basically a rave. It had a huge D.J. booth, (my friend Mitch was the D.J) overlooking the dance floor with big red velour couches surrounding the main area. We always ended the night on the fourth floor; it was another place to sit down and trip a bit while doing your drug of choice.

I went with my buddies. We did ecstasy, some cocaine, and we danced and drank the night away. We left the club around 2:00 am. Tianna invited me to come back to her hotel room and meet her after the Porno awards. I did accept this invite, so I showed up to her room around 2:30. I will not go any further indulging any more information.

The next morning, Tianna took me down to *Nina Hartley's* hotel room and introduced me to her. She is the Grandma of Porn. Nina was the actress who played *William H Macy's* wife in the movie *Boogie nights*. Every man who has ever watched porn will know who Nina Hartley is. Even I was impressed to meet the infamous Nina Hartley. When we showed up, she was there with her husband just getting out of bed. We all ended up going out to Malibu to Nina's house. We went horseback riding, a BBQ, and had a very eventful evening.

Home Improvement, the T.V. show starring *Tim Allen*. Another actor I have been told that I looked a lot like. Glenn was invited, and of course, he brought me, his trusty party buddy along. The party was at the *Century City Hotel*, and as usual, Glenn and I had to get primed. We stopped by our grungy hangout, the Coach and Horse on the Sunset strip. The two of us began with whiskey and Jagermeister shots to loosen us up for the party.

We eventually made our way to the wrap party. Of course, we arrived a little late, and a little buzzed from the jaeger shots. As soon as we arrived, we met Tim Allen for a bit and *Patricia Richardson,* who plays his wife. It was not long after being introduced to the rest of the cast that our stop at the Coach and Horse began to affect me. I was beginning to get fairly drunk, and my coordination was a bit off.

It happened right in the middle of the party while strolling along beside the pool with my good friend Glenn. My balance gave way, and into the pool I went. While the party was in full swing, executives and various celebrities scattered about. There was yours truly, being pulled out of the pool by my trusted inebriated friend Glenn.

We never laughed so hard in our lives, and I have to add that we were not the only ones laughing. I believe our laughter began to spread like a contagious virus. People were laughing, instead of being in awe or upset because of the ordeal, they took it light heartedly. In the end, our gut splitting laughter lightened the situation. Glenn and I had to depart the festive event because I was soaked to the bone, dripping wet. I was too buzzed to feel embarrassed, or shameful. To Glenn and me, it was just another night in Hollywood, doing what we loved to do, party and enjoy our lives. The sad thing is in the next three chapters there is no enjoyment in the partying; the end result is devastating and shocking.

Another wrap party we attended was for the T.V. show *Growing Pains* starring *Kirk Cameron*. Once again Glenn and I attended. I must add we were not as primed as we were for the *Home Improvement party*. This party was held at the *Pacific Design Center*, an amazing place located in Hollywood. Things were going well; as usual, we met the cast of the show because Glenn was a bit of a celebrity himself.

So with introductions and meet and greets aside, and after having a few drinks, we made our way to the bathroom. This is where the *"things were going well"* changes. A little guy with long hair shows up in the bathroom; he is a roadie for the band *Metallica*. He calmly asks the two of us if we would like to do a line. Glenn and myself answer with a, we would love to, so he lays out a couple of lines on the beautiful marble counter top.

Up our noses the powder flows. About 1-2 minutes later we come to realize that this was not Cocaine; it was speed/crystal meth. This is bad because I had a 7:00 am crew call for a *Pillsbury Dough Boy* commercial the next morning. Forget about sleep, because it does not take much speed to keep you up for a day or two. We decide to leave the party and go to *Johnnie Galecki's* place to hang out.

Not a wink of sleep, the sun is coming up, and I am on my way to *Paramount studios* where we are filming the Pillsbury commercial. It was one of the worst days of my life, no sleep and a ton of prop rigs that day. The first shot of the day, we had 12 biscuits on a baking tray, and the shot was for the biscuits to be slid down into a basket. The challenge was for one of the biscuits to fly out, and land on a plate with fresh fruit on it, right onto a very specific spot. Are you kidding me!

I took mono/fishing line, and sewed it into a biscuit, and then on cue, I had to pull it at just the right time, so it landed on the plate, in the exact spot. It took a lot of takes until we had it right. I was sitting there under the hot lights, dripping sweat because the speed was still running through my system. Don't forget that I had zero hours sleep the night before.

The actual little dough boy comes in an air compressed case. There is a stand that the body, which is about 5" tall, slides into. I would attach the head to the body, slide it into the stand and presto; there is the dough boy, ready to go to work. I then set him in place next to wherever he should go for the shot. It could be beside a plate of biscuits, or next to the *Hero box*, (you remember what hero means). They later superimpose the figure, so when you see the commercial, it shows him giggling and bending over. Watch the next time you see a Pillsbury commercial.

That was just the first of many prop gags that day; I spent the whole day doing all these effects, and rigs. It was the longest day of my life. We thought it was cocaine, not speed, or I would have never touched the stuff. I have no idea how I made it through that nightmarish day, where once again, I made another bad choice in my life and paid dearly for it.

All right, the last little bit on the Glenn and Dwayne Hollywood saga. I want to wrap up with a quick story about my very first brand new car. It, of course, had to do with my dearest and best friend, Glenn. He had a brand new BMW M5 series from Center BMW in the Valley. I was working, making lots of money, and I never had a brand new car in my life. So I was going to treat myself to something very nice. I was looking at Land Rovers, or maybe a Mercedes wagon. I needed a vehicle with room in the back for props and effects equipment.

Glenn suggested a BMW wagon. He was good friends with the manager at Center, so I went to meet with him. We talked, and I received the best deal ever on a two-year lease for a BMW 5 series wagon. Before my talk with the manager, while we were looking through the lot picking out a car, we ran into *Gene Simmons,* from the band *Kiss.* His wife and former playmate *Shannon Tweed* was also in the market for a new beamer. While I was looking at the selection, Shannon pointed out a black 5 series wagon to me, and in the end, it was the car I ended up getting.

My very first car was an $80,000 BMW 5 series. It was, and has been, the nicest vehicle that I have ever owned in my life. Gene and Shannon were very nice, down to earth, and helpful. I also want to mention that Shannon is Canadian. Imagine that, a Canadian celebrity who is down to earth. What else would you expect?

In some of the stories to come, I will be talking about Jenell and Alyssa. As I have mentioned, the book will be out of chronological order until the beginning of chapter eight. It is there that I will explain the beginnings of our relationship. Let's head to *Stings* house in the *Malibu colony* for 4th of July. Yes, Sting, from the band *The Police*, one of the most successful musicians in the world.

I was with Jenell at the time, and she was working with Tom, the Malibu dentist. I will expand on Tom and his antics in the next chapter. Sting was a client of his, as well as every other celebrity in Malibu. He was invited, so off we went, to Stings house in the colony to celebrate the 4th. His house was like a big yoga studio in Bali, Indonesia. It was two levels, very open with bamboo everywhere, and sheers blowing in all the open windows. He had these incredible wooden planks for the flooring; it was beautiful, the house must have been worth a couple of million dollars, and it was right on the ocean in the Colony.

There were a few other guests at the party, all the clients from the Malibu recovery center *Wavelengths* were there. It is a very expensive place to go to. If you were not really well off, then you would never be able to afford it. I want to mention that this is where Glenn went while he was trying to clean up.

One client, who was there with his ankle bracelet on, was *Robert Downey Jr*, from the *Iron Man movies*. This would have been around the time Robert was going through his addiction to alcohol and crack cocaine. He was sentenced to a three-year stint at *Corcoran State Prison* in California, but he only did a year before being released.

This is another reminder about the effects of drugs and alcohol; addiction is not picky. It will make its way into your family, into your neighbor's family, into your work relations, and even the rich and famous are not immune from addiction. Here is one of the most successful actors in Hollywood, a movie star, who was sentenced to prison, all stemming from addiction.

I am not sure if the prison sentence was after, or before the party at Stings house that day. With all the clients from Wavelength being there it could only mean one thing; a sober party. At this point of my life, I was heavy into my drinking, and smoking weed. I wanted a drink the whole time I was there. My body was screaming for one.

In the depths of my addiction, I went through Stings entire house. While everyone was downstairs, out on the huge wooden deck area, sitting on the beach enjoying the day, I was searching high and low through the house, looking for booze. None was to be found, and it was devastating. I accepted the fact that I would not be able to fill my body with the liquid poison. I decided to accept the fact that there would be no drinking until we left later that day. It becomes a mind game, but I fought the cravings. Eventually, I was able to put my addiction behind me.

Jenell and I spent some time talking with *Robert Downey Jr*. I had a lot to share with him about addiction, and recovery. I had tried to clean up a few times, going in and out of treatment centers. Alyssa was around a year old then, and Robert must have held her in his arms for about an hour, as we all sat around talking. For the remainder of the day, I took my focus off the booze and eventually began to enjoy the company and conversation.

While I was living in L.A., I did a lot of traveling around the world. I would like to share a few stories with you. I will also intertwine some of the women in my life which I dated, and spent time with. Please remember I am jumping around a bit, but we will get back into chronological order in the next few chapters.

Why not start with a famous director's daughter, who I dated for around six months. The wonderful *Sasha*, her father, is *Peter Bogdonavich*, he directed *The Last Picture Show* in 1971, starring *Cybill Shepherd*.

In later years, she became his partner. The film also starred a young *Jeff Bridges*. Peter also directed *Paper Moon* starring *Ryan and Tatum O'Neal* and *What's Up, Doc?* starring *Barbara Streisand*.

Their house was a mansion; right out of the movies. When you see a show, and it is featuring huge mansions in L.A., this would look like one of them. Sasha actually lived in Santa Monica, but we frequented the mansion at times to visit her parents, and sometimes to have dinner. I had an amazing relationship with Sasha, but after the infamous six-month period, she said; "*quit drinking, or the relationship will come to an end.*"

You are going to read the phrase *Six Months* a lot in the remainder of the book. It either signals the beginning of something, or, more often, it will signal the end. As always, I chose the booze, and she left me. This will spin us off to one of my trips I took years later, but trust me; it will tie back in with Sasha.

The trip was to *Costa Rica*, during the Christmas holiday season with Jenell, and my very good friend Christian. In the movie industry everything shuts down around Dec 15- Jan4. This is when most people, including myself, would take the big vacation. We would stay at the best hotels, at the best resorts, and everything would be top of the line. I would drop around Ten thousand dollars for our Christmas and New Year's adventures. There were always travels to exotic and foreign lands.

Costa Rica was definitely a very tropical destination; it had amazing rain forests, beautiful sandy beaches, and an active Volcano in Arenal. Our vacation did not start out all touristy. It started out with cocaine. Since Colombia was only two countries away, coke did come to mind.

The first night in Costa Rica, we went to a local bar and met an American girl who lived there and was the bartender. The conversation leads to finding, and locating cocaine. Well, she knew just how to get it. She made the call, and a gentleman showed up in his car. All three of us hopped in the car and went for a little ride. I was smart enough to bring the American with us; you need to be as safe as you can in third world countries. This definitely applies when you are doing something as stupid as scoring cocaine.

You guessed it. The dealer, and supplier of the coke, was none other than one of the local policemen. He had all the coke. I guess he had a little business set up on the side to make a little extra cash for him. The coke was in these yellow plastic straws. In case you don't know, coke usually comes in a bindle, where a small piece of paper is folded up in a certain way to hold coke. This was new to us all, the straws were around two inches long, and crimped at each end, holding pure Colombian cocaine. There were around twenty of these crimped straws full of coke in a baggie. We asked how much; the price was so low that we bought the whole bag of goodies.

This was not good. We made our purchase; then we were off with one of the locals we had met at the bar. He owned a huge Costa Rican style house, with a massive straw roof. Everything is open air, as any house is in a tropical setting. Bamboo stairs and railings, with ceiling fans everywhere made from banana leaves. When we arrived, it was time to dig into the Colombian coke. The first thing our new friend did was set up a Bunsen burner, like the one in chemistry class. A plate was set on top of a little rack above the flame; then he poured the coke onto the plate. The reason for this was the humidity. It was so humid there that the coke could dissolve.

We did so much coke that night. I can remember being outside his house, standing in a field; in my cocaine haze, there I was, staring at the trillions of stars. Looking up to the skies above Costa Rica, on a crystal clear night. The view of the sky and stars is still embedded in my mind.

We also went to some clubs and beach parties. We did coke for three days straight. On the third day, in unison, we clued in. We all looked at each other, and said, "what are we doing"? We came here for a vacation, not to be high out of our minds for the trip. So we dumped the remainder of the coke into the toilet and actually began to really enjoy all Costa Rica had to offer.

We did not stay in San Jose, the capital of Costa Rica, with millions of people. We had that in L.A.; so we stayed in *Samara*, a small town on the opposite side of the country. Nearing the end of our stay, we made a three-hour drive to Arenal. There is a huge lake that is world famous for windsurfing. The other famous attraction besides the rain forest was the active volcano. At the foot of the volcano, there was a long trail that we could walk along. It was where the run off from the lava flow had taken place a few years earlier when it erupted. We made our way through the rainforest, up to a wooden lookout.

The lookout was not a huge tourist attraction; actually, not a lot of people knew it even existed. The only reason we knew about this little gem was because we brought a local with us we had met in Samara. So we got up onto the wooden platform, it is about 30″ x 30″. As we are admiring the view, I saw three women standing at the other end. I walked over towards them, and when one of them turned around, it was Sasha, my old girlfriend. She explains that earlier that year they were filming the movie *Congo* in and around the area. She had been working on the movie, so she brought some friends from L.A. to see some of the locations. Here I am in the middle of Costa Rica, in the middle of the rain forest, on a little wooden lookout, and who do I run into. Sasha! We really do live in a small world.

Since we are on the topic of a small world, I would like to tell you about two other trips I took. You will see just how small our world really is; as if the Sasha story does not do justice to the small world analogy. A trip to *Moscow, Russia*; the trip was once again during the Christmas break. The reason for this trip was because of an amazingly hot Russian girl, whom I meet on the boardwalk rollerblading in Santa Monica.

Her name is Sveta. We met about eight months prior to the trip. We dated, and she eventually moved in with me for around six months. I brought her with me to work a few times so she could get the experience of being on a movie set with all the people, lights, cameras, and the energy you feel when working with a film crew on a Hollywood movie set. I thrived on this energy, walking onto a huge sound stage for work; there is no feeling like it.

Again, my drinking was a problem, and Sveta asked me to stop drinking, or she would leave. My addiction was so strong that I would once again choose the bottle. This was a recurring issue with 99% of the women I dated. She went back to Russia, but over time, we rekindled the relationship. I told her that I would love to fly to Moscow for two weeks and see her again. She was happy and excited about the concept of a visit. So, it was off to Russia for a Christmas vacation.

I brought my travel partner Christian with me. You may remember him from the *Costa Rica trip*. We had previously taken a few trips to *New York* together so this would be my fourth adventure with Christian. His Father is known as *Drew*. He designed the movie poster for the original *Star Wars* movie. His other works include *Indiana Jones, Back to the Future, Rambo,* and many more. He also designed the original *Industrial Light & Magic* logo for George Lucas's company.

When a movie studio has completed a film project, they will hire out a company to design the film posters, billboards, and the trailers. A trailer is the previews that you see on T.V., or in the movie theaters before it gets released. The studios do not do this in-house, but rather hire outside companies. Christian now has his own company in Hollywood, doing design work for the movie studios. I must say he is very successful.

O.K, sorry to side track a bit there but let's get back to our trip to Russia. It was just the two of us, on a plane, going to see my Sveta and the very cultural city of Moscow. Money was not an issue, so we stayed at *The Hotel National*, just of *The Red Square*. The National was simply a beautiful four-star place to spend our vacation. It was a touristy trip; we were interested in seeing some of the spectacular attractions Moscow had to offer.

I tried to stay sober in Moscow, but they have vending machines where you get a plastic sealed cup full of vodka and another cup containing orange juice, out of a vending machine. Are you kidding me. What help was that? My attempt at a somewhat sober vacation failed. I did O.K. until the last few days. But for the first week and a half, we filled our days and nights hitting the city, enjoying all it had to offer.

Our first night was spent at the world famous *Bolshoi Theater*, a 17th-century building which has been restored. It is famous for operas, and the Russian Ballet company performs there. We had a balcony seat which was breathtaking, rich red velvet curtains surrounded the place, and the inside was restored with original Imperial décor. We attended the opera that evening, and I want to say that I am not an opera guy. It was the experience of a lifetime, to actually be sitting on the balconies of the Bolshoi Theater watching an opera.

We spent a few days walking through the *Red Square*, which was originally designed for ceremonies, and occasionally used for the coronation of *Russian Tsars*. Also located in the Red Square is *The Kremlin*, a fortified complex in the heart of Moscow. It is the official residence of the President of the Russian Federation.

One other thing I do not want to forget, is another structure located in the Red Square, *Saint Basil's Cathedral,* which is now a Museum. The church was originally built around 1558, on orders from *Ivan the Terrible.* It has eight side churches that surround the central core. The architectural means of exterior decoration, and the elaborately sculptured sacred symbols and ornaments are hard to put into words. You will have to *Google* it to really understand.

Also while on our vacation, we attended the famous *Moscow Circus*. There are two buildings with various acts; one building has animals, like an old style circus. The second is more about acrobatics, and trapeze artists, sort of a Cirque Du Soleil type of show.

New Year's Eve was coming upon us, and we were truly blessed. While in the very ornate hotel bar, at the National, we met a Canadian man who owned a night club. It was called *The Hungry Duck*, and he gave us V.I.P. passes to his club for the New Year's Eve celebration. There were hundreds of people partying. and the place was full of unbelievably beautiful Russian women. I was smoking weed with a bunch of guys in the washroom of the club; I don't think things would have gone very well if I was caught in Russia, smoking weed in the bathroom of a nightclub. We were fairly drunk by the end of the night, but I had an incredible euphoric experience after we left. Almost heavenly!

There was a group of us laughing, drinking, and walking through the Red Square around 3:00 am. The world famous Red Square was totally empty. All of a sudden in the middle of the square, a silence fell upon all of us. We stopped, and just looked around, surrounded by the Kremlin, Saint Basils Cathedral. An amazing peace overtook me. The snow was falling; the square was covered with a pure white sheet. I mean it was majestic, heading back to our hotel in Moscow, on New Year's Eve, walking through the Red Square in Russia. It is hard to explain, but a surreal feeling came to mind, another truly amazing night in my life.

It was the day before we were supposed to leave, and we decided to go to the *Gum Mall*. It runs the length of the Red Square and is nothing like any mall you have ever been to in North America. The massive mall was more like the inside of a castle. As we were leaving the mall, walking through the Red Square, who do you think is walking towards us?

It was none other than *Chuck Norris*, surrounded by four bodyguards. The crazy part of this is Christian happened to know him from L.A. We began to have a conversation, once again, standing in the middle of the Red Square, chatting with Chuck Norris. He was in Russia over the holidays because he owns a Casino in Moscow. Chuck was very nice, and he invited us to stop by later that night to hang out at his Casino. Unfortunately, I was beginning to get the flu really bad; a combo of too much Vodka and not enough food. We never made it to Chucks Casino, because I was curled up in a ball on the couch in our hotel room, sweating like a dog, running back and forth to the washroom.

That is not the worst of it. We had to fly the next day from Moscow to New York. This is a very long flight, and I was so sick, curled up on a little airplane seat, cramped, sweating, with a few trips to the washroom. It was by far the worst flight out of all the flights I have been on in my life. We arrived in New York and spent two days with my friend Mary. I remember going out to dinner to an amazing restaurant. We were going to go to a few clubs, but I was still violently ill so I could not partake in the New York nightlife. We eventually made it back to L.A., and I did recuperate.

I would like to end with something real; I came to realize that after having a few conversations with Sveta during our stay in Moscow, that there was never a time in her life she or her family could ever afford such luxuries. She had spent her entire life in Moscow, but she had never been to the Bolshoi, or the Circus; never shopped at the Gum Mall or visited any of the attractions we frequented. I was blessed enough to be working and making good money at the time. It opened my eyes, and softened my heart; it was a blessing to be able to provide for Sveta. It led me to see how spoiled we all are in the West, and how we take so many things for granted. We are so blessed with all we have, and we need to be more grateful for all God has provided us. The most Sveta could provide was a meal of Borsch at her grandma's village, in a very small house. Bless her heart.

I did mention two trips, and I did not forget about the small world topic. This time, it was off to *Tahiti*, actually *Bora, Bora*, a little island just off Tahiti. This vacation included Jenell, my travel buddy Christian and his girlfriend. Again it was during the L.A. Christmas break, which always included New Year's Eve. I have been blessed enough to have spent New Year's in *Moscow, Costa Rica*, three times in *New York, Norway*, twice in *Lake Tahoe, Nevada* a few in *L.A.* and *Bora, Bora*. We spared no expense as usual and stayed at a place with their own little island. A ten-minute boat ride, just off *Bora Bora* called *Le Meridian*, a four-star resort. We flew to Tahiti, and then took a small watercraft airplane ride for about twenty minutes to Bora, Bora. After the plane landed in the lagoon and pulled up to the dock, we then had a ten-minute boat ride to the luxury resort.

When we arrived golf carts drove us out along the plank way to our bungalow. We were staying in over the water bungalows, held up on stilts, with *plexiglass floors*. When you are standing in the main living area, you look down through a plexiglass floor into the lagoon; it was like staring into a salt water fish tank. I had never seen water this crystal clear before in my life. The accommodations and restaurants were all four star, with top of the line service. Every morning they had a breakfast buffet set up beside a black bottom Infinity pool. Next to it was a perpetual waterfall that flowed into the lagoon, simply breathtaking!

While we were there, we went snorkeling, surrounded by huge coral reefs, with little baby sharks swimming around us. All the fish of the ocean were there; clown fish, yellow tangs, puffer fish. I can go on and on naming all the fish and sea life that was in abundance for our snorkeling tour. Another day we rented a boat and cruised around the local islands, boating past all the other luxury resorts surrounding the area. We ended up on the little island of Bora, Bora where we rented little two-seated, three wheel cars.

We circled around the island, and of course in our travels, with me being an addict, I sought out some local guys hanging out by their huts, smoking weed. It is crazy, but addicts seem to be able to find drugs anywhere they travel, in any city, any country. The addict manages to seek and destroy. I am in *French Polynesia*, on a little island, in the middle of the Pacific, and I still manage to seek out, and find drugs!

We hung out with the locals, smoking weed, as they cooked up some local delicacies. I was the only one smoking. Jenell, Christian, and his girlfriend did not indulge. I was not drinking at this point in my life. In addiction, we substitute one for another. I replaced my drinking for pills. It does not always have to be a drug; some people may stop drinking, and work sixteen hours a day. There are many addictions; food, gambling, relationships, drugs, alcohol, porn- whatever it may be, we are continually striving to fill the void.

I was hooked on *Vicodin*, not prescribed by a doctor. I had my own pharmacist in L.A. Let's say drug dealer that would be more appropriate. Vicodin is a very strong opiate painkiller I was addicted to, so

I was sober but not clean. The difference between *clean* and *sober* is sober means you are not drinking, and clean means you are not doing drugs. (Now you know the difference between the two).

Bora, Bora was a place where you would like to retire and spend the rest of your life; Marlon Brando has a huge place there. The end of the trip was coming upon us, so we packed up, and took the twenty-minute flight to Tahiti. We spent one night there before flying out the next day. Christian had a meeting in L.A., so he had to fly out a day earlier with his girlfriend. Jenell decided since it was just the two of us, we should go somewhere real nice and swanky for dinner.

It was our last night in Tahiti, and I agreed that it was a great idea. Jenell got all dolled up, looking like a super model from one of Peggy's photo shoots. We headed out to this real nice outdoor restaurant, and while we are sitting there, enjoying a drink and some appetizers, you will never guess who walks in with a couple of bodyguards. Good old *Chuck Norris* was coming into the same restaurant for dinner that evening. He sees Jenell at first, a stunning 5'11" California blonde; hard not to notice. Then he sees me, remembering our brief meeting in Moscow, from Christmas past. Chuck walks over to our table, says hi, and I asked him if he was following me around. He laughs, and we chat for a bit before he made his way to his table.

Are you kidding me? Now do you get the small world analogy? First Sasha in Costa Rica, and now I have Chuck Norris following me around every Christmas, Ha ha. Really, what are the chances of running into him the year before at Christmas in *Russia*, and now at Christmas, in the middle of the Pacific, at a restaurant in *Tahiti*? I guess the chances are pretty good. We live on a very small planet, and we are but a speck of dust in Gods glorious universe. But, we are not small; we are huge in His eyes.

O.K, before digging into some events that happened while I lived in L.A., I would like to mention a few other women who I was blessed with having in my life. I am reminded of roller blading on the boardwalk in Santa Monica. As mentioned, I met Sveta while roller blading, and there was another amazing woman I also met while blading on the boardwalk.

Her name was Eva; a model from Japan. While I was cruising through S.M. with a buddy of mine, I saw her and a friend strolling along; we made eye contact, and the rest was history. I ended up dating Eva for around six months; then my drinking began to be a problem. It was par for the course when she said, "*either stop drinking, or I am leaving you*." Once again I was making wrong choices in my life, I choose the bottle over the relationship, and once again, I lost another amazing woman because of my addiction.

Lill was a model from Norway who I met at a club called *Vertigo* downtown L.A. Lill came to L.A. so she could pursue a modeling career. I had a few friends from Norway, who worked in the business and were friends with her. We went to the club, and at first, I had no interest in her. As the night went along, after we all had a few drinks in us, things changed. Lill came up to me, and asked me to dance; I declined at first, but then felt obligated to hit the dance floor.

The next thing you know we are kissing and cuddling. It was not long after Lill ended up moving in with me. It was for around six months, and yes, the ultimatum came soon after. She said, "*stop drinking or I am leaving*." Once again my addiction had a strong hold on me, I was powerless, and I chose the bottle instead of this amazing Norwegian woman. So, she packed her bags and was gone, like all the other women.

The twins were from Portland, Oregon. Mary and Mara; both Pamela Anderson lookalikes. Again, a friend who I went to high school with in Canada was living in Phoenix, and he came to L.A. for a visit with the twins and another girl. Mary and Mara were going to University in Phoenix, and they were both Catholic girls.

We all went to a club, and again, I paid no attention to Mary, as I did with Lill. I seem to have no sense if a woman is interested in me, and it also seems they have to make the first move. I truly believe it is fear of rejection, so I never have made the first move. In all my life, the woman has always had to approach me. This may stem from my upbringing. On this particular night, I was more intrigued with her friend. Later in the evening, Mary came up to me, sat herself down on my lap, and said straight out, *you are supposed to be with me, not my friend*.

Mary and I ended up dating for around six months, but she did not move in with me. I would fly Mary and her sister from Phoenix to L.A. on a Friday, and they would return on a Sunday. I used South West Airlines because they had a special that friends fly for free, so it cost me $89.00 to fly both Mary and Mara out to L.A. for the weekend. This was a great time in my life. Mary and Mara were so much fun, and the bonus was that they were both the spitting image of Pamela Anderson, so guys would always be staring at the two of them. We would all go shopping on Melrose, or going out to clubs, and I would always take them to nice restaurants for dinner.

The fun lasted the traditional six months, Mary in true form, gave the familiar ultimatum, "*stop drinking, or I am leaving you.*" It boggles my mind, just how powerful addiction is. I mean over and over again it has taken every good woman I have ever been with. The problem is the disease; let's not forget free will and bad decision making. We cannot beat addiction on our own; we always come up with a master plan for sobriety that never works. There is an answer; that *someone* is what we need in our recovery. At this time in my life, I did not know this *someone*; we will get to the answer a little later. I am an alcoholic, and with no solid foundation, the booze won. I lost another wonderful woman.

In all my years living in L.A., I dated a lot of actresses and models, ones who you may know or have seen in a magazine, or on T.V. I choose not to give any names, let's call them anonymous. I worked on a Michelob beer commercial with the Michelob girls and ended up dating one of them, for yes, six months. Another commercial, this one for Budweiser, I again hooked up with a Bud girl, and dated for, six months. They both left me because of my addiction to alcohol. One of the many things addiction wants is to crumble relationships. It was winning.

After a few years, I swear to God, I made a pact never to date any models or actresses again. I didn't, they are very insecure and needy. Not to put them down, because they are still wonderful, and amazing women. Maybe I should have made a pact with myself, and quit drinking. Here I am in denial, always blaming someone else, and not taking onus for my actions. This is a major defect for people in addiction.

The Jen phase of my life; I dated four Jennifer's. One was an actress, one a model, and the other had a job outside of the industry. None of the Jen's moved in with me, but we all dated the traditional six months before, well you know the ultimatum they had for me, and you know what my choice was. I was an alcoholic, and in my selfish ways, I always choose the bottle.

The fourth Jen impacted my life. She is an incredibly beautiful Jewish girl who was an Art Director. I fell in love with Jen, and we spend almost every night together. I would stay at her place, spending time with her two cats, have dinner, and sometimes go out and enjoying the L.A. nightlife. Every morning we would get up, get ready, and head our separate ways, to whatever film studio we would be working.

We traveled, and had an amazing relationship; she would always call me Dwayne Denial! I never did get a grasp of what that meant till many years later. She was so right, I was living my life in denial, and I would continue to live that way for many years. Sadly Jen, whom I cared deeply for, dumped me after six months, because of my drinking. We remained friends, but the loss of Jen affected me for a long time.

I was never a one night stand kind of guy; I never went out clubbing to find a woman for the night like most guys do. I was very picky about the women I dated. I would go for months on end sometimes, before meeting another woman. I never cheated on any of my girlfriends; my feeling was that this is the one I had chosen to be with. I did not want anyone else because I was content with the woman I was with.

I dated women from all walks of life, from all over the world. Asian, Russian, Norwegian, Dutch, Swedish, Spanish, Japanese; I can go on. They were all amazing women who I had great relationships with, and many are still friends to this day. My problem was an addiction to alcohol and very bad choices. These are the reasons why I am not still with any of them. They all meant a lot to me; Rhonda, my first love, I married. The rest, I dated for my record of around six months. But this brings to mind one question?

How much could have they really meant to me? When in the end, I always choose the bottle over the women. I was a very sick individual to say the least. When I was in the depths of addiction, my decision making is skewered; I am wired differently. What kind of a person does that? It causes me a lot of pain and distress when I think back to how messed up I was, and what my addiction took from me. Normal people do not pick a bottle of alcohol over a truly amazing woman.

I would like to end the chapter with my involvement in a few human disasters and natural disasters during my years in L.A. Let's start with the L.A. Riots, *The Rodney King Riots*. It was unbelievable. Simply put, it was a war zone. The city was in chaos, fires were burning everywhere, rioting, looting in stores, with sections of the city on lockdown.

It is hard to believe that this can happen here on our home soil, in North America, in a city like L.A. I lived in the Hollywood hills during the riots, so everyone in our building was up on the roof. There was a view of the entire city from way up in the hills. We were situated above Hollywood Blvd. At first, the sky was clear, and then we saw the fires start along the Boulevard.

The first fire was at Fredrick's of Hollywood, and then at the corner of Hollywood and Vine. Soon enough most of the buildings were burning. It did not take long until we began to see fires burning throughout the city. Eventually, the whole skyline was a dark brown, almost black, from all the fires. We were on the roof with helicopters flying overhead, and we heard gunshots. Some gang members were a few blocks away shooting at the helicopters. It was out of control.

The whole city was on a curfew, and no one could be on the roads after 6:00. Well, I always had a problem with authority figures and being told what to do, (true addict behavior). I disregarded the curfew because a friend of mine was having a party at his house in Malibu. I hopped on the 101 freeway, and there were only a few cars on the road. A very surreal, eerie feeling overtook me as I was driving. I could feel the tension from all the rioting in the air. Of course, I did not do the speed limit because there were no police. They were busy trying to maintain all the looting and rioting. Normally the trip from Hollywood to Malibu would take 45 min; I made it to my friend Cyril's house in 25 min.

The next day I did something really stupid. Inglewood is a predominately black neighborhood, and the looting, fires, and rioting were in full flow there. I had the bright idea to grab another white friend of mine and we drove into the pits of hell.

We saw a huge mall to our right, with streams of people running in and out with stolen merchandise. Black people are on every corner, with fires burning everywhere. All of a sudden, while sitting at a red light, in a major intersection, a beer bottle smashes against the side of my car. Then another one lands and smashes on the hood. I look over to see a mob of around ten black guys walking towards us. Some were carrying bats; some were throwing beer bottles, screaming and yelling at the two stupid white guys who thought it was a good idea to cruise through Inglewood during the riots. As I mentioned, my mind is wired differently from the normal person.

I threw the car into gear and punched the gas. We were out of there like a flying bullet, speeding all the way back to Hollywood and up into the hills to my place. This was by far one of the most stupid things I had ever done. If they had made it to the car and yanked us out, who knows what could have happened. I am guessing that I would not be sitting here writing this book.

Two men who got themselves into trouble were O.J. *Simpson* and an acquaintance of mine *Mr. Robert Blake*, who starred on the T.V., show *Barretta*. Both were on trial for murder. I can't say much about O.J; I just happened to be living in L.A. while they were closing down all the freeways, as he made his joyride all over the city.

Robert Blake is a different story; I was living in Studio City the last few years of my stay in L.A., with Jenell and my daughter Alyssa. Robert Blake lived about six blocks from our house. During those days, I would go to a local grocery store in the morning to get my bottle of wine so I could begin my day. I saw Robert there on numerous occasions, and we got to know each other fairly well. The next thing I knew, on the T.V. news, I see he is being charged with murdering his wife. After he had hit the news, I did not see him anymore at the local market.

Two natural disasters that took place while I was in L.A. were the earthquakes. There is no feeling of riding out a major earthquake. The first quake was the *Whittier Quake*. It happened at 7:42 am, and had a magnitude 6.0, a blind trust earthquake. I was living up in the hills at the time; being in the hills eases the quake a bit. I did not feel the effects as much as I would if I was living down in the city.

This is not saying that everything on the walls did not come falling down. Table lamps, and anything that was not locked down, shock and fell. We had massive cracks outside the building and lost all power that morning. At the time, it was the strongest quake since the *1971, San Fernando Quake*. It shook the whole building, and the rolling effect is trippy. I mean the ground under my feet was rolling, and everything was shaking around me. I believe I can get a little more descriptive when I talk about the other quake that rocked my world.

The *Northridge Earthquake* was a massive quake. It was registered at 6.7, and it lasted approximately 10-20 seconds. The earth trembled and shook. It had felt like an eternity before the nightmare stopped.

I was with Jenell, and we were in bed sleeping when it hit. An enormous jolt threw us out of the bed, across the room, slamming into a dresser. The rolling and shaking was so bad that it took us forever to stumble our way through the debris to the door frame in our bedroom. They say when a quake hits, to get outside. Or if you can't make it out, stand in the door frame, because it is the strongest part of the structure. This way nothing can come falling down onto your head. Of course, that is if the whole roof or building does not come collapsing down all around!

Later that day, I went with Glenn out to Northridge where his manager lived. On the way there everything we saw that was made out of brick had crumbled to the ground. All the brick fences along people's property were knocked down. Our brick chimney had crumbled in, and we never used it again after the quake. There were thousands of other chimneys, houses, and highways that were demolished from the quake.

It is the aftershocks that send fear ripping through your body. At first it is calm, then out of nowhere, the earth begins to rumble and shake; everything is rolling. I mean the earth was rolling under our feet, and we didn't know when it would stop. It is hard to put into words, so maybe you need to move to L.A., and wait it out till the next quake?

This concludes the chapter. The previous three chapters have been informative, encouraging, and have shown many of my achievements and accomplishments. I have explained my journey to L.A.; the acting, and the work behind the scenes. I have listed many celebrities I worked with, and a lot of my travels. I have included some of the women in my life and the loss of women in my life because of my addiction.

It is time to get brutally honest with you; in the next three chapters, things will not be so good. Along with the honesty, there will be a lot of misery, suffering, and pain; there will be the total destruction of life. I call the first three chapters on L.A., the good chapters; they covered my journey to the mountain tops and covered my successes.

The next three chapters will open your eyes to unthinkable darkness, it will rattle your brain, and it will soften your hearts. In the end, you will have experienced my despicable acts of selfishness, and the unimaginable power addiction can have over one person. I will cover the absurd effects that bad choices would have, and how just one bad choice altered the course of my life.

I will explain where drug and alcohol abuse leads to, what addiction will do, and what addiction will take from you. I truly believe in my heart, that addiction is Satan's number one tool in our society to bring anyone as close to the pits of hell as possible. When all else is lost, when there is nothing left, and all hope is gone, all addiction wants to do is kill you. Satan gripped his claws so deep into me, he wanted to take everything and anything of any worth away from me. The truth is he won. Satan succeeded; he knew my weaknesses, and he used them to destroy what took fifteen years to build.

CHAPTER 7

The beginning of the end

L ET'S BEGIN WITH my first DUI. In the states, it is called driving under the Influence. This is how most normal DUI's happen. While you are driving, a cop usually pulls up behind you, hits his lights, pulls you over, gives you a breathalyzer, and arrests you. This was not the case for me. I was going through a major time of depression. I was living in fear, full of anxiety, isolating, and at a bottom in my life. *Every bottom has a basement,* so when you think you have hit one in your life, remember, it can always get worse.

I was living up in the Hollywood hills, life was crumbling all around me, and my addiction was slowly getting the better of me. It was 1995, and I was having a serious problem with Vicodin at the time. It is an opiate, a very strong pain killer, and highly addictive. I had a fractured L5 S1 in my lower back. The wear and tear from playing sports all my life eventually caused a fracture. I was dealing with a tremendous amount of lower back pain.

On this particular day, I was drinking whiskey, and taking a lot of Vicodin. Not a good combination. No one should ever mix the two. I was broken, and felt hopeless; I was going through a bit of a mental breakdown. Tears streamed down from my face; fear ripped through my body. I needed help. I was alone, in despair, sitting at my place going through hell. All I could think of was to drive to Cedars-Sinai Hospital in Beverly Hills and get a rapid detox.

My good friend Glenn had previously done this. They basically drain all your blood, and then pump fresh blood back into you. All the chemicals and alcohol get washed away by flushing the system. This is not treatment; it is not recovery, and in no way will it help you with sobriety. All it does is clean you up, a quick fix so you can go back out with the same mindset; nothing has changed. It is a physical fix, but in the end, you will just go back out and use again. It is a waste of time.

My thinking told me this was the answer to all my problems. A rapid detox would cure me, and it would make me a new person. I was crying uncontrollably, and taking huge drinks of whiskey from the bottle. The Vicodin was streaming through my body; the day would not end well. I was a total mess, desperate, and was reaching out for help. I needed *someone*!

I picked up the phone, called a friend, no answer. I felt hopeless and alone, so I grabbed my keys and hopped into my car. I was fairly drunk, and should not have been driving. But off I went; drunk, crying and lost. I began the journey flying through the canyons, making my way up to Mulholland drive. After making it to the top of the hill, I stopped where Mulholland meets Laurel Canyon. I needed help, feeling I could not go on; I made a call to another friend, no answer.

I was reaching out, but there was no help to be found. I was a mess as the car made its way through Laurel Canyon and down into the city. I was about two blocks from Cedars Hospital; to the left was the Beverly Center, a huge mall across from Cedars. This is where things really began to heat up. A guy cut in front of me, almost hitting my car at the intersection and flips me off. This would not have been the right day or place to have pulled such a move. Let me share a bit about road rage.

I pulled up next to him at the red light, got out of my car, and walked around to his window, which was about halfway down. I grabbed it with both hands, and ripped it out. Glass shattered all over the place, my hands were cut open, and blood was everywhere. I then grabbed him by the throat and started smashing my fists into his face. I can clearly remember saying, *you picked the wrong f-ing day to mess with the wrong f-ing guy*. I continued my brutal assault; I was so full of anger and rage. I must have hit him 3 or 4 times directly in the face. Did he really deserve this violent attack? I think not, but in the end, I definitely did some damage. I walked back to my car, hopped in, and peeled out through the intersection making my way around the corner alongside Cedars Hospital.

My head was clouded, and my thoughts told me to park five or six blocks away so no one would find me, or my car. I saw a secluded parking spot. As I got myself out of the car and made my way the five blocks to Cedars; my mind was spinning out of control. I had no sense of time, or what had just happened. I felt like I was going insane.

Now here comes the mind-bender, this unexpected chain of events was about to happen! I walked into Cedars Hospital. To get to the elevators that took me up to the area where they do the rapid detox I had to walk past Emergency. I stumble in, took a look to my left as I was walking past the emergency, and what do I see? Two police officers pad and paper in hand, taking notes and talking with a guy. This guy's eyes are all swollen up, and blood is covering his face and shirt; you will never guess who the mystery man was?

It was the guy whose window I had torn out and beaten. There he was, standing with two cops. They looked over and saw me staggering toward the elevators. All of a sudden the guy yells out, points at me, and says, that's the guy who beat me!

I was done. The police walked over to me, saw my fists all cut up and covered with blood. It did not take a brain surgeon to see how wasted I was, and that I was the guilty party. The next sound I heard was a click, click, on with the handcuffs. I was under arrest for drinking and driving, and assault. Not only was this day a total nightmare, it was also very expensive. I ended up paying the guy $3000.00, and Charlie, my lawyer, $5000.00 to defend me for the DUI; it was an $8000.00 day. This was the first time I used Charlie, but it would not be the last.

As I mentioned it was 1995, and for the next five years things slowly began to fall apart. In the next little bit, I want to continue to cover some of the catastrophic events that occurred. Weed, marijuana, pot, whatever you want to call it, I smoked it every day for twelve years.

For my entire career, designing sets, doing props, or special effects, I was high. Every morning, in the afternoon, in the evenings; I would smoke weed all day long. I was what you would call a functioning addict, a functioning pothead. I smoked so much weed that I was not really getting high, I was just maintaining. I needed it, and if I did not have it, I could not function; I would get irritable and snappy if I did not have my weed.

Why did I need to be high all the time? I clearly remember a friend asking me, *"Dwayne, why do you always have to be high?"* He was right, and it got me thinking. I always had to be on something.

If it was not weed, it was Vicodin, alcohol, or some other drug, always something to alter my thinking, to numb whatever I was trying to mask. I was not capable of feeling any kind of emotion, because if I was high on something, I did not have to feel. I would not have to face the demons that were tormenting me. What was my underlying problem? Why did I always have to be high? I was missing that *someone* who could heal to pain!

I functioned as any normal person in my day to day living, but what I did was not normal. I would get up in the morning, and grab my bong, a device used for smoking weed; loading it up around 6:30 or 7:00 a.m. so I could start my day. On the prep days, I would go to the production company to begin the day with meetings. I would start off with a few hits off the bong to level me out, and then it was off to my meetings.

My eyes never got red, so I would throw in a piece of gum and spray a little air freshener to get rid of the pot odor. The director, producer and three or four people from the ad agency would be there; as well as three or four clients, representing whatever the product was for the particular job. There were always a large number of people. I would sit down, and we would go over the design, budget, and layout. Whatever props and effects were needed, basically all the work required from the art department. I would be sitting there, after doing a few bong loads of weed, going over a hundred thousand dollar budget.

Right out of control. I did this job in and job out. I was a functioning pothead, and no one could ever tell if I was high. It would not change my behavior, and my personality did not alter. The effects of weed are definitely not like booze, cocaine or the opiates. All of them will alter you in a way that people will notice. They will see a change in you, and that would be unacceptable in the business. Weed is fairly prominent in the industry, a lot of people ranging from directors, producers, grips, wardrobe, makeup; people smoked weed. I don't want to say it is accepted, or that everyone smokes, just saying a fair number occasionally do.

I came up with a very clever idea of how to smoke weed on location. Let's say we were filming downtown L.A., where there are trucks everywhere, lining two city blocks. We had the film crew walking all over the place. So how could we smoke our weed without everyone smelling it? When anyone smokes weed, it gives off a very pungent odor that can be smelled for blocks, but my creative addict mind found a solution.

In the back of our 5-ton art department truck, we would take a paper towel roll, and stuff three or four bounce sheets into one end. Then we took the pipe loaded with weed or the bong; lite it, and took our hit, or drag. After we inhaled, we would blow the smoke into one end of the paper towel roll. The smoke would flow through the bounce sheets, coming out the other end. Our truck smelled like a Chinese laundromat, but hey, it worked like a charm.

Weed was a big part of my life. I am in no way saying it is ok, or that it is good. I truly do believe it led me to other drugs. It did not happen right away; it took many years until it was not enough. It could be a month, six months, or a year, but one thing I can promise, it will eventually not be enough, and it will take you to the harder stuff. After that happens, you can kiss your life goodbye.

I was a weekend warrior, meaning I mainly partied on the weekends. I would work all week, and when the weekend hit, it was on, and it was time to party. We would go out to clubs doing various drugs. One weekend was *cocaine*, at *Truth*, downtown L.A. Sometimes *ecstasy*, and it was off to a *rave* in Hollywood. Maybe *mushrooms*, and out to *Palm Springs*, going deep into the desert, and tripping out.

It was all about the weekends for us, and I came up with an ingenious plan to get into the clubs in L.A.; it was magical. I put my creative, mischievous addict mind to work, and came up with an idea. I always say that alcoholics and drug addicts are borderline genius when they sober up, clean up, and put their minds towards accomplishing any goal. When we put as much energy and time into achieving a positive goal as we do planning our ways to score our drugs, and to survive out in the world; we could be running corporations.

There are always lines and waits to get into the big clubs in L.A. I have a pet peeve for lines. As you know, I hate waiting in them. I needed to work on my patience a bit; this is one of the nine fruits of the spirit, so I had better learn how to apply it in my life.

The plan went something like this. A group of friends and I would pick a club, and then I would work my magic. Let me use one of the massive clubs on *Santa Monica Blvd* called *Arena* as an example. This is a true story. I did this same routine all the time, every weekend, for a year or two. I really should not be telling you this, showing you the tricks I came up with, but why not? I am sharing my whole life with you, so why leave this little gem out.

I would pretend to be a manager (For models and actors), and came up with a fake management company, RD Higgins & Assoc. I would use my real name; because they are going to want ID at the door. The key to all this is your mental approach and the way you speak. Always remember that whatever club you are calling, the person answering is usually some young lady just doing her job. It is not the owner of the club, or the manager answering the daily calls; it is an employee answering phones.

This is where the mindset comes into play. O.K, here we go. I called *Arena*, during the day around 2:00 pm; it seemed to be the best time. They were having a grand opening that night, red carpets, lights, celebrities, the whole deal. I made the call and a female's voices answers. I mention my Management Company RD Higgins& Associates, and that I have a few clients and models coming into town from Vancouver.

I would always use Vancouver because so many shows were done up there; 21 Jump Street was my choice show to use. I would say that some of the cast and a few models were really interested in checking out their club, and they really want to visit while they are in town.

Now remember, this is just a regular person on the other end of the line, and, I want to add that I could sell snow to an Eskimo! But that's beside the point. I would have the person excited about my clients coming to the club, and in the end, their answer was always, we would love to have them be our guests. I would also ask if I could get them VIP. Then the person would ask how many? For this event, I said I would need seven of my clients on the list, including the VIP list. There are always two lists at clubs, one to get in, and the other for the VIP room.

We wanted to have a good time that night, so I had to have us on the VIP list. Clubs only need one name on the list so I would say Dwayne Higgins plus seven. We showed up, and there was a line up around the block. The bouncers knew nothing of the talk earlier in the day, or who I said was coming. All they have on the list is my name, plus seven.

So, we walk to the front of the mob scene, I give my name, show my real ID, they scroll down the list, and there I am plus seven. We go to the grand opening! The VIP lounge and free champagne, because yours truly, has a very creative addictive mind. I did this for so many clubs on so many weekends; it was genius. This was in the 90's, and I am sure procedures have changed.

I never drank or did any hard drugs when I was working with the exception of weed. It was a very challenging job, and I was committed; the film industry is a demanding business. I was a workaholic; this is also an addiction. Most people think that they only have one addiction; unfortunately, this is not the case. We never have just one!

To be honest, the number is usually three. Let's use me as an example, and count my addictions, #1-I was an alcoholic for twenty years. #2-I enjoyed doing speed, and having sex. #3-I was a workaholic. #4-I smoked weed every day. #5-I was hooked on opiates. There is an addiction to relationships, porn, gambling, work, coffee, shopping, should I go on? It is not only drugs, and alcohol. If you or someone you know is suffering from any form of addiction start counting, and I will almost guarantee three, or more.

I was living in Santa Monica on 5th st, five blocks from the Pacific Ocean, with one of my best girlfriends; she was just a friend, a platonic relationship. We partied all the time, and went rollerblading together after work; she was my dearest friend, Chrissy.

Here is the kicker, Chrissy was a stripper by night, and a financial adviser by day. She worked out in the valley at a few strip clubs a couple nights a week. Her boyfriend was a friend of mine who I lived with at the *Jungle House* in Santa Barbara. His name is John, my Russian buddy. Again, a small world.

One night I came home drunk and parked my car in the entry way leading down to the parking garage. The keys were left in the ignition, and it was blocking anyone from getting in or out of the underground garage. Thank God it was early morning, around 2:00 am, and Chrissy noticed it. She went out and moved the car. This was not the first or the last time Chrissy was there to rescue me while in a drunken stupor.

Before writing the book, I emailed Chrissy and asked if she could remember anything about our time together in L.A., some info for the book. She sent me a few things, and I felt it would be a good idea to attach her actual writings. Here is one excerpt she wrote to me, this is copied and pasted from her actual e-mail. Written by my little Angel Chrissy Snow, that is what I called her.

***** funny whether you were smoking pot, drinking or on Vicodin the unique thing about our friendship, is you were the big brother I always wanted. You looked out for me and protected me even if you were drunk or high!! One of my favorite memories is we were roller-blading to Big Dean's on the boardwalk on a Sunday afternoon; it was summertime, and I was wearing a bikini top and shorts and some guy (by the way he was huge around 6′2″) on a skateboard road by us and grabbed my ass. You skated after him pushed him off his skateboard and hit him over the head and told him never to touch me again. Then in only Dwayne fashion you looked at me with your smile that could light up a room and said "come on Chrissy Snow let's go to Big Deans and get a drink"... meanwhile, this big 6′2″ guy was on the sand bloody around the face... lol... that's one of my favorites because you always protected me

Thank you Chrissy for forgotten memories.

I have to be honest, I do not remember any of this, but reading it does bring back memories of the amazing times we had living together in Santa Monica. I also want to add that I am only 5′7″ 150 lbs. That has been my height, and weight since High school. I have only had three fights in my life, all of which took place in Jr High. I guess I will now have to include the one at the beach with Chrissy, so four fights.

I should have had my butt kicked hundreds of times, but God blessed me with a tongue that I knew how to use very well. In my past, growing up all over the world, and being short, it became my defense mechanism. I could talk my way into dangerous situations, but I could always talk my way out. Instead of getting a beating, I would end up sitting at the bar having a drink with the individual. Usually, in the end, we would become very good friends; this happened a lot.

I want to share one more letter from my friend Chrissy, once again written by her, then e-mailed to me as the above letter, in her words.

***** Our condo faced 5th street and the street had several large speed bumps, one night I was going to meet you over at "my father's office" that was one of our hangouts and so was Obrien's (we would always listen to young Dubliners play) anyway you called me and as I looked out my bedroom window I see your black BMW wagon get air flying over speed bumps and what I am guessing was over 100 miles of speed...all of a sudden I see oil coming out as you are flying by and before I can get out there I think your oil pan broke the car seized and stopped.

***** I used to blow in your breathalyzer

(There was a breathalyzer put in my car after my second DUI).

Thank you, Chrissy; it puts a smile on my face. I have to laugh at myself after reading her e-mail; I do remember the night Chrissy mentioned. I was pretty messed up, and was going to a bar up the street from us, but I did not have my ID with me so they would not let me in. Well, in my drunken state, I was going to show them. I sped off leaving the club making my way home to grab my ID. As Chrissy's letter says, I was driving fast, flying over the speed bumps, and then the bottom of the car slammed down. I blew out my oil pan, and the car seized up.

This turned out to be a very expensive night, because, for a new BMW 5 series, an oil pan was $800.00, American dollars in the late 90's. Oh, the joys of owning a new car, and the nightmare of addiction. Once again, my addiction had a grip on me, causing more destruction, and more chaos. It was doing what it does best, slowly breaking me, and turning my world upside down. Since we are talking about the powers that drugs and alcohol have, it may be a good time to share with you the story about my second DUI.

It was 1997 I was still living with Chrissy, and it was two years after my first DUI. I just want to say that I should have had hundreds of DUI's because I drank and drove all the time. I thank God for His mercy and grace, that I never killed anyone, or caused any major accidents.

Today my thinking tells me that drinking and driving is one of the most selfish acts one can do. Getting behind the wheel when you are drunk, and having no control of anything. In our addiction, we never think things through. We never focus, or think about the end result. It is always an impulsive thought from the enemy. We take the chance of killing someone and spending years in prison. We do not consider the consequences of our actions in addiction.

Why? When we are in that state of mind, we do not discern what is of God, or what is of the enemy. God will never give you the thought to go out, get behind the wheel drunk, and cause total destruction. What I can tell you, is that the enemy, Satan, will do all he can to get you behind that wheel. As I mentioned, one bad choice can alter your life, it can take everything from you. Addiction wants to kill you.

Speaking of not drinking and driving, I clearly was not following the advice I was just preaching about. I was at home with Chrissy, and I just happened to be propping a *Fosters Beer* commercial at the time. When you are doing props for a commercial, you always get lots of the product sent to you.

We had a few scenes where there had to be cases of beer stacked in a pool hall setting, as well as six packs of oil cans, (a name for the big cans of beer). Fosters had sent me cases of beer for various scenes and for the product shot. Anyway, I brought a couple of cases home with me at the end of one of the shoot days.

I began to drink, and drink some more, and was beginning to get fairly drunk. Here comes the normal reaction for many alcoholics. They get buzzed, or drunk, and then something kicks into the brain. This something does not happen to normal people because these thoughts are by no means normal.

These are basically bad choices, and usually, the outcome of that choice leads to irreparable damage. My thought was, *boy it would be a good idea to head downtown and score some crack cocaine.* Yes, this is one of those thoughts that is not of God, but it is definitely something Satan puts into our weak, powerless minds.

Do normal people, after a few drinks come up with amazing ideas like mine? Let's go get some crack? No, they don't, but in my case, my addictive personality says, I would love to get some crack to go along with my Fosters beer. The alcoholic mind begins to take control, and the thought becomes action. The next thing I know, I am on the freeway, with a ½ dozen oil cans of Fosters beer flowing through my system. Heading downtown to a place where normal people would never set foot. To a place where I have been many times before, where the Mexican gangs hang out, selling crack cocaine.

Let me explain a bit, just how things work when you enter into the drug-infested underworld of downtown L.A., and then we will get back to the DUI. I want to bring Glenn back into the picture because both of us would always drive into the pits of hell. We would frequent the little corner, where no one should ever go, especially at night, to score crack cocaine.

We would usually take the trip on Friday and Saturday nights, and then make our way back to Glenn's house up in the Hollywood hills and smoke crack all night till the sun came up. The way the Mexican gangs dealt their crack is something like this; first off they keep it in their mouths. They are small, flat, rectangular piece selling for $20.00.

We would drive up to the corner, and they would be in groups of four or five. We knew them all by name; you could call them friends or acquaintances. Either way, they were always cool with us. The probable reason for this was because we spent a lot of money over the years. As we pulled up, they came to the window of the car and asked how much. We would reply 120, or 200, meaning the dollar amount. They would spit the pieces out of their mouth, and hand them to us. Then we paid the cash and drove away. Quicker and easier than McDonalds drive thru!

One night I went downtown by myself, around 11:00 pm. This would not turn out well. Right after I scored my crack, and was pulling away, an undercover cop car pulled up behind me. The next thing I see in my rear view mirror is his lights flashing. The Mexicans scattered, and I pulled over; this was about 20 seconds after scoring. I was a well-trained addict, with a mind that can get me into, and out of trouble rather quickly, so a bright idea crept into my mind.

I threw the crack out the passenger's window, which was half way opened. The cops walked up to my window and asked me what I was doing in this part of downtown. My bright idea saved me; I responded that I was on a Location scout.

A location scout is when you are working on a commercial or a movie, and you are filming at various locations. There is a prep day, where the director, producer, and the key people from each department go to the locations to see them and set up how the shots will be done. I said I was on a scout for a commercial. I just made one up, let's say Pepsi. My addict mind is doing what it does best, *being mischievous, and lying*. I tell them that we were scouting a location not too far from where I was. While making my way back home, I got lost downtown, and I was looking for directions.

Well, being sober, and being in a brand new BMW helped. My gifted way of talking helped get me out of the predicament. If they found the crack, I would have been charged with possession of drugs. This would not have been good. In the end, I drove away, clean and clear, I am sure they doubted me, but what could they do? No drugs were found, and I was sober.

Here is where my addictive and psychotic way of thinking kicks in. After the undercovers had driven past me, I had the balls to go around the block and pull back up in front of the apartments where they are dealing. I walk up to the open door where the dealers and gang bangers live. Some little kids were running around playing, and I joyfully and happily played a bit with them, and then the dealer came out.

He knows what happened because it was a couple hundred feet up from where we made the deal. Here is the insanity of it all; I had the audacity to say to him, an 18th St Gang member, that I tossed my crack out my open window, and almost got popped. So I would like the crack back. He could have put a gun to my head and shot me, or they could have grabbed me and dragged me into the apartment beating me to a pulp.

As my dear friend Chrissy mentioned, with my persona, and a smile that could light up a room, he gave me the crack back, without extra charge. I shook his hand, and in Spanish, I said thank you and wished him and his compadres a good night. I walked back to my car, hopped in, and headed out of downtown, making my way home. Here is a prime example of the lunacy, and complexity of bad choices and wrong decision making while in the depths of addiction.

OK, let's get back on track. But hey, it was all related to the same topic. Mexican gangs and crack cocaine, it all ties in. Now getting back to the second DUI, I believe we left off with me having a few fosters. My addict kicked in, and I had the amazingly bright idea to go downtown and score some crack cocaine. I believe we left off with me in my car, flying down the freeway, making my way into the pits of hell.

I would be going back to see my 18th St. buddies. I arrived in the not so good part of town, pulled up to the regular spot, saw my regular Mexican gang banging buddies, picked up some crack cocaine, and was off and running. O.K. here we go again, addict thinking, and very bad choices. Here I am with all that Fosters beer flowing through my system, and $200.00 worth of crack on my console. Then another bright idea pops into my head, I need more booze. Let me explain the alcoholic mind:

Mental Obsession—The alcoholic mind tells me to pick up that first drink. That started back in Santa Monica with the Fosters beer.

Physical Allergy—There is an allergy, an abnormal reaction to alcohol in which my body creates toxins which decrease inhibition, and causes irresistible cravings for more alcohol. This is why I jetted across the solid double yellow line and flew into the liquor store parking lot.

Phenomenon of Craving—When I start drinking I develop the Phenomenon of craving, which is manifested in the allergy. The Fosters did not satisfy; I needed more, hence the abrupt stop at the liquor store.

Yes, after picking up my dope, while exiting downtown, I saw a liquor store on the left. Without thinking, I made a hard turn, crossing over two solid double yellow lines, and made an abrupt stop in front of the liquor store. As I am getting out of the car, a cop on a motorbike comes screaming up behind me with his lights flashing.

I am already standing outside the car, ready to make my way to the liquor store. I stop and turn to face him as he is getting off his bike. He walks up to me, asks for my license, which I had in my pocket, and he starts lecturing me about my erratic driving skills. Remember; I have $200.00 worth of crack cocaine sitting on the console! I had carelessly tossed my drugs there, not thinking of hiding it after I picked it up.

He smells the booze and decides to give me a breathalyzer test. We are standing next to the car, with $200.00 worth of crack sitting there in the open. Now tell me there is no God because he never looked into the car. All he does after I fail the breathalyzer test miserably is make me sit beside my car, on the curb. Then the sound of his radio echoes as he calls for a patrol car to come pick me up.

I know the drugs are there, so my immediate thoughts are to start up a conversation with him. I need to steer his attention from ever looking into the car, and it works. We chat for a bit, he chews me out for being such an idiot, and then the patrol car shows up. I am already handcuffed, so they throw me into the back, and the motorcycle cop hopped on his bike and took off.

This whole scenario could have played out much worse than just a second DUI; I could have been charged with possession of crack cocaine. That would have meant some prison time and a whole new mess of problems. Once again Charlie's services were required. This time, it cost me $10,000. At this stage of my life, I was just a believer, not a follower. God was still watching out for me, even in the pits of hell. He was there for me, and this would not be the first or last time.

So, I still had to work the next morning, and by now it was around 11:30 p.m. I was locked up at *Rampart Division* downtown. I made the call to my trusted friend Glenn, who was at the *Lava Lounge* in Holly-wood, having some drinks with the owner, who was a good friend of ours. As I talked to Glenn, I explained what had happened and that my car was sitting downtown with $200.00 worth of crack on the console. Glenn proceeded to say that if he could get the money to bail me out, the crack was his. I had no problem with our deal because by now it was getting late, and I still had to get to the set for work by 7:00 am.

I want to add that Glenn was getting deeper and deeper into his addiction around this time. He would have bailed me out whether there were drugs on the console or not. I think it was more of a joke. For some reason, I can't remember why, but Glenn did not have enough for the bail. So, the owner of the Lava lounge used money from the bar. He showed up at Rampart about an hour later and bailed me out.

Now I need to get my car because I have to get to work soon. We get there, and the parking lot is locked. Downtown L.A. is a little danger-ous at night in certain places. So there are ten foot, black metal fences, on little wheels that can be rolled into place. I could not get my car; it was locked in the parking lot, and the drugs were sitting on the console. Glenn comes up with this bright idea. He wanted me to climb over the ten-foot fence, and get the crack.

Two thoughts kicked in; one, if they came to tow my car, I would get popped for drug possession. Second, being the great friend that I was, and considering our deal we made on the phone, I began to shimmy my way over the metal fence. I made it over, walked up to my car, grabbed the drugs from the console, and climbed back over the fence and into Glenn's car. I handed him the drugs, and he dropped me off at home in Santa Monica. I called a work mate to come pick me up in the morning, went to bed, and was on the set at 7:00 am. Should I dare say, just another night in Hollywood?

I would like to end on a good note. My incredible ex-roommate and very close friend Chrissy made some changes in her life. I thanked God earlier for my narrow escape, but I also want to thank God for His amazing work. Today she is a stock broker in Century City, and she is a Christian. Chrissy and her wonderful twelve-year-old daughter, Taylor, are living an amazing life.

CHAPTER 8

L.A.—The Fall, Part One

CHRONOLOGICAL ORDER, WE finally made it. From here on in, the book will be written in sequence as my life unfolded. It was 1996, and I was living with Chrissy. This would have been around the time I met Jenell. She is 5'11", blonde, and incredibly beautiful. Jenell was the woman I would fall deeply in love with, and we would have a child together.

Once again, rollerblading on the boardwalk one sunny day with two friends, we saw Jenell and her friend coming towards us. We all stopped, and a conversation began. Not having much confidence, I thought to myself she was too tall and way too attractive for me; so I paid no attention to her.

Later that evening we all went out for sushi in Venice Beach. My one friend was with Lisa, Jenell's friend, and my other buddy is hitting on Jenell. The only thought going through my mind was to head over and see a friend a few blocks away, and get some Vicodin. Not caring about either of our two new acquaintances, that is exactly what I did. I left and went to score some pills, arriving back before the meal was done.

After sushi, we all headed to *Renee's*, a nightclub in Santa Monica. Everyone was drinking except me. I was sober at the time, but not clean; I was hooked on Vicodin. My friend is still hitting on Jenell, then, out of the blue, Lisa comes up to me and says, "*My friend does not want to be with your friend, she wants to be with you.*" I clearly remember the words, so I made my way over to Jenell, and we spend the whole night together. The rest is history. I would spend the next 7 years of my life with her.

On my first date with Jenell, we went to Malibu for a Sunday brunch at a restaurant on the ocean called *Pier View*. The only glitch was that a breathalyzer was installed in my car due to my second DUI. It is hard to put into words how embarrassing it was, to get into the car, and go through the whole process of blowing into it so the car would start. Jenell was sitting by my side, on our first date; not good. This should have been a huge red flag for her, dating a guy with a second DUI, and a breathalyzer, but she did not seem to care.

I quickly fell in love with her; she had a heart of gold, was kind to everyone she met, and would do anything for anyone. We traveled together to Costa Rica, Tahiti, Hawaii and Mammoths Mountain ski resort in California. We went to Bakersfield a lot because her parents lived there; it is about a two-hour drive from L.A.

A great thing for me was to experience what family was like, having Christmas, Easter, and other holidays, surrounded by her relatives, two sisters, and all their kids. Jenell had a big family. It was something I missed growing up, and it was healthy for me to see how normal people lived. In addiction, we do not have the chance to live a normal life. I needed some normality in my life, and she provided it for me.

I was living with Chrissy in Santa Monica while dating Jenell. After three months I moved in with her; it would have been in 1997. She lived in a very nice townhome in Beverly Hills, around Olympic and La Cienega Blvd. She was working as an office manager for a dentist in Beverly Hills. Going back a bit, remember Rhonda? She also worked for a dentist when we met, a little insanity here. What's with falling in love with women who work in the dental field?

After a year of living together in Beverly Hills, somewhere in 1998, I would move once again with Jenell.We made the move to a house in Studio City, on Fair Ave, about 5 blocks from Universal Studios. It was a beautiful three bedroom house, with a backyard, side yard, and a garage in a very nice neighborhood. I had lots of friends at the time, so we had BBQs in the backyard, house parties, and always had guests. Glenn would come by all the time, which led to some form of partying.

I was working all the time, and so was she. Money was never an issue. We went out for sushi all the time and went to all the nice restaurants in Hollywood. The two of us never really went to any clubs; we were more of a stay home couple, having friends over, or just spending quality time together.

We had amazing neighbors. Chuck lived in the house to our left, with his wife and kids. Chuck was a director, and he did a lot of music videos for some of the top musicians in the Industry. On our right lived John, his wife, and two kids. He was a writer on one of the top T.V. shows running in the late 90's. We lived in an area where pretty much everyone was involved, in one way or another, working in the film industry.

One neighbor who lived a block up from us was *Michael Biehn*, an actor who is famous for battling *Arnold Schwarzenegger* in the original *Terminator Movie*. He was also in the original movie *Aliens*. Michael became a good friend over the years while we lived on Fair Ave.

The year was 1999, and life could not have been better. I was working all the time, doing props and F/X with the biggest directors, and celebrities in Hollywood. I was making a low six figure income. I had a nice chunk of change invested, and some put into savings. My relationship with Jenell was so good, and the exciting news was that we were expecting a little girl in September. We were both so happy and excited about bringing a new life into the world.

We were living in an amazing part of town, in a house full of every material possession you could imagine. We lacked for nothing. Our bedroom was nicely decorated; plants and artwork everywhere. We had a $3000.00 Chattam and Wells mattress on our bed. One room was converted into an office for me, which had all the trimmings. The back yard had two sets of patio furniture and a hammock we brought back from Costa Rica. I should also mention the six huge pot plants, which were growing along the sunny side of the house. Lastly, I want to include the two $80,000 BMW's parked in the driveway. Yes, we had it all.

Everything the world tells me I should have, I had! The question is; was the Shalom shaped hole in my Heart filled? (*Shalom means Peace*). Was I satisfied with all that I had? Was I content, and at peace? God created us all with an empty space in our hearts, let's call it a void, and according to worldly standards that void should have been filled.

Well, guess what, none of the material things worked. Nothing would fill the emptiness in my heart. Jenell would not fill it, and having a baby girl would not fill it. Some catastrophic events were about to unfold in my life. Since nothing was working to fill the void, I had another bright idea, another way to fill that Shalom shaped hole in my heart.

My mind and smart thinking said doing more drugs and alcohol may just be the answer. Could this be the solution that I was seeking, the answer to ease the inner pain and the brokenness? Let me tell you how that worked for me; I will share with you what drugs and alcohol did. The *Enemy* had his claws embedded so deep into me. Just like addiction; *The enemy comes to steal, destroy and to kill.*

Just before the actors strike hit, there was something I said that still haunts me. I vividly remember word for word. I would never be able to take back what I said. It happened one evening in our kitchen. I was drinking at the time, taking pills, and inside I was irritated with life, and confused.

There was a routine for me. Up at 6:00 am, get the coffee ready, prepare breakfast, food or fruit, then bringing it to Jenell and Alyssa in the bedroom. At 6:30, I would be off to work when there was work. Then come home at the end of the day, clean up, take Juana home (our full-time nanny), come back, prepare dinner for everyone. Then, run the bath for Alyssa, back to the kitchen to clean up, and a quick about face back to the bathroom to tidy up after Alyssa's bath.

On this particular evening it hit, my mind was spinning out of control, and I yelled out, *"Is this it, is this what my life amounts to, a routine. This unfulfilling life I have, is there more to life than this? God, is this all that life is?"* Not being content, or grateful, I was crushed, dissatisfied with my life, and depressed about everything. *Depression is an inability to construct a future!*

I regret these words to this day. What the hell was wrong with me? At this time of my life, I had an amazing woman, Jenell, my daughter Alyssa, the cars, house, and money. The thoughts that ran through my head were not telling me how good it was. Well, God heard this comment, and so did the Enemy.

I was about to realize how my lack of gratitude for all the Lord had blessed me with would come to an end. This is exactly what was about to happen. Life as I knew it was about to change dramatically. The path of destruction that I was about to leave behind is unthinkable and incomprehensible. My bad choices, my lack of discernment, and my addiction were about to destroy everything in my life.

It was the year 2000, and L.A. was hit with an actors and writers' strike. The life I knew was about to spin in such an uncontrollable downward spiral, that it would take me to the deepest, darkest pits of despair. The grief, agony and the irreparable damage that I caused would break me. My heart and soul would be tossed around like a wave in the ocean. Everything I loved everything I cared about, all the material stuff; absolutely everything in my life would be gone.

I was not a Christian at this time, but something in me screamed out to God. I cursed Him and blamed Him for everything. I did not know Him so why did I do this? Why did I scream out to Him when my life was at its lowest? Yelling out *Why God, Why? I just don't understand.* What I have come to learn is He is patient, loving, and He cares deeply for us all. He always has a plan and a purpose for each of our lives. But before I could get on His path, I had to enter into the pits of hell.

I had to suffer, and endure unexplainable pain and go through such incredible loss. I made every wrong choice, and decision that was humanly possible. The next 2 years of my life would shake my inner core. My heart would shatter into little pieces. The loss I had to endure would throw my life into a whirlwind of disaster. I had no one to turn to, and I had lost all hope.

Let me explain some of the events that would alter my life because of addiction, and the actor and writers' strike. The work came to an abrupt halt; the whole industry shut down. There was no work for about eight months, and this was not good.

My monthly costs just to survive were around $5000.00. We had Juana, an amazing lady who was our nanny. She took care of Alyssa five days a week, $400.00 a week times four weeks, was $1600.00. Plus, the rent was $2000.00, car payments, insurance, cell phones, and credit cards. This did not include food, going out, or my $600.00 a month weed bill. The cost for all the drugs and alcohol that I was about to consume would be out of control. As I mentioned, my life was about to come crumbling down all around me in a way that I could never have fathomed or imagined. Put your seat belts on, because it is going to get real bumpy!

The first issue was my drinking and smoking weed; both became a daily ritual. It caused a lot of strife between Jenell and me. Not too long into the strike we would have a baby. My daughter Alyssa would enter into this world on September, 8th, 2000. I almost missed the birth of my child because of my addiction. It almost won! But by the grace of God, He put an angel in the hospital room. A little later in the book you will see how God used another angel, in another hospital; to save my life!

Jenell was in labor, and I was sitting there in the room. My addict was saying that I should run down to the liquor store a few blocks away, grab a bottle of booze, and come back. Really, I mean what was wrong with me? I was putting the bottle before the birth of my little girl; this makes me sick!

There I stood in front of the love of my life, and she was about to give birth to my daughter. Thank God the nurse (an Angel) was very persistent in telling me No, I couldn't go. She calmed me down and helped take the selfish thoughts of alcohol from my messed up mind. She said Jenell could give birth at any time. She had been in labor, and that is just what happened. Within ten minutes after my thoughts of leaving for booze, my beautiful daughter came into this world; she was healthy, alive and well. I was so proud when I cut the umbilical cord and watched Jenell hold my little girl, whom God had fearfully and wonderfully made. He wove and knit Alyssa together in her mother's womb, and I was the happiest man alive. But this would not last very long!

The family, Jenell, Alyssa, and Dwayne

Two days after Alyssa was born, I was 30 and was walking into my first treatment center, Brotman Hospital, to participate in a 28-day program. My drinking was out of control leading up to the birth of Alyssa. I was burying my sorrows and had no hope for any kind of a future. I could not cope with day to day life. The time came when Jenell could not take it anymore. She had enough and was caring for a two-day old baby; she did not need to take care of another one.

Brotman is a medical center in Culver City, with the detox taking up the whole 6th floor. Back in the day, *Lionel Barrymore* would go there to sober up. I believe he frequented Brotman so often they had an office set up for him so he could work. It was around $30,000 for the 28-day stay. Thank God for Motion Picture Insurance! I was treated like a king, sleeping in a hospital bed, ordering whatever meal I wanted each day. They medicated the hell out of me when I first came in.

When I come off booze, when I abruptly have to stop drinking after a run, my system shuts down, and I get, let's say, a bit crazy. I am not myself; things usually start to really fall apart on the second day. I begin to get out of control, my vision gets blurred, violence becomes an issue, and my thinking is skewered. Life just spins around in my head; my thoughts are making no sense at all, and I black out, not remembering anything.

What I do remember is the first day I was there, Jenell came by with Alyssa. I was holding my daughter in my arms, and she told me I need to clean up for Alyssa. My reply was yes, I have a baby now and need to be responsible and provide. After Jenell and Alyssa had left Brotman, I began to sob uncontrollably. I was discouraged, and the separation from Alyssa caused such loneliness that it was unbearable. I was shaking and trembling as the tears rolled down my face.

Like clockwork, the next day I began to spin out of control. I was getting violent, and the staff had to contain me. Off I went to the psych ward. When they brought me into the ward, I decided that I was going to run. Not sure where I would go, but being out of my mind, I ran straight into a metal door and split my head open above my left eye.

Blood was streaming down my face, and my head had a three-inch gash in it. I started yelling at a nurse; I was not very nice to say the least. The next day I came to with 13 stitches above my eye. I had calmed down from all the medication they had me on. They basically sedated me for the better part of my 5-day stay in the psych ward.

I did my 28 days at Brotman, was sober, and went home to be with my family and try to find some work. Lastly, I went and bought a huge bouquet of flowers, went back to the psych ward at Brotman, and gave flowers to the nurse whom I mistreated. Everyone was so happy to see me sober and doing well. Too bad it didn't last.

Jenell's earlier comment about sobering up for Alyssa would not work; this was not the answer. The problem is you cannot ever get sober for anyone, or anything. The only person you can do it for is *yourself*. You must be a bit selfish, you have to clean up for you, and for no other reason, or it will not work. Not for your wife, your kids, your job, your parents, none of these reasons will keep you sober. You must be at a point where you are sick and tired of living the life of addiction. You need to be willing, and completely ready to surrender everything to get your life back on track. God knows I tried it for every other reason, and it would take years before I realized that I needed to do it for me.

I would go to three or four A.A. meetings a day. L.A. has thousands of meetings; the problem was that I was smoking weed, always having some before a meeting. After, I'd come home, hang out because there was no work, get high, and go to another meeting. I could not stay sober for more than a week or two before I would start drinking again; this process went on for a few years.

Jenell later told me something else that hurts me to this day. During the rough times in 2001, in the evenings, I would sit in the living room drinking my Jack Daniels. We had an amazing surround system hooked up to the big screen T.V. While in my state of self, being only concerned about me; I would drink, get drunk, and watch movies with the system cranked up.

I did not have any thought of Jenell having to go to work in the morning, or my infant daughter sleeping in the bedroom. I had the audacity to stagger down the hall in my drunken state, open the bedroom door, and curse and scream at Jenell. She later told me she would lay in bed holding Alyssa, crying uncontrollably, with fear and anxiety running through her body at night. To this day, it makes me sick to think about my behavior and my actions. I did not care about the woman I loved or my infant daughter. All that was important was the alcohol!!

When in our addiction, we are blind to the devastation we are causing all around us. In our minds, we believe we are not hurting anyone else. It is only after the fact that we see how much pain and suffering we have caused others; then we wonder why no one trusts us. In addiction, it takes time for our family and friends to rebuild their trust. We need to be patient and remember the trail of destruction that we left behind.

It is the people closest to us, those we really love, that we hurt the most. I hate addiction so much, and anyone that says they like it for whatever reason needs to go see a psychiatrist; so they can get their head examined. There is absolutely nothing to like about addiction. It is a lifelong disease, and all one can do is maintain a *spiritual program of recovery*. I was helpless and powerless, and it was controlling my life.

Not only was alcohol controlling me, but my addiction to Vicodin was insatiable. I needed them every day. An opiate combined with booze is a very bad thing! It was causing a great deal of destruction in my life. My addict had another great idea; don't you just love it when an addict has a master plan? I can say from experience; our plans *always* end in failure, and we fall flat on our faces.

I would hide my pills in Jenell's car, in her trunk, while she went to work. This way I would not have them, trying to go through the day without any pills. This was my brilliant idea and my attempt at cutting back. She did not know, and I would be pacing back and forth, waiting for her to get home from Malibu at 4:00 pm. Whenever she came home late, if it was not right at 4:00, I would lose it on her. I would be yelling and screaming because she was late. Jenell did not know I was waiting for the pills that I hid in her trunk. She would walk away from me, grab Alyssa from Juana, and go to the back yard. She was confused and hurt. I mean really, she was working all day, and then came home to a drunk, yelling and screaming at her. Once again, we don't see it while in the depths of our addiction, but we hurt the ones we love, and we don't realize it at the time.

It is painful writing these stories; actually writing the *Fall* is tearing me apart from the inside out. My actions in addiction caused me so much guilt and shame. I sit here crying, as I am writing about how I was, and the horrific ways I was treating Jenell. As I am writing, I am somehow trying to find the good in all this. It is therapeutic for me; it opens my eyes to my addictive behaviors and all the reasons to find a solution. I needed to find something more powerful than addiction, something to overcome my powerlessness. The answer was coming, that *someone* was waiting, but it would take more time and a lot more suffering and loss until I would let that *someone* in.

Saturdays were Jenell's day off, and Juana only worked during the week. It was my day to have Alyssa. Let me share something despicable, an act of someone desperately in need of help. This is how messed up I got in my addiction. It sickens me.

On my one day alone with her, I would walk Alyssa in the stroller up to the 7-11 on the corner and grab a bottle of wine. Having my liquor in hand, it was off to the park, and I would play with her on the swings and slides. Every 5 minutes, I snuck back to the stroller, taking huge swigs of wine out of the bottle; in the middle of the playground.

I would drink too much too fast, and within an hour, the bottle was done, and I was fairly drunk. My system could not take it, so we would walk over to one of the local restaurants, and go to the bathroom. I would lock the door, then turn Alyssa's stroller, so it was facing the other way. I then knelt in front of the toilet, throwing up my breakfast and all the wine. There I was hiding out in a bathroom, in a local restaurant, with my one-year-old daughter, puking my brains out on a Saturday morning. The insanity of it all! I would go back to 7-11, and get another bottle of wine.

All I can do is end with a question mark? This happened a lot, and it was not just one Saturday, it was many Saturdays. By the afternoon, I would be drunk. Jenell would have to take Alyssa from me. I would not be capable of caring for my daughter, because of my addiction. I am by no means proud of this story. It causes me such grief and despair; but in the end, there is an answer. It will all make sense, just give me some time.

I was in the depths of my addiction, smoking weed every day, drinking, doing cocaine, and taking Valium and Xanax at night to sleep. I was a mess and touching back on the vomiting; my drinking was so bad I did it every morning. I would wake up, go straight to the bathroom, and throw up. Yes, yellow bile, from drinking the night before. No food, just bile, and phlegm coming up.

It burned so badly as I leaned over the porcelain god, the pain and rawness in my throat was unbearable. I did this every morning for almost two years. All my molars and most of my back teeth are rotted down because of the acids. Years later, I had a Barium and a scope done on my stomach because I was throwing up my food during the day. I was told that I could not handle red meat or deep fried foods because the alcohol had done so much inner damage. So for the past 8 years, I have not eaten red meat, deep fried foods, or eaten at a fast food restaurant.

Four ways addiction breaks us are; *physically, mentally, emotionally* and *spiritually*. In this case, it was physical. The short, and the long-term damage and effects it caused will last a lifetime. To this day, I still have issues pertaining to my stomach, and throwing up. As I have mentioned, when the waves calm down, and you get your head on straight, you can look back and see the trail of destruction.

My father came to L.A. for a visit while I was deep in the storm. It was 2001 and things in my life were not so good. The good news is there was some work while he was visiting. I took my dad with me on the movie set; it was a commercial for *Snickers*, the chocolate bar. We had sets built on stages at 20th Century Fox. He was able to experience the lights and excitement of the film industry.

Now remember, my dad is a military man and an undercover drinker. One night when we were having dinner, my dad went up to Jenell and said these words, *"Why are you with Dwayne? He is a loser, and you could do much better than him."* Are you kidding me? My own father is saying this to the woman I have been with for 6 years, and we just had a child together? I mean, this really upset her; she came up to me and told me what my father said. I think at the time I blew it off, knowing my father, and the way he was. Years later I would remember my dad's comment. It hurt me really bad. Why would my father say such a thing?

It is now, as I am writing this, it hurts me most. Right now, as I am hitting the keyboard, I am going through some emotional distress. I feel deep sorrow, and I have to admit there is some anger flowing through me. There is only one thing I can do. I need to forgive my father for the hurt he caused me. I need to pray, and let it go; I need to give it to God, because if God can forgive me, then I need to forgive others. And, I need to forgive myself; I love my dad dearly.

It is time to share about a catastrophic day, a particular day so tragic and devastating. It was a day that would change my life forever.

I will never forget, for the rest of my life, that day. Jenell had it; she had taken as much as any woman could possibly handle. Living with a guy who was drinking every day, hooked on Vicodin, and getting cocaine delivered to the house three or four times a week. A guy who was hooked on Valium and Xanax, smoking weed morning, day and night, was not working and spending our savings on drugs and alcohol. This nightmare guy was me!

It was a Friday afternoon; Jenell told me to find a hotel room, a place to stay for the night because *she was leaving*. She and my daughter were moving out of the house; they were moving out of my life. *I was losing my family because of addiction.* She did not want me to be there while she was packing everything up.

In my brokenness, I told her to take anything and everything she needed. She found a two-bedroom place in Calabasas, a suburb of L.A. I stayed up the street, at the *Beverly Garland Hotel* that Friday night, and drank. Jenell, being the angel she was, came to the hotel that evening with Alyssa. As I am writing, I clearly remember being on the playground out back of the hotel. I was sitting on a slide, holding my daughter Alyssa, who would not be there when I walked through the door of our house.

They left after an hour, and I sat and cried all night, with a bottle of Jack Daniels in my hand. The grieving really started the next morning, when I went back to the house and opened the front door. Someone get a gun and shoot me now because that's how I feel at this moment, as I am writing this; how do I put this into words?

It was devastating, to say the least, to walk into a desolate, empty, lonely house. It was like the absence of God, there was no light, it was dark. The energy was off, no joy or peace. I walked through the house; there was the big screen T.V., the surround system that caused Jenell so much grief, and my wooden sleigh bed. My office was intact but other than that; everything was gone.

What caused the most pain was the absence of my daughter Alyssa, and the love of my life Jenell. I was lonely and ashamed of myself. My actions and decisions took away the two most important people in my life. I was overtaken by fear and anxiety, and I broke down and began sobbing uncontrollably.

I fell to my knees, then to the floor, laying there in a pool of tears. It was the worst day of my life. My choices and my addiction just took my daughter and Jenell. It was not like I had plenty of chances. Jenell, for a year or more, said these most powerful words," *quit drinking or we are leaving.*" They left!

What kind of a person has the choice between a newborn child, and an amazingly beautiful, wonderful woman, *or alcohol*? It blows my mind; it is incomprehensible. Here is the choice Dwayne. Either you quit drinking, and live a wonderful life with your 2-year-old daughter Alyssa and Jenell. Or you can take that bottle of Jack Daniels, throw the child and the woman away, and spend your days in misery with drugs and alcohol.

My addiction was incredibly powerful. My mind was so twisted and fragmented because of all the drugs and booze I had been consuming. Satan had his claws dug so deep into me that I actually said these words; "*I will take the bottle over my infant child and her mother.*" If I can be honest with you, I am trying to come up with words to describe a decision like that. What words can I use to explain how I picked a bottle of Jack Daniels over my daughter Alyssa, and Jenell? None! Addiction *will* take everything you love or care about away, and in the end; it wants to kill you!

After this grueling and painful experience, I checked back into Brotman. This would be my 4th time visiting the treatment center for alcohol and drug addiction. I was off to another 28-day program that would never work; 28 days is not long enough for any kind of recovery, or any kind of spiritual healing.

There is no time to do any type of work on yourself for healing in any way. The program is enough time to get some food into you, get you healthy, and jam a bunch of recovery into you that you cannot process at all because you are still in detox mode. Let me tell you why there is a 28-day recovery program. Why across Canada and the States the number 28 seems to be the recovery number.

The insurance companies had their little board room meetings and the powers to be decided that medical insurance would only cover 28 days. Yes, because of that decision, 28 is the magic number needed to get an alcoholic or addict back on their feet. Give me a break! I had been to Cry Help, Daniel Freedman, The Green House, and Brotman Institute. I went to seek help numerous times, and to be honest, over a two year period, I must have gone to treatment 12–15 times.

Yes, that is a big number, but there are a few problems, a few reasons why there was no success. Why none of the programs worked;

why I didn't work. The first reason is that in my heart, I did not want to sober up; my mind told me that treatment would work and that after 28 days I would be good. Every time like clockwork, I would be drinking within a week or two. It did not help that Jenell drank her wine in the evenings. I would stand firm, but as I mentioned, it only lasted a couple of weeks until I gave in, and drank again.

There is another reason why 28 days is not remotely enough time. I had 18 years of drinking behind me, and at this time in my life, it would be around 6-8 years of dabbling with the hard drugs. O.K, take all that time I have been building and working on my addiction. Now, you tell me that 28 days will take care of all those years of using and drinking? This makes me laugh. The first month is just enough time to get back on your feet, and let your mind clear a bit. It is the next six months to a year that will get you standing on solid ground.

I will dig deeply into that in a few chapters, but for now, I want to talk about the last woman who I would spend time with in L.A. Her name was Cori. I cared deeply for her, but she was an alcoholic!

I met Cori while I was in treatment at Brotman. The wrong place to meet women is definitely in a treatment center. Two broken people can't fix each other; it just does not work. Do the math, one alcoholic hooking up with another. What do you think the outcome would be? We did hope for a happy, fun loving relationship, and a chance to rebuild all the wreckage from our past. None of this is plausible. Unfortunately, two alcoholics or addicts together do not work; it is just a matter of time until one slips, and the other follows.

The year leading up to meeting Cori, I had already lost my daughter, Jenell, the house, the cars, and all my material possessions were gone. Most of my friends were gone, and my career had come crumbling to the ground. I had nothing left in my life when I met Cori. This is a list, a very sad one, of what addiction does. It wants to take anyone and anything you care for or love; anything you own and destroy it.

It was not too long after we left Brotman that I moved in with Cori at her place in Santa Monica. Cori's dad is a top laser eye surgeon in Detroit and is a millionaire a few times over. They live in Gross Pointe, Michigan, where the car maker Henry Ford had a mansion, as well as many other influential people. All the homes have a front yard the size of a football field, and every home is worth millions of dollars.

Cori's dad did anything and everything in his power to see her sober. She went to Wave Lengths in Malibu, where the monthly cost is exorbitant. This is where my best friend Glenn went before he was kicked out and came to stay with me; I will talk about that in a bit.

She had a town car, with a driver who was there for us every day. We would have him take us to lunch, or the liquor store, which happened daily. She and I had some sober times together; we would go to A.A. meetings and hang out with people in recovery. All it took was for one of us to fall and to make the decision to drink. Then, the other would follow, and we would both be back on the bottle.

The both of us were involved in a few very reckless times, and some insane things happened with her and me during our relationship. I was having suicidal thoughts for the first time in my life; I wonder why? After the year I had been through, all I wanted to do was die.

I remember driving down PCH and wanting to jump out of the car while it was doing 100 mph down the highway. One time while being fairly inebriated, I opened the door of the car and tried to launch myself out. By the grace of God, Cori was able to grab the back of my pants, which in turn held me in the car. She proceeded to grab the door and slammed it shut. I was inches away from splattering my body all over the highway.

Weeks later we were in her apartment one evening drinking which in turn lead to an argument. The big problem was that I was still in my suicidal mood. I clearly remember sitting there, lost and hopeless. I was in a daze, staring at the huge plate glass window in her living room. I got to a point of anger and frustration. In my self-pity and drunken state, I told her I felt like I wanted to jump out the living room window. Her reply *"Go ahead and jump through it."*

Like a bullet coming out of a gun, my mind snapped. I threw the bottle of vodka to the floor, and I leaped up onto the coffee table. Using it as a springboard, I ran the length of the table, and dove head first through the massive window. Glass shattered, it was everywhere, I landed out in the courtyard, all cut up, with blood streaming from open wounds. My mangled body laid face down on the ground, surrounded by blood and shards of glass. I came to and was confused, but not really hurt; nothing was broken.

She came running out, held me, then brought me back into the apartment. During the chaos, one of the neighbors called 911 and before I could blink an eye, the paramedics, and police were there. I thought I could manipulate everyone. I said to the police that I was walking by the window, and fell through. They had a look and a grin on their face that said I was out of my mind. The glass was shattered all over, inside and out. There were fragments of glass lying about 10 feet out from the window. With all that evidence, and the cuts and blood covering my body, the only possible answer was that I thought I could fly. It did not take a CSI unit to figure it out. I was locked to a stretcher, and it was off to the psych ward, again.

My second trip to the psych ward, and it would not be my last. I have a problem with being held down and contained; I basically lose it when I am subdued. They put me in a straitjacket when I arrived at the psych unit of the hospital. I did not like that at all!

They put me in a room, and I began to work my magic. I twisted and turned, and within a few minutes I had worked my way out of the straitjacket. They had an IV tube in my arm, and I believe this was a big deal according to the following chain of events. The door was not locked, so I began to make my escape. The nurses saw me and were astonished that I had broken out of the straitjacket.

I began my sprint down the hallways, making my way to the exit. The problem was I had company while making my escape. Three security guards were hot on my tail; they kept screaming about the IV tube, and they wanted it. I made my way to the exit of the hospital and ran outside to freedom. In an instant, I grabbed the IV tube from my arm, pulled it out, and threw it to the ground. To my astonishment, the guards stopped the chase, grabbed the IV tube from the ground; and walked back to the hospital.

There I was, outside of the hospital, a free man. I was standing in the parking lot wondering what my next move would be? My quick-witted addict mind tells me, call a cab, and get a ride back to Cori's apartment. I arrived, we hugged and kissed. We are so happy to be back together, and in the midst of the ran-shackled apartment, we begin to drink. After all that happened! I made it back to Cori's, so I could pick up the bottle and start drinking again. The insanity of addiction is mind blowing!

One more Cori story for you; my birthday was coming up, and I thought that we should fly to Detroit and see her parents, a nice little vacation. I called the airline and booked our tickets for the trip. We were going to fly out in a few days, and the flight was at 9:00 pm.

The day arrived, so we decided we should have a few drinks before leaving for the airport. Being the alcoholics that we were, we began drinking around 2:00 in the afternoon. By the time we called the driver to come pick us up, we were, to say the least, a little drunk. We had a few more drinks in the town car on our way to the airport. This was not a bright idea because the last thing we needed was more alcohol flowing through our systems.

We arrived at LAX, made our way to the gate to board the plane, and once again we were squabbling about something. I can't remember about what, but we boarded the plane, and we were tucked away into our seats. The next chain of events is something I have never experienced on all my flights.

She and I were drunk, and we were yelling and screaming at each other. The plane began to pull out from the terminal. We must have made it about 100 ft. when the plane stopped. The US air marshal showed up at our seats, and the plane began to make its way back to the terminal. The air marshal informed us that we are getting kicked off the flight. The plane re-docks and Cori and I are escorted off the plane and led back into the terminal.

This was a once in a lifetime experience. Nothing remotely close to this had ever happened to me in the hundreds of flights I have been on. The airline staff was very nice and said to go home, sober up, and catch the next flight at 8:00 am the next morning. We obliged, and went back to Cori's, took a little nap, and made the flight next day.

Cori was, and is an amazing woman; we had a lot of good times together. She helped me when I was at my lowest, and she was always there for me during the six months we were together. Obviously, because of the alcohol, we had some very trying times, and in the end, we broke up. I moved back to the Valley, about a block from the house that I lived in with Jenell and Alyssa. What drew me back to the same area, the same place, where the *fall* began?

CHAPTER 9
L.A.—The Fall, Part Two

IT SEEMS THAT all of the places I moved to in my later years in L.A. something horrible took place, or was going to take place. I moved about a block from our old house in the Valley, living alone, and drinking. I was checking into one treatment center after another, always leaving after a week or two.

There were many times, and these are not good times, where in the mornings after waking up from a night of drinking, I would have to go out back to the parking area. The first reason was to see if my vehicle was there. If it was, what a blessing! The second reason was to check for blood. I would walk around checking to see if there was any on either side of my front bumpers.

There were times I was so drunk the night before that I would not remember driving home. I would not know if I crashed into another vehicle, or hit someone. While in my drunken state, did I run someone over, killing them, not knowing?

Is this any way to live life? How much more messed up could I have been? I had no control over my drinking at the time. I would always drink and drive, even after two DUI's. I definitely did not learn anything from the past drunk drivings. The first DUI cost me $5000.00; the second cost me $10,000.

I used the most amazing lawyer named Charlie. I got myself into a lot of troubles due to the DUI's. In the end, Charlie got me off; I walked away from both of them. I thought, what would have happened if I did not get off? Maybe I would have learned a lesson? Could I have possibly stopped drinking and driving? The honest answer is "No," I was not willing or ready to surrender.

There was nothing at this point in my life that could have told me, or showed me, to stop drinking and drugging. Addiction had it claws dug so deep into me. I was caught in a vortex, continuing my downward spiral. All the loss and suffering I had to endure so far weighed heavy on me. Still spinning down, and down, there was more bad news to come. When you think you have hit your bottom, always remember; *every bottom has a basement*. There would soon be another call to Charlie.

There is this one event that was going to take me again to the pits of hell. Glenn; yes, that is how I will start. Glenn, as you remember, was my best friend; he was on Rosanne back in the day. At this point of his life, he had been fired from the T.V. show Angel because of his addiction.

As I am telling you my story, I want to share a bit about what Glenn had. He was a successful actor, working on *Angel*, and making a ton of money. He had a huge house in the Hollywood Hills, just under the Hollywood sign. He had a brand new M series BMW, and the love of his life was Aimee.

There was a small problem; alcohol, cocaine, and heroin. Glenn was battling his own demons. He had it all, but in the end, he was missing something, that *someone*. Once again, addiction performed as it does, triumphing; and taking everything from Glenn. The house, the cars, and the money was all gone!

I have told you many times about addiction, what it does, and what it will do to your life. If you have any doubts, please take a look back and see what it has already done to me. If looking back is not enough, and you think you have drugs and alcohol under control, go back a few lines, and see what it had taken from my best friend, Glenn.

A famous, wealthy T.V. star, someone you would think, after reading one of those stupid Enquire magazines or gossip newspapers at the checkout telling you what an amazing life celebrities are living. Well, here is a *real hardcore*, down to earth example of how addiction is not picky. It took everything from Glenn, all the material things, everything he loved was gone; and he lost any hope he had for a future.

The real sad part of the story is that it does not end here; addiction was not quite done with him. The day came when he called to see if he could stay the night. He needed a friend and a place to stay. A couple of hours later he was at my door, and I invited my best friend into my apartment.

As I write this, I am going to try to somehow put it into words. Making it as real as it was, and letting you know some very personal emotions and feelings I went through as I try to explain this momentous event. Glenn showed up to my place around 8:00 pm in a rental car. He is in shambles, a broken man, who was trying to deal with all life was throwing at him. As you know, I was going through some catastrophic events of my own. We were both deep into the darkest storms of life that only addiction can cause. We took a trip to the liquor store to pick up some relief, something to help ease the pain we were both dealing with.

Glenn had lost everything, and he was just kicked out of Wavelengths, a treatment center in Malibu, for using drugs. We arrived back to my place, and in no time after a few drinks, we were both in good spirits. We put the misery and despair behind us. Neither one of us wanted to confront the emotions that were set before us. All we wanted to do was bury everything, to stuff the pain as far down as we could.

We drank, and talked about some of our adventures; we laughed and actually turned a nightmare into a better time. It was around 11:30 pm, now I am going to share something that I have never told anyone. Glenn called me into the kitchen and asked me if I wanted to try something new. Being an addict, I was game. I said yes, not even knowing what it was.

He opened up a bindle, and inside was a gram of heroin; now, I had never done that in my life. I have experimented with pretty much every drug out there, but I had not entered into the world of heroin. He asked for some tin foil, and then he proceeded to put a line on it. You burn the foil from underneath, following the line as it burns. Then you take a straw, and hold it above the heroin, inhaling, as you chase the line.

Satan's smoke is flowing into your temple, hence the phrase *Chasing the Dragon*. I did one line of the heroin, and that was all. He did a couple of lines, chasing the dragon because that is what heroin is; a dragon who wants to kill you. It was quite an experience. The first time doing it in my life, sitting together talking, drinking and being high. I have never mentioned this to anyone until now. I have always left this part of my story out. But this is a real, honest account of my life. It was about 2:00 am, and I was getting tired, so I said goodnight to Glenn, and went to bed for the night. He was going to crash out on the couch.

The next morning, I woke up to a day that I will never forget. This would be another day in my life that would shake my inner core, and send my life spinning out of control. As if I have not had to deal with enough pain already! I got dressed and was going to head out to do a few errands. As I walked by the couch, I saw Glenn laying there.

He looked like he was still sleeping, but the odd thing was he had thick saliva, a mucus type drool running down the side of his face. At the time, being ignorant of what heroin does, I thought nothing of it. Assuming he was still sleeping, I headed out; it was around 9:30 a.m.

I arrived back at my place around 11:00 am, and walked in the door. Glenn was still lying there, in the same position. I walked over to him grabbed his wrist and at the same time, I yelled out, "*Quinny its time to get up.*" Those were the last words I ever said to my best friend.

Glenn's wrist was ice cold, so I took my other hand and placed it on his neck. This too was ice cold. I let go with both hands and took a step back. There I was hovering over the dead body of my one and only best friend. Now here is the honest, dark truth. I did not know what to think, I did not break down crying. It was as if I had no emotion. I was numb; there was no real sense of sadness or tears; I didn't understand this. Where was the grief that I should have been experiencing? There he was, lying on my couch, dead, and I can't muster up any feelings; this confused me.

I grabbed the phone and called 911. It was about 10 minutes later when the fire dept. showed up with the paramedics. They checked his body and reaffirmed that Glenn was dead. Within minutes, the police showed up and did a check of the apartment. They looked over the scene and waited till the detectives arrived. By this time the fire dept. had already left.

About an hour later the detectives showed up. The police can now leave. All the while, Glenn is laying there lifeless, with nothing covering him. I had been looking at his ice cold, lifeless body lying there the whole time. I got a bed sheet from my room, and the two detectives took it and covered him up.

In L.A. the fire dept. does their thing, and then the police do their thing, and lastly the detectives arrive, and they have to stay till the coroners show up. I found Glenn around 11:00 a.m, and after all was said and done; it was around 12:30. There I was, in the apartment with two detectives, and my best friend dead on my couch.

I needed a drink. The next thing you know, I flew out of my place and made my way to the liquor store to grab a bottle of tequila. I arrived back around 1:00, and I remember putting on Africa Serengeti, a documentary on the big screen. I was drinking, hanging out with two detectives, and Glenn, watching an African documentary waiting for the L.A. coroners to show up.

There are only so many coroners in L.A. So the wait was long; they finally showed up around 5:00 pm. I spent the whole afternoon in the apartment with Glenn lying there covered with a bed sheet; it was traumatizing. When they arrived, they asked me to wait outside so they could put my best friend into a body bag. I did as I was told, and waited outside. When they were finished, I came inside, and they said they had found two syringes under his body when they rolled him over. He died from a heroin overdose.

There was no flood of emotions. I am sitting here wanting to tell you how I was feeling and what I was going through, but I can't. I was just numb, it was like a nightmare, almost as if it was not real. I did what I have done my whole life. I just stuffed it way down deep into my soul burying the pain. I have never dealt with feelings my whole life. This was because I used alcohol and drugs to deal with all my emotions. I lost my best friend because of addiction, and my best defense was to bury it with alcohol.

To close, I want to give you some info. The drool coming out of Glenn's mouth was actually vomit. One of the ways an addict dies from a heroin overdose is from choking on their own vomit. You may think it is from the heart-stopping, which it does. Your whole body turns blue, and you end up on your back, because, in an overdose, that is how you will be.

What happens is you begin to vomit during the overdose, and since you are on your back, you choke on it and end up dying. The other crazy thing is by 6:00 pm that evening; I received a phone call from the *Enquirer*, offering me $10,000 to give them the story. It was about twenty minutes later the *Globe* called, making the same offer. I was filled with uncontrollable rage, the audacity of them to call me for a story a few hours after I found my best friend dead on my couch from an overdose. They wanted to know what happened for their stupid, mindless magazines.

Glenn was a celebrity, and they were calling for the story. I cannot write the words that I said on the phone to both of the parties involved. It would turn this into an X-rated book, but I declined all offers. After giving them a verbal beating I hung up, continued drinking, burying all emotions and feelings deep into my soul. I drank myself into oblivion, all alone, late into the night. I missed my best friend!

Addiction took everything from Glenn. I also told you what addiction wants, it only wants one thing, and that is, in the end after it has caused enough pain and loss, it wants to kill you. In the end addiction accomplished its goal; it killed Glenn!

Remember earlier I mentioned making a call to my lawyer, and I would probably be in need of Charlie's services again, for the third time; this would not be good. It all started on a beautiful day in Malibu. I was taking care of Alyssa while Jenell was at work. After she separated from me, around 2002, she still permitted me to see Alyssa. We were never married! Jenell clearly stated that "*if I quit drinking then we would get married*." Even this offer was not strong enough to conquer the goliath of addiction.

Jenell was dating, and I think she had already gone through two or three guys. It bothered me a bit that so soon after our break up she would be out on the prowl. I guess they call it *a rebound*, after a breakup. You seek someone else; you seek companionship. My only relationship was Cori. Other than that I was too busy destroying everything in my life. I did not have time for women. In the end, who would want to be with a guy like me on the road to hell?

I took my incredible daughter for a ride through Malibu canyon, then back to Calabasas where Jenell and Alyssa were living. I decided that we should go to a local Mexican restaurant that we frequented. We went in, and I ordered a margarita on the rocks, with a double shot of tequila. The restaurant was fairly empty. The two of us were running around playing hide and seek. We knew the staff, and they did not mind our playfulness. After playing some more, I ordered another, and eventually a third double margarita.

After an hour of drinking and playing, sushi sounded like a good idea for dinner. We drove two blocks up the street and ordered a bunch of sushi to bring back. The not so good news was someone in the

Mexican restaurant noticed my drinking and driving with my daughter. So they called the police.

I was not privy to such information, so we drove to the sushi restaurant, went in, and ordered. While we were waiting, I had a couple of sake shots, and a Sapporo beer. We picked up our order, walked to the truck, and hopped in. Alyssa was full of energy, and did not want to sit in her baby seat; she wanted to stand in the back seat. Being a bit drunk, I thought nothing of it. Plus, I wanted to make my daughter happy.

I figured it was only about six blocks to their house, so I said no problem, play away my little angel. Being in my addiction, with alcohol flowing through my system, I had no thoughts of putting my sweet little innocent daughter's life in danger. So I pulled out of the parking lot to make our way home. I was blind to the fact that there was a police car sitting there, watching and waiting for me to get in my truck. I began the short journey home, and almost immediately I saw flashing lights in my rearview mirror, so I pulled over. The cop walked up to me, saw Alyssa bouncing around in the back seat, and asked me to step out of the car. He gave me the Breathalyzer test. Again, I failed miserably and was arrested for drunk driving.

I also picked up a child endangerment charge for having Alyssa in the car; she was only three years old. The police called Jenell to see if she was around so she could come get Alyssa. Thank God she had just finished work and was driving through the canyon on her way home. About ten minutes later Jenell showed up. I clearly remember sitting in the backseat of the police car in handcuffs. I was sobbing uncontrollably as I looked out the window and saw Jenell standing there, holding my three-year-old daughter. She had a look on her face that I would never forget. She was disgusted with me. Jenell was so angry and ashamed that I was Alyssa's father.

We are definitely making our way to the end of the nightmare I was living. You have read about all the pain, suffering, and loss I have had to endure. My bad choices and my addiction were on a path of destruction; I was out of control. My life was totally unmanageable. I have been referring to addiction as some sort of an entity. Yes, it is, and the entity is Satan. Here I am with a third DUI, and a child endangerment charge. My life was about to end as I knew it. As we will soon see, this bad choice would alter my entire life.

Before the driving mishap with Alyssa, I had an accident; I was so drunk one day that I slammed into the side of another car while driving at 80 mph, down the freeway. After I hit them and was still driving, I flagged the person to pull over at the next off ramp. As we approached the off ramp, they exited, expecting me to follow them. But at the last minute, I pulled back out onto the freeway and took off. I sped my way back to my place, pulling the truck around back, into the parking area out of sight. There was a lot of damage to the passenger's side of my truck. I never did get caught. No one had taken my license plate number during the incident.

This is another time that shame and guilt overtook me. My destructive behavior and my addiction has now ruined my new truck. Once again, I turned to alcohol and buried any emotions and feelings I was having. About an hour later, I drove to get more booze, came home and drank my fears away!

One last incident happened when I was at a liquor store in Malibu. I was leaving the store with booze in hand, after a morning of drinking. Without thinking, I jumped into my truck, hit the gas, backed out, and ran the back of the truck into a two foot round metal pole. Crushing the back door into that familiar V-shape; I could not open it after that happened. Addiction always has a plan to destroy everything; relationships, careers, and material possession. I had crushed the back of my Montero, and the passenger's side was all torn up because the accident on the freeway. The destruction we leave behind is endless.

Here is the sick part of it all. What would have happened if some kids were walking to their car? I would have backed into them, probably running them down, and possibly killing them. This sends chills down my spine. I could not imagine doing something like that. By the grace of God, in all my days of drinking and driving, I never killed anyone. I believe if I kept going the way I was, it could have easily happened.

Someone was sick and tired of my driving under the influence. This someone, who we will call anonymous, was about to put an end to it. They called up some people, who just happened to be part of a Latino gang we knew. They worked out a deal for them to come and steal my truck. I was back in another treatment center when this occurred. I left my truck in a place I believed to be safe. They knew where the truck was, and one night our Latino friends came by and stole the truck.

What happened next is a bit crazy. The gang members drove downtown L.A., stripped the truck, put it on blocks, and proceeded to burn it to the ground. When I got out of treatment, I noticed my truck had been stolen, so I called my insurance company. They already knew what had happened. The truck was a lease, so my insurance settled the claim. Anonymous did not tell me until a month later that the whole event was planned. This put an end to my driving, either sober or drunk. My vehicle was gone, toasted as you could say. Sometimes God works in mysterious ways; I truly believe this was one of those ways.

Malibu court, my third drunk driving within seven years; this is a very bad thing in the states. They wanted 2½ years in prison for the drunk driving and the child endangerment charge. It was time to call Charlie. This third DUI would cost me $15,000. Remember this was in 2000, fifteen years ago; it was a lot of money. I have to add a comment; don't you just love addiction, and all the wonderful things that go along with it?

I believe it was worth every penny. I did not want to go to prison for 2½ years. There were a couple of factors on my side. First Charlie is one of the best Lawyers in L.A. as far as drunk driving goes. He actually goes to USC and UCLA to instruct future lawyers on how to defend people with DUI's. The second bonus was that we would be going to court in Malibu, and my case was with Judge Myra.

If you remember the *Pam Anderson* and *Tommy Lee* case, the *Charlie Sheen* case, and *Robert Downey Jr.* All these people were before Judge Myra, in Malibu. Charlie just happened to be very good friends with him.

Ted Knight, the actor from the T.V. show *Too Close for Comfort*, had a son who was involved in a huge drinking and driving incident, and the case was before Judge Myra. Charlie defended Mr. Knight's son. During this lengthy trial, Charlie became, and still is, very good friends with Judge Myra. In the long run, and through a couple of court cases, Charlie worked his magic. I did three months in a treatment center and lost my license. But other than that, I was cleared of all other charges, and there was no prison time. Thank you, Charlie!

A few months after this, things would continue to go downhill, as if my life was not spinning out of control. I mean, was there anything left to lose in my life? Even though it may be hard to comprehend, it was going to get worse. My addiction did not want to stop. It was on a mission to devour, steal, and to kill. It had a few more storms for me to walk through. As I mentioned, every bottom has a basement, and I was about to walk down into that basement with a shovel so I could dig a little deeper.

While I was living in the valley, I stayed in contact with Cori. She had moved to a new apartment in Santa Monica. She liked to meet people, sometimes street people. She felt as though she needed to care for them. Cori would invite them over to her place so she could have drinking companions.

I went by one day, and she had two guys and a girl there. Things went real bad, an argument ensued, and I ended up getting into a very violent fight with both guys. One guy was huge and during the struggle her place was demolished. The big guy smashed me in the face so hard that my eye socket was shattered, and my left eye had swollen so much that I could not see; it was like a balloon.

The neighbors called the police. They arrived rather quickly; which was good for me because I was not winning the fight. They arrested the big guy, and me. The police took me to the hospital emergency to have my eye checked out. The doctor took an x-ray and examined my ballooned eye. He said it needed to be cut to release the pressure building up. It reminded me of the Movie *Rocky* when Stallone says *cut me*. Well, this was the same thing. They cut the lower part of my eye. Whatever it was came oozing out, and I could see again. Prior to that, it was swollen shut.

After my visit to the hospital, I was brought to the Santa Monica Police station, to a holding cell. While I was there, they ran my info and saw I had breached my conditions because of my third DUI charge. After spending five hours in the cell, I was off to a place that will be very hard to put into words, but I will try. It was about 4:00 pm and they loaded me up, along with three other guys. It was off to *L.A. County Jail.*

The Twin Towers Correctional Facility is the biggest jail system in the world, and one of the most violent and troubled facilities in the U.S. They call it a windowless dungeon in downtown. It has an average daily population of 18,000 inmates; this is not a typo or an incorrect number. When you hear about jails and prisons in Canada with 1500 or 2000 inmates, you think, wow! Even prisons in the states only house up to 4500 tops, and that is considered a lot.

Now think about it, L.A. County Jail has an average of 18,000 inmates going through the system on a daily basis. Here are a few more bits of info for you. The ACLU of Southern California has documented overcrowding, unsanitary conditions, and extreme abuse of inmates at the hands of deputies. The hell I was entering into was unlike anything you could or would want to experience. Let me share with you about my journey into the pits of hell, and it was hell.

Upon arriving at the massive facility where I was incarcerated, they took me into one big holding cell; there must have been a hundred-fifty guys in there. After spending hours waiting, they took me down a long corridor; they then split us up and put me into a smaller cell. There I got to wait some more before being called to a window, where I sat, and my file was run.

After this, I went back to the cell and waited some more. Eventually, I was called, lined up, and proceeded to make my way to a bigger cell. This is where I stripped down out of my street clothes into the beautiful orange inmate uniforms. Here is the astonishing moment, and I remember it clear as day. They led me down another long corridor. At the end, I came around a corner, and all I saw was an ocean of orange. The area was massive, with 8–10 huge cells. There must have been somewhere around 600–800 guys, all sitting and waiting. To top it off, air conditioning was pumping through the whole place, so it was very cold. I spent two days waiting until I was called.

So there I was, little old Dwayne, a 5′7″ 150 lbs white boy, surrounded by Crips, Bloods, and 18th St, gangbangers from all the surrounding areas of the city. Murderers, rapists, and hardcore criminals; this was by no means Disneyland.

They kept me waiting in these massive holding cells until my time came to go to medical. Every inmate must go through a process before they get sent up to the pods. I had a bit of a bonus, and you think how in the heck can I have a bonus? Well, let me tell you; my huge ballooned eye, still puffed out, and black and blue was my ticket.

I walked into the main holding cell with my messed up eye. All the inmates immediately assumed the Sheriffs did it. Right away they began to get angry with them, thinking that either out on the street or when I came into county, the police gave me a beating. I am not stupid; I was in the jungle surrounded by wild animals. My witty addict mind kicks into play; and rightly so, I agreed with their comments. My response was, yes; the sheriffs kicked my ass. If there was ever a time in my life where a little white lie might save me, this was the one. They all sympathized with me, and I fit right into the jungle.

Here is a little more info for you. From the time I came into L.A. County, went through the process of meeting with the medical intake worker, and being sent up to my pod, took three days. The average time to process into county takes around three days; now that is insane!

I have one more bonus to add, a saving grace. I just happened to be taking Wellbutrin at the time, a mood stabilizer. So when I met with the medical intake worker and mentioned this little gem of info, it saved me. I was sent to a medical pod, and not into the general population. In County, they segregate the gangs, the homosexuals, and medical inmates. We had yellow uniforms; general pop is blue, and so on. Everything is colorized.

They go one step further and segregate us as to where we were arrested. For me, it was Santa Monica. This meant everyone in my pod was from around that general area, and everyone in my pod was on some type of medication.

This was so much safer than the general population, but it was by no means a nonviolent pod. There were fights almost every day. I watched as an inmate was almost beaten to death by two gang bangers for ripping them off. During my stay, I saw more than one inmate taken out on a stretcher, barely alive, and hardly breathing from getting beaten. I also witnessed a man get stabbed with a plastic pen. One thing I learned in my life was how to be street smart, and not to be stupid. In an environment like county, you definitely don't want to be an idiot or rip someone off. In there, it could get you sent to the hospital, or killed.

The overcrowding is a huge issue at county; our pod had 12 two man cells along the bottom, and 12 two man cells along the top. So obviously, it was designed for 24 inmates. This was not the case. We had floor sleepers and bunk beds on the main floor. There were 48 guys in our pod; it was overcrowded and dangerous. I don't miss the midnight shakedowns, or stripping naked in front of correctional officers, and having a body search done.

I had never felt like such a criminal, being shackled, both hands and feet when I left the pod for whatever reason. I was treated like dirt, and the sheriffs could not care less about me. We had an older man in our pod, and he had a heart attack. He laid there for a day before he was stretchered out. L.A. County Jail is by far the worst place I've ever been in my entire life, and I've been to some pretty bad places.

I witnessed torture and beatings at the hands of both inmates and staff. The local drink in county is called pruno. They make it with orange peels, potatoes, and anything with sugar. It's a wicked blend of fruit that ferments and turns into alcohol; let's call it jail house moonshine. Crazy as it was, I never drank any of it when I was in county. I was smart enough not to drink, or get drunk in the presence of the company I was keeping.

Here is some good news about my stay in paradise. Being the smart, witty guy I am, I made friends with a couple of the main inmates in my pod. I would buy them calling cards from the canteen, which was once a week. You could order chips, soup, soap, very basic necessities. I continued to buy my new friends calling cards, so they could call their sugar mama. This is jailhouse slang for a girlfriend, or wife.

Three weeks into my stay, as we were all sitting around the spider tables waiting for a count, something happened. Three times a day everyone must stand at their cell doors, or be on the main floor sitting at one of the spider tables. Spider tables are stainless steel and round, with four seats attached, made, so they do not come apart and are bolted to the ground. Everyone was sitting around waiting; it could take an hour or two, depending on whether the sheriff's felt like getting it done, or they made us wait, just because they could.

One of the big black inmates, who was a buddy, came walking from outside the pod up to the main door which enters in; accompanied by a sheriff. The pod is surrounded with huge glass windows looking out to the middle of the complex. In the middle is the bubble, where the sheriffs can sit and see into all six surrounding pods. They walk up, and the black guy bangs on one of the window, and points in my direction. I pay no attention. Then the bang happens again, and the guy next to me says, "hey, he is looking at you." I look up; he points at me, and signals for me to come to the pod door. I oblige and walk to the door. The sheriff opens it; I walk out, and my black friend says, "Come with me, you are now a trustee."

This would turn out to be a life saver; a trustee means freedom. I was able to leave the pod at 8: 00 am, and return around 8:00 pm.

The job of a trustee included cleaning the pods after they were empty and everyone had gone to court. We would also feed everyone; the meals would be brought up to the 6th floor, and dropped off by the kitchen staff. We would go from pod to pod with the sheriffs, who would open the door at each one. Inside the inmates are lined up, and one by one you hand them their meals.

The bonus was that we had access to a T.V. in the rec room, and food; this is a huge commodity in Jail. There was bread, meat, and peanut butter; it all came packaged up. So what I would do was stuff my pants full of food after my shift finished. I would then walk to the pod door, and the sheriff in the bubble would buzz me in.

Now, here comes the smart move. I would go from cell to cell, sliding food under the doors so the guys could have a night time snack. I did not have one fight or any problems during my three-month stay. They called me by my nickname; Canada. Everyone wanted to come to Vancouver with me when they were released. One reason was because it is an amazing city; the other, the three strike law in California.

As I mentioned, there were fights, and a lot of insane unexplainable things happened during my stay there. I never was approached, or threatened, because of the circle of friends I made. Hey, I am not stupid, and I did what I had to do so I could survive my time in county. A smart addict, who puts his mind to use, can survive anywhere, with anyone.

This chapter is called the *fall II*, which means exactly that. You may be getting an understanding, after reading this chapter and the last two. Seeing the wreckage, loss, and life experiences I had to endure because of addiction, you would think, O.K. Dwayne? This has been quite the downward spiral, to say the least, after everything that has happened, and being in the pits of hell; how could it possibly get any worse? Well, let me tell you. Unfortunately, I am not done. There is one last thing, one last piece of the wreckage I have not shared with you.

The call came for me to go downstairs. I had no idea what it was for, but I was escorted through the long unending corridors, down to the main floor, to a holding cell. L.A. County is so complex, and so big, that if they unlocked all the doors, and said I was free, I would not be able to find my way out. I sat there for hours, thinking what could it be, am I being released? In county, you do half time for nonviolent crimes. So I thought I was being released because it was three months;

that's half of my six-month sentence. This was not to be the case; the thought of freedom and fresh air was still a long way away. I was taken from my holding cell into the immigration office in county.

They proceeded to tell me that I had three DUI's within seven years, which I also want to mention, were only misdemeanors. I had no felony charges. The fight at Cori's caused me to breach my probation from the third DUI. They did the tally and told me; "*I was being deported back to Canada.*" My heart stopped, and I was speechless. I was being deported! I was in a state of shock; then they said that I would be transported to Long Beach, to the Immigration Detention Center.

Within a week, I was brought down to the holding cells, waiting to be transported to Long Beach. How many white guys do you think were in the cells with me awaiting deportation? There were fifty guys in the cell, and, you guessed it, I was the only white guy in the whole bunch.

I can't count how many guys asked me, what was I doing there, and why and where was I being deported? Eventually, it was goodbye L.A. County, and hello Long Beach Immigration. I arrived there around 5:00 p.m. Once again I was put in a cell, and I changed into the orange inmate uniforms. Then we were escorted to the massive dormitory, where again there was an ocean of orange, and bunk beds as far as the eye could see.

It was one huge dorm room, full of guys from all over the world, fighting their cases, trying everything humanly possible to stay in the states. I was taken to my bunk, and there were 250 guys in this one area. People scattered all about, on the pay phones, huddled up in groups, talking and planning. Some had paperwork stacked to the roof, all fighting to stay, even though most did not have a chance.

I had a chance, but this is where I get brutally honest with myself. I go before the judge, and she tells me that I can fight the case, and probably win. I respond that I don't have the $5000.00 to fight the case. So out of the blue, she says, well, I will lower it to $3000.00. In a split second, I have the most incredible moment of clarity; almost a revelation! An honest evaluation of the past two years flows through my mind, and I come to a conclusion.

As I stood before the immigration judge, thinking of my case, and my life, I became very humble; I crushed what little pride and ego I had left. It was an honest, selfless moment. I began to go over all the storms, trials, and the insanity I have gone through. I think about the irreparable damage I have caused. I felt completely broken as I thought about the ones I loved, and cared for, and the complete hell I put them through. As I continued to run the past two years through my mind, my heart was softened; I became very emotional, and sadness overtook me.

I made very bad choices, and while being so deep in my addiction; I did not have any power over my choices. The first step was to *admit that my life was unmanageable and that I was completely powerless.* If you are not sure what that means, I want to share with you what a powerless life looks like. Let me give you a rundown of the unmanageability in my life.

First Jenell and my daughter left me; they were *gone.* I did not have them in my life anymore. *Second* I lost the house on Fair, *gone,* where I lived for the first two years of my daughter's life. *Third* My BMW, *gone,* and the truck I leased was taken downtown and burnt to the ground, *gone. Fourth* all the material things that I possessed, *gone,* auctioned off at the storage facility. *Fifth* the career that took 15 years to build, *gone, Sixth* I found my best friend dead on my couch from a heroin overdose, *gone. Seventh* I just did three months in *L.A. County,* basically hell on earth, and here I stand before an *immigration judge* being *deported* back to Canada. I pray this list opens your eyes to the incredibly destructive power of addiction!

I clearly told the judge that life as I knew it was over, I had endured about as much pain, suffering, and loss that a human could handle over the past two years. I said, "*Just deport me,*" and I would pay for my own plane ticket to expedite the process. Within a week, I was handcuffed, shackled, and put in the back of an immigration van. Then I was driven to the tarmac at LAX. I exited the vehicle, was unshackled, given my duffle bag of clothes, and then escorted up the metal stairs to the plane. As I made my way in, the immigration officer gave my passport to the stewardess and told her to give it back to me when we land in Canada.

Rev 3:20 tells me *someone* was knocking on the door of my heart. I am on the other side, and all I have to do is let Him in. To open the door, and let Him into my life; I needed that *someone.* The question; was I ready to open the door and let Him in? Was I done doing it my way?

CHAPTER 10

Back To Canada

I WISH I COULD say that all was good. I came back to Canada, went into treatment, and I found that *someone* who heals the pain and brings freedom. I went back to work in the film industry and rekindled my relationship with Alyssa and Jenell. I stayed clean and sober and began to put my life back together.

NO! I am sorry to say, this was definitely not the case. Unfortunately, when I came back, things only continued to get worse. After all I had endured; the most insane thing was my addict telling me to keep driving the bus, to do things my way. Is it possible God was not done allowing specific situations to occur in my life? He was at the door knocking, and I should have opened it and let Him in. I believe the problem was that I did not know Him, or was it because I wasn't ready?

Does this make any sense to you? How much more does a person in addiction need to suffer until they ultimately decide to change? I ended the last chapter with a long list of an unmanageable life; this would not be enough to change me. Why? I will try to answer this question a little later, for now, more chaos and destruction.

I would like to add something that is very prevalent for the rest of the book; it is my use of the word *addict*. An alcoholic is someone who is addicted to alcohol; an addict is someone who is addicted to drugs. I cannot write throughout the whole book, alcoholic/addict when referring to someone in addiction. So when you read the word *addict* from here on in, it will refer to both alcoholics and drug addiction.

The year 2004, I was 37 years old, and this would be my 22nd move. It was back to Canada, to a small town called Innisfail. This is where my mom lives, just outside of Red Deer, Alberta. It is the city where I spent my High school years. I came back about as broken and shattered as any human could be. I had lost everything in my life because of addiction. Now, I had been clean and sober for 3½ months, because of my time spent in county and immigration. It did not take long, while in my broken state, to find something to help ease the pain. My mom had a back problem, and she was taking an opiate painkiller called OxyContin. Well, wouldn't you know it, my addiction kicked in, and I began stealing oxy's from my mother.

The news was out that I had arrived back from L.A., but no one knew the reasons why. I never told anyone about the horrific events that had taken place prior to my coming back to Canada. The local newspaper and high school got wind of my arrival and wanted me to go to my old high school and do a speech for the students.

I might as well start off with something positive before we begin to dig into this chapter. I received a few calls from the paper, and my school, to arrange for me to come by. A date was set, and I went back to Lindsay Thurber High. I made a powerful speech about the ups and downs of life, pursuing your goals, following your dreams, and shared some of my positive life experiences.

I inspired the students to *go for it, pursue your goals and dreams*, and not to let anything stand in their way. If your heart was telling you to pursue a career or goal, then take a leap of faith. Reach for it, and put all you have into turning that goal into reality. After the speech, the local paper did an interview with me and put an article in the paper. No one knew about *The Fall*, and there is something else I need to share with you. I did the speech while I was high on OxyContin. I know, you are thinking to yourself, Dwayne you are right out of it! But as I mentioned, this is a real story, and as you already know, I am not holding anything back.

My bright mind and intelligent thinking wanted to get back to work in the film industry. Canada has two cities where the film business is busy. The closest to where I was is Vancouver, which would have been a one-day greyhound ride, or Toronto. I choose to go to Toronto, on the other side of the country.

I only stayed with my mom for about two weeks, and then it was on the greyhound bus to make my way across the country; final destination, Toronto. A small problem occurred while on my travels. Our dear friend, Mr. Addiction, showed up in full force. I began to drink again; a three-day ride took me about a week. Whenever the bus made a stop, I would seek out a local bar, get some booze in me, and then make my way back to the bus. Something happened on more than one occasion. I was not allowed back onto the bus because I was too drunk. So I would have to wait, sober up, and catch the next bus. Sometimes it would not be until the next day.

I made it as far as Windsor, Ontario, and for the life of me, I don't remember why I decided to hang out there for a while. The first night I had nowhere to stay. I wandered up to a local church where someone told me they had a shelter. I arrived around 10:00 pm, and it was closed. My thinking told me I would need to spend the night on the streets of Windsor.

As I was wandering, alone, lost, and a bit inebriated, another person was walking along, and he mentioned the Salvation Army had a matt program where I could stay. Together we made the journey to the Sally Ann, grabbed a couple of matts, and slept on the floor of the gymnasium for the night. There must have been around 75 street people there, suffering from homelessness, mental disorders, or addiction. This was my first experience in such a place, and I'm sorry to say; it would not be my last.

The next day started out innocently enough, but it would end up like no other day I had ever experienced. After having breakfast, I left the shelter. I did not want to be with anyone, wanting just to isolate myself from the world. Still reeling from all the loss in L.A., sleeping on a matt, being surrounded by people I had never been around before. I was slowly beginning to lose my mind; being so broken and alone was having its toll on me.

I found myself wandering in a city I had never been to. I had a few dollars in my pocket, so to mask the grief, loneliness, and the fear; I went to the liquor store. I bought myself a bottle of whiskey; this would be my first mistake. It is amazing how *misery finds company*, because I ran into a few other lost souls, and spent the afternoon drinking with them on a park bench.

It was around 5:00 pm, and I had enough of the company I was keeping. I was at a point where the alcohol was only making things worse, so much worse. I was like a lost sheep that strayed away; I was a broken person and was a mess inside and outside. As I wandered around aimlessly, I saw a construction site downtown Windsor; they were half way done building an apartment complex.

With bottle in hand, I squeezed my way through the fence that was supposed to keep people out, and I walked up to the second story of the building. I found myself standing on the edge of an uncompleted balcony, looking down to the ground two stories below. I began to cry. As I stood there I had so many emotions rifling through my body; anger, sorrow and a complete loss of hope. I had been through too much for one person to endure. I began to think about my daughter Alyssa, and the sight of seeing Glenn lying on my couch, dead, flashed through my mind.

I could not carry the weight of the burden any longer, all the suffering I had been through, and the failure. I did not want to live any longer, I just wanted to die; I wanted to kill myself. I took a few steps back, set the bottle on the unfinished concrete floor, and in an instance, everything inside me shut down. I began to run and dove two stories to the ground. There I laid; a tragic lost soul, unconscious in a pile of rubble.

This would be my first suicide attempt. I awoke, or came to consciousness in the emergency room; there I was, alive after jumping two stories to the ground. The only real damage was a broken wrist; once again, *God had His hands on me!* From the emergency room, it was off to the psych ward. Oh no, not again! I would spend three days there until my head cleared. After my release, I choose not to stay in Windsor, so I made the two-hour trek to London, not England, but Ontario. I would spend four months there, and it would be the beginning of something disastrous. On a very good note; I would not touch another drop of alcohol for two and a half years.

I arrived, this time in London, with nowhere to stay. The hospital staff told me about the men's mission near downtown. I made my way there, talked to the staff, explained my situation, did the intake, and there I was. My new home and this was a first for me. In my past, I was not privy to such an experience.

It was a men's 146-bed facility, housing people suffering from mental illness, homelessness, and addiction. I would like to add something; most people are one paycheck and one bad choice away from ending up in such a place. I was surrounded by men with no jobs, no family, and most were deep into addiction, struggling with alcohol or drugs.

Was I better than any man in there because I came from Hollywood? I think not! You have read the *fall*; I was right where I was supposed to be at this point in my life. I truly believe two very important statements: *First*, absolutely nothing happens in God's world by mistake. *Second*, no matter where you are living, or what you are doing, it is exactly the way it is supposed to be at that moment in time. God has a plan and a purpose for each of us; and always remember, in the end, God will bring about good. In my case, unfortunately, it was going to take a while.

So, in 2005, I was homeless, penniless, and staying in a men's mission. Well, guess what? That is exactly the way it was supposed to be! My thinking was not as clear back then as it is now, so of course, these were not the thoughts I was having at that moment in time.

I began to get to know a few guys, and they let me in on a little secret. They informed me about a doctor at a clinic not too far away, who had no problems prescribing opiates. I had received a small dose of OxyContin back in Windsor for my broken wrist, but I had already gone through them. I called and booked an appointment. Since I had my back problem in L.A., with my L5 S1 having been fractured, I had an MRI and a CAT scan in hand.

With my reliable paperwork and some acting experience, I went to see the doctor and walked out with Percocet's. A lower dose of Oxy-Contin, Percocet's are 5mg, and you should take 2 every 4-6 hours. Now, I am an addict, so my mind tells me to take 4-6 pills every 2 hours; the twisted mind of an addict. As I mentioned, this would be the beginning of something disastrous. You see, I continued to pay a visit to my new friend, the doctor, every two weeks.

It all started innocently enough with Percocet's, but, in a very short time that would not be enough. The problem with opiates is they make you feel very good. Any grief, any emotions that you are dealing with, are all put to the wayside. The opiate has an amazing way of masking all your problems.

During our second meeting, I told the doctor the Percocet's were not doing the trick, and I was still in pain. Well, being the script writing doctor that he was, he prescribed me 20 mg OxyContin. At the time, it was like striking gold. I would give it another two weeks; go back in, same story, same giving doctor, but a different script. This time, it was the 40mg oxy. I eventually graduated up to the monster of OxyContin, the 80 mg pill. This was very bad, because I am an addict, and having a weekly script for 80 mg OxyContin could only go one way.

We call it a crossover, to substitute one for another. It is when you change your D.O.C, which means your Drug of Choice. Mine was alcohol, even though I dabbled in every drug out there while living in L.A. I made the switch, and I substituted one for the other. I crossed over, all the while still staying in addiction. I became a pill popper, an opiate addict.

Something you should know about people in addiction. We are adrenaline junkies. We are addicted to it. There is the possibility that an alcoholic in recovery may turn to stealing. Why? Because of the rush; we seek adrenaline in our lives. We change our D.O.C. because it is a different form of adrenaline. It gives us a rush that we are not accustom to, but all the while, we are still hooked in the world of addiction. You may ask yourself why? Why does someone in recovery, who has a month, six months or multiple years go out and use? They sabotage everything they have worked for.

The addict will get a job, a relationship forms, and things get going really good in their lives. What happens? One big reason is *self-worth*! The addict feels they are not worthy, not good enough to have acquired all the blessing that come with sobriety and clean time. We are used to a scattered messed up life; a normal life is uncomfortable. We want the rush, and we want the chaos we are addicted to. *We are more comfortable when we are uncomfortable.*

During my time in London, I was just maintaining, and not living a life. I managed to move out of the mission, and by the grace of God, I found myself waiting tables at a fairly reputable restaurant. I could do my pills and function; maybe I was a little too high energy, because for me, doing the pills jacked me up. I had energy, was personable, and I could keep going. It gave me an adrenaline rush, and any emotion or pain in my life was masked by the opiates.

There is another problem with taking opiates. You don't eat; there is no craving for food. This is the main reason for a profound amount of weight loss among addicts on opiates, cocaine, crack and speed. The drugs make you lose your appetite. I survived on Vector cereal for months. I would get up, pop my pills, and go through the day popping pills every 2-3 hours. Eventually in the evening, around 7 or 8, I would have a bowl or two of cereal, and do it again, day in and day out.

My life in London was a waste; I did nothing productive. I waited tables until I was fired for selling drinks and pocketing the money so I could afford my drug habit. I moved two more times while living in London; the last place was into my drug dealer's house. He wanted me to work for him selling pills. I want to give myself some credit here. I declined, because I had never done anything like that before, and my heart told me no, don't go down that road. What I did decide to do was continue on my journey trying and get back into the film biz. This move would take me to Toronto.

Toronto is one of Canada's biggest cities. I researched out a place to live before I moved. I found residence with a local prop master who worked in the film industry named Axel. I was still addicted to Oxy-Contin and had my prescription forwarded to a pharmacy close to our house. I would continue down my path of destruction with an insatiable appetite for opiates.

I did manage to find an agent in Toronto to represent me, to help find some work art directing, or doing props. My addiction was so bad that I did not really pursue any type of work in the industry. This probably was a good thing considering the state I was in. My three-month stay in Toronto was filled with depression, loneliness, and boredom; this is very dangerous ground for an addict. I was so low at this time in my life that my thought was to get into recovery.

I managed to make an attempt at cleaning up. I found a detox/treatment center a few miles from where I was living. I checked in on a Monday morning, and by Tuesday I was very sick, dope sick; this is a horrible feeling. I will explain a little later about being dope sick, but it is something I do not wish upon my worst enemy. My addict kicked in, and I came to realize my refill for my oxy's was sitting at the pharmacy.

I decided to sneak out after breakfast, walk to the bus stop around the corner, and take the bus to the pharmacy. I arrived, picked up my script, popped a couple of oxy's, caught the bus, and snuck back into the facility. Now, does that make much sense? Did I really want to get well? Of course not, half measures avail nothing. I ended up leaving the next day. What was the point of being in detox with a bottle of pills?

Sometimes I don't understand the love of God. I was so deep into my addiction, and God stilled poured out His mercy upon me. I received a phone call from Jenell, and she told me that she and Alyssa would be in Vancouver the following week. I was overwhelmed with joy. The following day I bought my ticket to fly to Vancouver and see my little girl.

As I have mentioned, Jenell was working in Malibu for a very successful dentist named Tom. Well, he moved fast; after our breakup he moved in on Jenell, and they started dating. By the time Jenell and Alyssa came to Vancouver, he had already whisked her off to Mexico, and they were married. They were all coming to Vancouver to attend a dental convention because he had invented a product called *The Isolite*.

I want to add something that Jenell would end up telling me only a few years ago. It was Tom who had me deported. He hired an immigration lawyer and made sure I would be kicked out of the country while I was in L.A. County jail. He had the fear that if I was around, there would be a chance that Jenell and I could get back together. Well, he made sure that would never happen. If it were not for his actions, I would never have been deported for misdemeanor charges. So I have to ask myself, am I mad at him, do I hold a resentment; or do I forgive him for his actions, and move forward with my life? I chose to forgive him and keep running the race, to persevere, and keep pushing forward.

The next week I was on a plane, on my way to Vancouver to see my daughter. I have to say that I had the most amazing time with Alyssa; she was four years old at the time. I took her to Grandville Island, Playland, shopping, and to the beach; sharing some quality time with her. Jenell hung low at their hotel for the better part of the vacation, and Tom was busy at the convention.

I was still hooked on OxyContin for their whole visit, and one night while we were all out at dinner, I had a breakdown. That evening I was so high on my pills, and I was dealing with the grief of them leaving the next day. My emotions caught up with me at dinner that night. It did not go well, and it scared Alyssa. The next morning, I took my daughter, and spent my last three hours with her before she had to fly back to L.A. It was so hard to be happy and uplifting with her, knowing she would be gone again a few hours later. I did my best; I just tried to be the best dad I could be at the time, being with her, loving her, and in the end, we did have a wonderful time together.

Let me share something that is incredibly heartbreaking. *I have not seen my daughter since that morning in Vancouver 2004. It has been*

11 years since I have held my daughter, picked her up, or given her a kiss on the cheek. *I have not* been able to tell her how much I love her to her face. *I've never* taken my daughter to school or picked her up. *I have never* been to a school play, *never* seen her dance, or taken her on a vacation. *I have never* had lunch or dinner with my daughter, *nor have I ever* tucked her into bed, and left the light on for her. *I have not* seen Alyssa since she was four. My incredible daughter is now fourteen years old.

Can you try to imagine what that is like? Do you have a child? If you do, just try to envision not being with them. Imagine that at the age of four; they were taken and kidnapped from you. Well, addiction kidnapped my four-year-old daughter, and I have not seen her since! Not being able to hold and love Alyssa for eleven years. I have not had the chance to see my daughter grow up. I truly believe this is a huge part of my addiction. I have been using drugs to kill the pain, to help bury the emotions that come with the loss of a child.

You try to carry this kind of baggage around for eleven years, because I have, and it has been killing me. All I knew was to jam it as deep into my soul as I could and bury it with alcohol and drugs. That was the only answer I knew. I needed help bad, a way out of this life. Unfortunately, that *someone* or something had more suffering and more torment for me to go through. I would eventually find that *someone*, but first I had a pile of bad choices to make. I would continue to live this devastating lifestyle for another three years.

It tears me apart inside as I am writing this, because as of this very moment, I still have not seen my little girl. I text and talk to her almost every day. I have to be accepting that it is good enough. In my past, I must have buried all this so deep into my recesses, trying somehow not to feel the anguish and the misery I was enduring because the loss of my only child. I do love my daughter more than anything. I yearn for the day when I can see her face to face, and tell her that her daddy is so sorry, oh so sorry, for not being there for her. She had to grow up without a father because I was stuck in the vortex of addiction.

To this day, I fall apart when I see fathers with their kids, walking in the park, or riding bikes together. It pains me seeing parents with their kids at the market or coffee shop. I see them playing, being together, and I am overwhelmed. My heart breaks, and I tear up; I never had that experience with my daughter. Seeing kids smiling and laughing with their parents, it paralyzes me inside. All I can feel is despair, and failure, because the loss of Alyssa.

When I see this; I want it to be me with my amazing daughter. I don't want to come across selfish, but the pain it causes is at times unbearable, and it shatters any sense of dignity I have. I see it day in and day out, parents being with their kids. If you have kids, I pray you count your blessing, and be grateful you have children in your life. You have the chance I never had, the chance to be the parent God created you to be. Make sure you love your kids, treat them like gold, and *tell them you love them*. There are people like me who would give anything, to just have ten minutes of what you have.

I hate addiction; I hate my bad choices, and I hate the fact that because of it all, I have not felt the heartbeat of my child on my chest for eleven long years. If you are reading this, and you are struggling with some form of addiction, here is another example of where it will take you. It has taken my daughter. I have talked about Glenn, and in the end, yes, it killed him. I have written 60 pages on the *fall* in L.A. If you do not see a pattern here, if you cannot see clearly what addiction will do, and what it wants to do, you need to get real with yourself.

I just told you about the loss of my little angel, about what addiction did, and what it has done. It took everything away; because of my bad choices in my addiction. I have lost everything! Sorry to be so blunt, but *Get it together*, *stop*, and get some help before your life begins to crumble. Addiction will haunt you like a plague, so please get some help, before it is too late.

There are detox and treatment centers you can go to. The most important part of getting your life back on track is that *someone* whom I have been speaking about. I truly believe you need to have a relationship with that *someone*. Without that *someone*; there is no long lasting success in recovery. If you are questioning this *someone*, your questions will be answered soon. He will be revealed in the next chapter. Until then, let me continue to share with you how bad it can get when Satan has his claws embedded into your soul. You may be feeling some emotions because Alyssa's not in my life; it is traumatic, but what's to come, will send your mind into a tailspin.

I would arrive back in Toronto the next day. I had spent a week in the most beautiful city in the world, Vancouver. The winters in Canada can be incredibly cold, but Vancouver does not have very bad winters.

It has the mountains and oceans, it is clean, and I fell in love with Vancouver the moment I landed to see Alyssa and Jenell.

Within a week of coming back to Toronto, I had my bags packed, wrapped up what business I had, and was on a flight back to Vancouver. I decided to make another move, number six since arriving back from L.A. I was going to make a pit stop on my way to Vancouver; I would fly to Calgary, Alberta and spend a week with my mom. I was 39 years old, making my 28th move to the most beautiful city in the world. But for me, it would literally turn into hell on earth.

I landed in Calgary; mom picked me up, and we drove to the little town of Innisfail. There is a reason for mentioning this pit stop. One of my best friends from high school invited me out for dinner; his name is Wade. We had dinner at a very nice restaurant with his wife and kids, and after dinner, he said he would drive me home.

During our dinner, I had let them in on the nightmare I had been living, and what happened in L.A. I want to add that Wade is one of the top oil executives in Calgary. He has started up more than one successful oil company, and these are multi-million dollar companies. On the way home, he said that he wanted to help me. My buddy from High school knew I was moving to Vancouver and attempting to start a new life.

I had no idea what was to come next. His words were; "*I want to give you some money to help you get back on your feet.*" His next words sent my head spinning out of control; he said he was going to give me $10,000.00. I was stunned, and he pulled through on his word and gave me $7000.00 at first, and he would get the rest to me in a few weeks. This was to be the only good thing to happen to me, because, over the next two years, my lifestyle would take me to the pits of hell.

It was 2005 when I arrived in Vancouver, and I would spend two and a half years there. It would turn out to be the worst years of my life. I bought myself a car with some of the money from Wade and found an apartment in Burnaby, a suburb of Vancouver.

I was still hooked on OxyContin, and it was quickly ruining my life. I needed a way to get my pills because I needed them every day. I had no drug contacts in Vancouver, well not yet, but once again, my brilliant addict mind kicks in. At this point, it was about survival, and I figured out a way to score my oxy's.

The emergency rooms in the hospitals of Vancouver would be my answer. I had my MRI's and Cat scans from L.A., and the x-ray from my crooked doctor in London. I was equipped with all the paperwork, and I needed my academy award acting to get the job done. I would limp, and slowly ease my way into the emerge, giving tell-tale signs of how much pain I was in. I would play it off that my back had given out, and I could hardly move.

My acting was so good that I was always put at the top of the priority list to get in before the not so serious cases. They usually offered me a wheelchair; because they saw the pain I was in. I would sit squirreling in agony as I waited. I would finally go to the doctor, show him all my paperwork, and explain the incredible amount of pain I was in. Then I would come up with some story that I fell off a ladder, or slipped on the stairs at home and blew my back out. When all was said and done, I would leave with a big fat prescription for OxyContin.

I was known as a drug seeker; that was the label for people like me. My acting was so good they thought I was suffering from a devastating back injury. Now, of course, I did not slip, or was I in pain, none of it was real. The only real thing was that I was an addict, doing whatever it took to score my drugs. All I was doing was feeding my addiction, to get high and stay high.

I eventually was kicked out of the place in Burnaby, and moved closer to the downtown east side, this time to Fraser& 29th. The owner was alcoholic, and the two other people living there were addicts. This would again turn out to be another very bad choice. By this time, I needed money, so I found a job driving escorts around Vancouver to their dates. So, here I am broke, driving call girls around Vancouver, taking OxyContin every day, and I then began to smoke crack with the girls. Well, it gets worse; a lot worse if you can imagine.

I am so ashamed to share one of my next moves with you. I was out of money, and I had not received the remaining $3000.00 from Wade. I was so sick, so selfish, and such an inconsiderate, greedy bastard, that I had the audacity to call Wade, and ask where the other $3000.00 was.

Are you kidding me? It sickens me; the things we do and our actions while in addiction are disgusting. When Satan has his claws dug so deep into you, we do things that we would never imagine doing clean and sober. When in addiction our choices are, how do I say, gray, not logical, we make very bad choices. It is the addiction that takes control, and our brains do not function properly; we are wired differently from the normal person not struggling with addiction.

Satan knows each of us better than we know ourselves, and He knows what works for each individual. He knows where our weak spots are; drugs, alcohol, porn, or gambling. Whatever it is, Satan knows where to hit you and me. He will work overtime, and put demonic forces on the job to drag us into this fallen world. He knows my weak point is the opiates. This is where He will attack me, and tempt me. He wants me to fail and fall flat on my face. As if I am not already there; but he had plans, and he was not finished with me. I am so sad to say that it worked; he would grab a hold of me, and drag me through the fires of hell.

I had been doing OxyContin for around six months; ah, the infamous six months, are you still counting? The day came when I ran out of money, and I could not get any drugs. I was sick, dope sick, curled up in a ball on the couch at the house. I was crapping my pants, vomiting, shaking like a leaf, and sweating profusely. The joys of drugs and the joy of being dope sick.

The next chain of events changed everything. My roommate came home with his prostitute girlfriend, and they saw me lying there, sick as a dog. He says he has a cure for my problem; he invites me upstairs and proceeds to pull out a bag of heroin. I have only done it once in my life with Glenn.

He puts it on the foil, and I chase the dragon, inhaling the long line of heroin. Within a minute, my sickness is gone. I am back on my feet again feeling incredibly good. This would lead to a major problem. My addict mind said; I really like this stuff. I don't need to drug seek at hospitals or doctors' offices anymore. All I had to do was make a call, and have it delivered. The other bonus is that it was cheaper. I would be hooked on heroin for the next year and a half.

I was eventually kicked out of the house because I would always have the escorts I was driving around over in my room. We would be smoking crack and heroin. Things got a bit out of control at times, to say the least, so I had to move again. I moved to a basement suite about a block away, but this did not last more than a month. Again, I did not learn from the mistakes I had made at my last place of residence. I was a typical addict doing insane things. The definition of *Insanity: doing the same thing over and over again, expecting different results.*

I would move again, to the upper part of a house, with a guy who was hooked on speed. He worked at a printing shop and maintained his life the best he could. He smoked speed all night and worked during the day. By this time, I had stopped driving escorts around and found a job with a sign installation company. We put up billboards in town and installed the metal bus stop shelters around Vancouver. I started to smoke speed, as well as heroin.

I had a plan of action. Every morning my roommate would leave for work, and I figured out a way to break into his room from the outside patio. I mustered my way through his window, and would climb through it into his bedroom. Addicts think like addicts, so it did not take long to find his hiding spot, the place he kept his speed. I would do this every day, but my addict mind went a step further.

He had a couple of hundred DVDs and video games in his room. So I would call my drug dealer every morning. I would break into the room, open the door, and invite him in. It was like the shopping network. I would tell him to pick out three or four movies, and a play station game in exchange for a point of heroin and a forty rock of crack. What was I thinking, this was so messed up? Obviously, my bad choices were in full swing, along with my addiction.

This went on for about two and a half months until my roommate became suspicious. To top it off, there was one other thing that I was up to. Every morning while my roommate went into the shower before he left for work, I would sneak into his room because it was open. I would quickly scan the room, find his speed, take a little bit out so he would not notice, and run back to my room. He would get out of the shower, and head back into his room not knowing what was happening; so I thought! I would do a couple lines of speed, smoke a little heroin, and go to work for the day, installing big glass metal bus shelters, and hanging billboards around the city.

One morning as I was planning my dash into his room for my daily fill of speed, he had a plan of his own. I lay in bed as normal, heard the shower turn on, waited for one to two minutes, and then walked into his room. As I was rummaging through the room, I turned to see him standing at the door. I was speechless, and he was livid. He yelled at me about all his DVDs and play station games being gone. He was pissed that I was stealing his speed, and he gave me the ultimatums. Either I had to be moved out by the time he came home from work, or, ultimatum number two, he would call the police, and have me charged with theft. He turned away and walked out the door for work.

Things got bad, real bad; my mind was spinning in all sorts of directions as I stood there in a state of shock. I had been on a bit of a run. I was smoking heroin, speed, and I had not slept in four days. I was in a drug-induced psychosis, and a state of paranoia was filling my mind. Nothing makes sense when the addict has been up for days; our thinking is warped, and nothing you say to the addict at this point will ever sink in. We become incoherent, and I will go one step further; we actually become a bit psychotic in our thinking. If you are dealing with someone in this state, it is best just to agree with their insanity and walk away.

Here comes the addict in full force. There was booze in the house, and it has been there the whole time I was living there. My addict tells me that a shot of whiskey would be the answer, just one shot to ease the pain, to help clear the haze I was in. Now remember, I have not had a drink since Windsor, it had been around two and a half years. I walked over, grab a bottle of whiskey from the cabinet, and took a shot.

Come on, I am an alcoholic; there is no such thing as one! I proceed to drink the whole bottle of whiskey within 30 min. In an instant, everything goes dark, there is no light. I felt alone; anxiety overtook me like nothing I had ever felt. There was no joy or peace in my life; it was filled with resentments and misery. The drugs and alcohol were flowing through me, I was in such despair, and I had lost all hope.

Once again, I felt life was not worth living. My mind and heart told me just to end it, to kill myself. I walked to the kitchen and pulled a knife from the butcher block. I held up my left hand and quickly sliced into my wrist. I saw the skin split open, and blood began to pour out. I then exchanged hands, took the bloody knife, and sliced open the other wrist. I remember standing there, looking down at my wrists, blood was spewing and shooting out in all directions. I dropped the knife, and it fell to the floor. My mind and vision began to grow dark. There I was unconscious, high, and drunk, lying on the kitchen floor, slowly bleeding out, waiting to die.

I woke up in Vancouver General Hospital with 16 metal staples on my left wrist, and 18 staples on my right. If it were not for my roommate coming back home because he forgot something and finding me on the kitchen floor in a pool of blood; I would be dead right now. Once again, *God had His hands on me.* This would be my second suicide attempt, and the second time I picked up a drink in 2½ years.

All addiction wanted was to provide and feed the empty hole in my heart with drugs and alcohol. Satan filled the *shalom shaped hole,* with once again, the wrong topic of worship. Satan and addiction wanted to kill me; to end my life. God said, *"No, not now, it is not his time; I have work for this young servant of mine."* I did not know what that work was, but I would find out later.

After all this, I decided to go out to Surrey, another suburb of Vancouver, with a lot of gang violence and drugs. I went to a recovery house with eight other guys, and while I was staying there, I continued smoking heroin. I can't figure it out; I had been to at least six detoxes in Vancouver, all to get off heroin, but to no avail. I have tried to commit suicide twice, but for some reason, I was stuck. I could not break free from addiction, and my path of destruction would continue.

I was kicked out of the recovery house for using heroin, and once again, something life-changing was about to happen to me. I packed my bag, not bags because I did not have enough material possessions in my life to pack more than one. As I was walking to the sky train station, I ran into a, shall we say, an acquaintance. We began walking and talking, and he informs me that he has a bag of heroin; an overwhelming feeling of relief came over me. I knew it would ease the depressive state I was in, being so lost, and not knowing where I was going.

We made our way to the Scott Road sky train station. There is a grass lawn under the platform, we sit down, and he proceeds to pull it out, along with a couple of syringes. He mixes it and draws it up into the syringe. I mention that I have never put a needle in my arm, or shot dope in my life. My addict kicks in; it tells me that this would be a good way to soften the grief and misery I was dealing with. Here I was, forty years old, under a sky train station platform, with an acquaintance, injecting heroin into my arm for the first time.

I was done; I was hooked on the needle. I would become an I.V. drug user for the next year, and it took me again to the depths of hell. Trust me; you do not want to go down that road. I want to add, that if you are using drugs, and you get to the point where you put a needle in your arm, you will never do drugs any other way again. You will be hooked on the needle after the first time, and in the end, it will kill you. Let me explain.

Things would only go downhill from here. I was shooting heroin, and I ended up in the *Downtown Eastside of Vancouver.* The Eastside is famous, but not for the fame you and I think. The DTES is the most drug infested area in North America. The infamous corner Hastings and Main; where you can score any drug, at any time. Poverty and homelessness are rampant; it is one of the worst problems in the DTES. It is estimated that 40% of the people down there suffer from mental illness. The DTES has the poorest postal code in Canada and is one the most dangerous and violent neighborhoods in Canada. The DTES has the highest crime rate in Canada; it is also the oldest neighborhood in Vancouver, full of junkies, panhandlers, and prostitutes.

It is common to be walking down the streets and see people smoking crack and speed. There are always people sitting on the corners, or in the alleys, injecting themselves with heroin. The DTES has one of the highest rates of suicide and overdoses in Canada; should I go on? You get the picture; this is not where you want your sons or daughters to end up. But living in a fallen world, living the lost, lonely life of an addict, and after making very bad choices; I would spend 1½ years living in the pits of hell.

If you want a little taste of this, go to *Google*, enter in *Vancouver Downtown Eastside*, and hit *images*. Take a look for yourself. It will open your eyes, and I pray it softens your heart for all the hopeless and lost souls living down there. I was one of them.

I checked into a place called the *Cobalt Hotel*, about 5-6 blocks up from the infamous corner of Hastings and Main. This was a grungy, dirty hotel, with filthy carpets, and peeling wallpaper; it also came with an assortment of bedbugs and cockroaches. I would sit in my room, feeling detached from the world. I was disconnected from life, no communication, isolated and sticking needles into my arm.

It was like I was dead. I had no friends, and I had no one in my life that I could spend time with. We are social creatures created to love; that is the way God made us. The problem was I did not know love. I could not stop using drugs and every day I would wake up to the same nightmare, having to live it again. I was in a rut, to say the least, needing money for my heroin, or I would get sick, dope sick.

I was dabbling with crack and cocaine, as well as shooting heroin, living in a rundown hotel, with drug dealers, prostitutes, and people in the hallways shooting up. Satan had his claws dug so deep into me, it felt as if the tips of them were etched into my bone, searing into my soul. I felt that there was no way out. I was stuck in my addiction. It had taken me to places I could never have imagined.

I had a routine for survival while staying at the Palacious Cobalt Hotel. Labor Ready was around the corner, a work placement center. I would go in, sign up, and sit around and wait until they called me when a job came up. It was usually stacking things at a warehouse, unloading trucks, working on construction sites; basically mindless, meaningless jobs that needed to be filled.

I would work an 8 hour day, and after taxes, I would make, maybe $70 or $80. Then I would go down to Hastings and Main, and buy a $40.00 bag of heroin. This was not my only problem; I would also buy a $20.00 piece of crack, a $5.00 pack of smokes, and $10.00 for some food. My one and only meal for the day; do the math, I am broke again.

This was an ongoing routine for a couple of months. After work, I scored my dope, and would shoot up anywhere I could. There was a McDonalds a couple blocks from my hotel. I would go and shoot up in the bathroom stalls all the time. Try to remember the McDonalds bathroom, because later in the book, it will have a major impact. A lot of times it would be in the bathroom at Tim Hortons or Starbucks; basically, anywhere I could find.

The lifestyle I was living is unexplainable; living in the DTES, surrounded every day with people who had lost everything. They had no hope left in their lives. Addicts, alcoholics, and prostitutes; it is just all kinds of wrong. I have seen people get stabbed and beat down violently. Girls held in hotel rooms hooked on dope and then being prostituted out. I have witnessed people dying on the streets from an overdose, people sleeping in their own puke and urine in alleys.

Addiction is not picky; it will be your best friend and lover until it starts to borrow and take everything from you. It does not care if you are the CEO of a company, a doctor, mechanic or a greeter at Walmart; it can get you, and it will destroy you. Satan would like to have everyone living in the DTES if he could, but thank God this is not the case. I want to add, when you get stuck in the DTES, living down there in addiction, it is very hard to get out.

God had taken my craving for alcohol away since coming back from L.A. I drank on two separate occasions, and each time I tried to kill myself. The problem now was my craving for heroin; it was out of control. My insatiable appetite for the drug would drive me to do anything to score. I never stole; I was never a thief that could go into a store and lift a stereo or T.V. like some of my acquaintances.

With opiates, you need them every day, or you get violently ill, and it gets very expensive. When you have the daily need, it takes so much time and work, to find and score your drug. I was on welfare for about 2 years from 2006-2008, during the time I was living in Vancouver. Part-time work and welfare were nowhere near enough to cover the cost of my addiction.

So, I started to call my mom for money, maybe once or twice a month, which progressed to once a week, then to almost every couple of days. I lied to my mother. I would tell her I owed money or a bill was due, or that I needed food, that was a big one. I had hundreds of manipulative, disgusting ways of misleading, misguiding, and cheating my mom out of her money. I would do whatever it took to make sure her money ended up at the Western Union, Payday advance, or direct deposit into my checking account.

So many times I would call, and she would be broke, not having enough money for herself. I would still manipulate something, anything out of her, as long as I could get my fix. I look back, and I want to cry, I want to hurt myself, for some reason thinking to cause pain to myself would help. I am so disgusted and sickened by my actions. I wonder how I could ever pay her back, or somehow make it up to her.

I think back as to how my addiction could be so strong, so powerful, and unrelenting, that I would cause so much pain to my mother. I remember a time when she was crying so badly because she was hurt, and all I wanted was money. She got to the point where she did not want to answer the phone when my number came up because all I would do was ask for money. This made my mom an emotional wreck. At the time, being so deep into my addiction, I did not know how much pain and torment I was causing her.

We as addicts think we are only hurting ourselves, that when I get high, it only affects me, not the people around me; my friends, people at work, and family. We do not see it; we think it is innocent enough. What a misconception. We do not see the amount of pain, suffering and worry we cause to the ones around us. It is always the ones we love that we hurt the most.

My mom worried all the time about me and do you think I cared. Do you think it mattered to me that my mom was crying, and broken? No, I would still try to manipulate money out of her, so I could go out and get high. Not caring one bit about how broken mom was or how she was up night after night, worrying if her son was alive or dead. Wondering If I was in the hospital or the morgue.

It is the worst of all my actions in addiction. Out of the county jail time, ripping people off, detox's, dealing with other addicts, loss of jobs; they were all very trying. I did bad things in my life, but the ordeal and total devastation that I caused my mom is the most heartbreaking.

As I am writing this, I think back, and it just sickens me, my stomach is in knots, and I just want to die. The worry, pain, and the nightmare I put my poor mother through are unexplainable. If you are reading this, and you are doing the same thing, please stop killing your parents. Stop thinking they are a bank; they are not and you can stop the pain right now. You need to go and get some help. If you are the parent in this situation, you need to stop being the *Enabler*; stop fueling your kid's drug habit. It is called *Tough Love*; please stop killing your kids, and stop providing for them; you may just save their lives.

The craziest thing is it can only come from the love of a mother, and it is hard to comprehend. In the end, all my mother wanted was a clean and sober son that she could be proud of. It is not the thousands and thousands of dollars I manipulated out of her; she is not concerned about any of that. From the addict's point of view, this is hard to understand. It is hard to figure out that my sobriety was what meant the most to my mother. This has been so hard for me writing this, to think back, and in detail, remember the devastation I put my mom through, thinking what a selfish, arrogant, untrustworthy human being I was.

The incredible power addiction has and the temptation that Satan puts in our path turns us into *the people who we really are not*. What it all boils down to is real bad choices, and when we are deep in our addiction, it is at times hard to make the right choices. I am not blaming anyone but myself. It simply is my bad decision making, my choices, and addiction that caused my mother so much grief and pain.

Mom, I love you more than anything on this earth, and I would do anything to change the past, but that is not possible. All I can do is bend to my knees, and ask you to forgive me for my despicable acts, and I want you always to be in my life. I am sorry, and I cannot believe the love you have for me, still to this day. There is nothing on earth as powerful as the love of a mother. Mom, I thank you for the love of a mother, and I am eternally grateful. I love you.

I just want to wrap up this chapter with a few other details about my time living in Satan's playground. I moved out of the Cobalt hotel to another place in the DTES, called the *Lotus Hotel*. It was actually very clean, and the upkeep was tops for the area I was living in. I made a go at trying methadone to help get off heroin; this was a very bad idea.

Hitler and the Nazis invented methadone back in WWII for their soldiers. I suggest you do not give methadone a thought if you want to stop opiates. It is a lot harder to come off than heroin, or OxyContin, or any other opiate. Methadone has a shelf life and soaks into the bone marrow; it is a nightmare. I suggest you go to treatment and go through the month of hell to get off whatever opiate you are hooked on as oppose to a lifetime on methadone.

O.K, enough of my drug counseling speech; while I was living at the Lotus, I met a drug dealer who offered me a job. Now, being so broke and desperate for money to feed my habit, I decided to take the job. It was 2008, I was shooting a lot of heroin, living in the DTES, and now I was selling/dealing heroin on the corner of Hastings and Main.

Let's do a quick recap just in case you have not been following along. In 2000, I was living in Hollywood, working for the biggest celebrities, and directors in the industry. I made a low six-figure income, and I had all that life had to offer. Here I am five years after being deported from the U.S, dealing heroin on the worst drug-infested corner in North America.

It should make you stop and think. The downward spiral I have been talking about, the devastating trail of destruction that I was leaving behind me was insurmountable. The damage I had caused myself and others are unspeakable. It was not a lightning bolt from the sky, and it was not a gentle nudge, but God whispered, and I said, *enough*!

I could not keep going like this; I could not live the lifestyle I had become accustomed to over the past 2½ years. I needed out, and I made the decision to get out of Vancouver, to go and clean up. I left Vancouver, flew to Alberta, and stayed at my mom's place to detox off all the drugs that were intoxicating my system. I needed to detox of the heroin, and the methadone. I was carrying around so much baggage when I left Vancouver. It was a bag full of pain, guilt and shame and I did not know how to get rid of it. It was going to be a nightmare coming off the drugs, but I could not go on any longer. I needed a change; I needed a new life.

Addiction says it wants to be your friend and lover, so we let him in. We, for some reason, choose to let addiction creep its way back in, thinking it will mask the pain. You have read chapter after chapter about the devastating effects of drugs and alcohol; this is one of the major topics of my book. I have shared about Glenn and what addiction did to him, killing him. I have also shared in rather graphic detail; what addiction has cost me.

I have lost everything, and it has taken everything from me, including anyone I have loved, or cared about. Addiction has tried to kill me twice, but, by the grace of God, here I sit. Addiction is cunning, baffling and powerful, and it is not to be taken lightly. If you or anyone you know is struggling with some form of addiction, I have an answer for you. All you have to do is practice one fruit of the Spirit, *Patience*; practice patience. Our only hope of escape is for *someone* else to take our penalty. Our nature is to rebel against God, and that's called *sin*. The answer is coming in the next chapter; that *someone* delivers light to the darkness hiding in our souls.

CHAPTER 11
Puerto Vallarta, Mexico

I WAS FORTY YEARS old, and this would be move number 32, back to the little town of Innisfail, just outside Red Deer. I was sick, very sick, coming off heroin, pills, and methadone. I was 128 lbs and looking like a skeleton; I am normally 150 lbs, so I was 22 lbs underweight, I was slowly killing myself while I was out there.

I know it has been a rough ride with the last chapter, and the *fall*; it has not been very positive or uplifting. What it has been is real, yes, as real as it gets when one is struggling with addiction. I am sorry to say there is one last event that I must share with you before things begin to get better in my life.

I had been at my mom's place for about a week, coming off the cocktail of drugs flowing through my system. I had not slept at all; opiates are one of the hardest drugs to detox from. While coming off them, there can be no sleep for up to a month. I will get into more detail a little later in the book about opiate detox, but I am sure you get the idea.

With no sleep, came sleep deprivation. I was beginning to hallucinate, seeing shadow people as they are called. My anxiety was through the roof, and I needed a way out. I could not handle the suffering any longer. I was alone, isolated, and laying around the apartment in a fetal position for most of the days and nights; and then my addict shows up.

The mental obsession kicks in. The first drink, I think once again, just one shot to help ease the pain. I obviously had not learned from

181

my mistake in Vancouver two years prior; this gives us an idea of where the first drink leads. My mom had one of those old bar globes (if you are older like me, you will remember). It is a three-foot round globe that pulls open from the top and basically splits in half once it is open. There are places for glass's, bottles and a container for ice.

I want to let you know the reality of addiction. When my addict mind snaps in and says, I am going to use, or drink as in this case, there is no stopping me. There will be no talking me out of it. When the addict makes up their mind to go out and use, to go on a run, nothing on God's green earth will change their mind. Maybe I should first clarify a run; it is not a jog, it is a stretch of time while the addict is in full blown addiction.

My mind was made up, I went and took a bottle of whiskey from the globe bar and poured myself a shot. This was my first mistake; I do not need to tell you that being an alcoholic, there is no such thing as one drink. No such thing as one shot. Within the hour, I had polished off the entire bottle of whiskey. I was not myself, things became very distorted, and I was losing it.

What happened next will make your head spin. I was detoxing off a lot of drugs, I had ingested a bottle of whiskey, and I had not slept for over a week. Satan had me just where he wanted. When God has a plan, and a purpose for our lives, Satan will work overtime to put an end to it. I believe He did not want me to write this book, I believe He did not want me to have anything to do with forwarding Gods Kingdom.

The feeling of distress became rooted in my thinking and coloured my decision making. I walked out to my mom's balcony; I set up her chairs and a table that led to the railing. I was broken beyond repair. I was so lost, there was no hope, and I felt there was no escape from the life I was living. I wanted to end it all, to die, to kill myself. I took a few steps back, and in my addiction, in my drunkenness, I ran, jumping from the chairs to the table, then my final leap, diving, and sailing through the air, falling four stories.

My body slammed to the ground below. I watched the world come through the dark side of the moon; I left my body lying in the sands of time. This would be my third suicide attempt while in addiction, but God had angels surrounding me that day. Addiction wanted to kill me, and I wanted to kill myself, but this would not be the case. It was only by the grace of God that I was still alive; once again, *God had His hands on me*, and I would spend the next six months in the hospital.

Our lives are but a span of a lifetime, it is what we do with it here on earth that matters.

. . .

I came to a few days later at Foothills Hospital, in Calgary Alberta. I awoke to a punctured lung, a broken pelvis, and all the ribs on my right side were broken. Now tell me God did not have His hands on me? I should have been in a coma, paralyzed, in a wheelchair for life, or I should have died. This was not the case, after diving four stories off a balcony; I believe I came out with minimal injuries.

I really wanted to die. Satan would have been in his glory. But No, God said, once again, *It is not his time; I have work for this servant of mine.* Here I sit, six years later, writing this book about my journey, about addiction, and about finding that *someone*. I don't need to tell you how amazing God is, and that He has a plan and a purpose for each of us.

The punctured lung was so painful because I had a tube running through my rib cage, into my body, the pain was excruciating. The broken pelvis is another story. Every day I would be wheeled from the sixth floor to the basement, where they would do x-rays, MRI's and Cat scans. I knew every piece of broken cork board on the ceiling running down the long corridors of the hospital. I was on my back, on a stretcher, laying there in pain, being wheeled to the elevator. As I made my way down the long hallways, I'd be staring up at the ceiling. After months, I had it memorized in my mind.

I would go through this process for about two months until they performed the surgery on my broken pelvis. The entire time I spent at Foothills, I was on a morphine drip for the pain. Every two hours I could press a button releasing it into my body; it helped to ease the discomfort and the agony I was in. After the surgery, there was no weight bearing on my legs, meaning I was in a wheelchair. I could not stand on my feet for another 2½ months. I would end up spending most of my hospital stay at Foothills Hospital. When the time came for me to begin the process of learning to stand and walk again, they transported me.

Around the 4½ month mark, they moved me to Red Deer, to the Regional hospital where I would spend another month and a half learning how to walk again. The atrophy in my legs was very bad. I had not used the muscles or stood on my legs for a long time now. They had a pool equipped with a machine that I sat in, and then it picked me up, swung me around, and lowered me into the pool.

Remember, I could not walk yet. I did this every day, supervised with a physiotherapist, doing exercises in the pool to help get my legs working again, and to strengthen my pelvis. I would go to the actual physiotherapy center in the hospital and do training there once a day as well. All this work and time so that I would be able to stand, and then walk again. It was rigorous and painful; it took every ounce of strength I had to get through all these exercises.

Maybe you wonder where God was in all this. Well, let me explain. A miracle was about to happen in my life. A nurse at the hospital, a young wonderful Christian nurse who was taking care of me, would change my life. We talked all the time about God and what I had been through, where I was emotionally, and how I made my way into her life. We chatted about my third suicide attempt; she was astonished that I would dive four stories of a balcony, trying to kill myself. She told me that I had so much to live for.

This touched my heart deeply, and stirred up my emotions, but I could not comprehend what she really meant by this powerful statement until a few days later. God will use people, places and things in our lives, to bring us to Him. God used this little angel; He used her to open my eyes. A few days later, she showed up with a picture of that *someone*, an 8 x 10 picture of Jesus holding a broken man. This is the picture she showed me that day.

It did begin a transformation in my life; the framed 8 x 10 picture had a bunch of scriptures from the Bible written on the back. I was by no means living any kind of life that had anything to do with God. Look where it got me, read the *fall* again, and the last chapter. Here I am, lying in a hospital bed, after diving four stories to the ground because of addiction.

It is in the tragic moments of loss and suffering, in the moments when we are most broken, that we realize how alone we really are. At that moment, The Holy Spirit causes the spiritual bandages to fall from our eyes. Then we realize God is our only source of power.

. . .

I am not going to preach to you in this book. What I am going to do is continue to tell my story, exactly the way it happened. This journey we have been on has taken us to some very dark places, but it is being used for good. In the end, there is light. God is using my past, and all the deep dark events, to bring about good. I can share Him with you, and about all He has done in my life. I pray God will soften your heart as we go on with the rest of the book.

This broken road prepared His will for me. It was not a bolt of lightning from the sky; it was not an automatic life changing moment. What it did was open my eyes. It gave me some clarity and showed me Hope. Something in my heart softened towards this God whom I had known about my whole life, but I never choose to acknowledge Him; I never let that *someone* into my life. That *someone* I have been touching on throughout this whole book showed up that day, in an 8 x 10 photograph, given to me by an angel, the Christian nurse whom God had so perfectly placed there. He orchestrates our lives; you can see it in my life. He has orchestrated everything in my life to bring me to this point.

God planted a seed in my heart and soul that day. You know the way a seed grows? It needs to be watered, and only God can water it. This was not like I was at a Billy Graham Crusade, heard the message, and I was saved. It would not happen right away; there was no conversion. My understanding and acceptance took place over the years.

The seed was planted; it was going to take some time before the seed was watered. The transformation was a process. Why not right away? I honestly do not know the answer as to why it did not happen right away.

When I saw the 8 x 10 picture of that *someone,* something amazing happened. It was unlike any other day in my life. Angels heard the news, something in my life was going to change; I closed my eyes to pray, and tears of joy streamed down my face, my eyes had been opened. As I stared into the picture, He showed me love, and a peace overcame me like none other. I wanted to surrender; I knew I wanted to give this God thing a shot, but it was not going to happen right away. God delivers light into the darkness hidden in our souls; this I truly do believe.

After six months, I was beginning to walk again, not only physically, but I would need to learn how to walk spiritually as well. The people at my mom's strata were not too pleased that her son did a four-story swan dive from her balcony, so they banned me from the building for three years. Being the nomad that I am I had nowhere to go, so I stayed with my friend Mike. He was one of my best friends from high school; he offered to let me stay at his place to recuperate and to detox off the opiates I had been taking while in the hospital.

I was in a wheelchair rolling around his house, trying to taper off OxyContin, and acting like a lunatic. I was taking way to many pills, so one night he hid them. I put my addict mind to work, and thinking like one; it did not take long for me to find them. He had them hidden way up in a cabinet in the kitchen.

I somehow in my determination to get the drugs, struggled my way out of the wheelchair, and held myself up on the counter. To this day, I don't know how I managed to reach my way up and get the pills. I was barely able to stand at this time. Anyway, I took most of the pills that night. He awoke to a doped up addict, sitting strung out in a wheelchair in his living room. Mike packed my belongings up and drove me to the Red Deer detox center; he could not take any more, honestly, who could blame him.

They called me *Wheels* in there; I would spend a month and a half learning how to walk again. There was also the battle to get me off the opiates. Dr.Keen was my doctor for the stay at the hospital; an amazing and caring man who worked overtime to get me cleaned up. He would come after his shift in the evenings, bringing me non-addictive, non-opiate medication to help me through my ordeal.

Something happened to me while going through all this. There was an overwhelming urge to serve, to give back. Every night I would stare at the picture from my nurse friend, the picture of Jesus holding a broken man. In all my years in L.A., with the money I made, I never gave to a charity or a church. Never served, or helped anyone else but me. God instilled it in my heart to do something, to give back, and to go help others.

My heart told me to do some mission work somewhere. So I hopped on the computer and began my search. Within a week, I had found Calvary Church in Texas; they had a team in Puerto Vallarta, about to design and build a school. I built a relationship with the people in Texas, explaining that I had designed movie sets in L.A. for years. My heart strings were being pulled, and I said that I could put my skills to use helping people in Mexico. My passport was renewed; I had only been up and moving for about two weeks. Let's say, I was still a bit fragile in my walking. But I pushed forward; I knew I needed to change my life.

I needed to give back, but I did not understand all this. It happened so fast, my heart and soul screamed for me to go, to do something for others. I feel God did not want me to understand, or to know why. He wanted me to walk by faith, even when I could not see, or understand. He wanted me to learn to walk by faith.

He has used everything that has happened to me to accomplish His purpose. He uses our circumstances for His own purposes, for our good, for the benefit of others, and to bring Him Glory. Two weeks later it would be move 33. I was once again on a plane, going to Puerto Vallarta, Mexico.

I arrived mid-day, and I would spend six months there, serving and giving back. I took a taxi from the airport to the church, or, shall we say, a converted store. It was a bottom level space in a two story complex with various shops and stores in the area. I met with Bill and Renee from the Calvary church; they were a delightful couple who had been there for years.

They planted a church, and they were helping the poor in an area called *The Dump;* and that is exactly what it was. It was an area full of poor families who were living and surviving at the Puerto Vallarta dump. This was not a mission trip; it was more of a humanitarian trip for me. At the time, I want to specify that I was not a Christian, but I was a believer. I was not reading the Bible, nor was I a prayer warrior. I was not there to go to church or to surrender my life to God. I was a man recovering from a heroin addiction and a suicide attempt. I went to be of service, to help the less fortunate in any way I could. Don't get me wrong, God was still at work in me. Little did I know; He was watering the seed.

At this time my life was very good; I was not drinking, or doing any drugs. I had been sober for seven months, living in Mexico, giving back. As I mentioned, God softened my heart, and I had a desire, a quest, to go and help. I found a place to live way up in the hills above the old part of P.V. The lady who lived in the house was a wonderful Latino woman, who had a husband who supported her, but he lived in the states. The views from the patio and balcony at her place were breathtaking; I could see up and down the whole coastline of Puerto Vallarta.

Normally, when someone goes to work for a church or to do mission work in another country, they stay at a complex provided for them. Or, they would stay with the pastor and his family. In my case; I did not stay with them. I stayed on my own, the story of my life. I was not connected with the other people there serving, I was not part of their night time activities, I just worked with them during the day out at the dump.

I would end up living in the hills for around 5 months. In the mornings, I would take my 15 min walk down to the bottom of the hill, where I would catch the rickety old run down bus. In Mexico, the buses and roads are nothing like back here at home. They had old worn seats; many areas in the bus were missing seats, and missing handrails to hold on to for the bumpy ride.

Every morning I would meet a group of people from the church who were there serving as well, at a specific meeting spot. It was the same meeting place every morning. I would arrive at 8:00 am, and from there we would load into vans, which in turn drove us up into the landfills of P.V. It would only take us around 10 min to go from the exotic beauty of Puerto Vallarta to get to the slums. It was a desolated horrific dump, where hundreds of children and families were living in conditions that you could not imagine.

It was astonishing to see children in torn, ripped up filthy clothes, digging through the dump. It was heartbreaking to say the least, families living in little shanty shacks, made from cardboard, rags, scraps of corrugated metal, and broken pallets. They used anything that would offer them some semblance of shelter. I saw kids with their parents living in the garbage dump, eating whatever remnants of food they could find. It tears at your soul when you see things like this happening a couple of miles from paradise.

Down from the dump are people in their luxury resorts, with buffets and tons of food. Comfortable beds and linens surrounded with all the amenities the resort has to offer. Then people have the audacity to complain because their food was not quite right, or the maid was late to clean up their room. *Really?* Why are we are so ungrateful in the West; always complaining and whining about silly stupid things affecting our day. I want to take a van down there, and load it up with a bunch of people from the West. To round up the ones who are lounging around the pool, complaining because the waiter is taking too long to bring their margarita.

I want them to experience what life is like for the people at the dump. To take them up to the landfills for an hour or two; that is what needs to happen. I can promise it would change their perspective on life. I believe it would stop the ungratefulness, at least for a while. I was fortunate enough to spend four months, every day, in the landfills, and garbage dumps of P.V. It helped change my life, my perspective, and it made me incredibly grateful for all God has blessed me with.

I think all North Americans need to spend a little time at the dump, or a couple of weeks in a third world country. I don't mean staying at the resort; I am saying getting out, and getting deep into the culture. This would mean going to the places that are not on your tourist brochure. We need to understand what being grateful means and to be thankful that we are American, or Canadian, having all God has provided for us.

Thank Him for your shiny new cars, your house, and a closet full of clothes. Be content with having a good job, and schools for your kids to attend. Thank God that you are not stuck living in a dump like some of the poor families in P.V. Could you imagine your child rummaging through trash trying to find their breakfast? It is time for a heart change and an attitude adjustment in North America. I do not see it happening!

I came to help, and to serve. When I saw this, when I saw how these people had to live and survive, I did everything in my power to better their lives. Whether it was buying food for families, bringing clothes I bought at the local markets, or soccer balls and games. My heart said it was more about spending time with them, giving hope and any type of encouragement that I could muster up from my soul. We all need a little help, and we all need love, without it, we have nothing.

This is a picture of what a family's home looks like in the landfills, and dumps of P.V.

In 2006, the mission discovered that whole families were living and working in the city dump. They knew no other way of life. Some families had been living there for many generations. The families would spend their days going through the dump, looking for bottles and cans. Recycling was their way of life; it was how they made money to survive and eat. Their children were not registered and were not able to obtain birth certificates. They had no official address, so the children could not go to school; their futures were bleak.

Well, that was about to change. Bill and Renee had a plan to design and build a school. It would be right in the heart of the dump, to help these children. It was a blessing for me to be able to put my skills to practice. The years spent in L.A., designing movie sets, was now being used to help children who needed a place to learn. The school would be there so it could be a part of their growth and also a place of refuge. In the end, what it did was give them something we all need; it would give them hope.

In my life, I have dealt with and had the feelings of complete hopelessness. I knew what it felt like. So being able to give the people and the children of the dump hope was very encouraging. I had an overwhelming sense of accomplishment. Doing things for others will do that for you.

There is no reward better in life than being able to help people less fortunate. I have traveled all over the world, but none of my travels were to help others, they were for me. This would change as the book goes on; you will see other countries and continents I was about to visit. The reasons were much different; it was to go and serve, it was about bettering people's lives.

It all started with an 8 x 10 picture of that *someone,* Jesus holding a broken man. When I look at that picture, I saw myself, broken and hopeless. Things had changed in my life, and I was serving, and giving back. This was something I never did until God planted that seed in my heart.

There was another group in Puerto Vallarta, who was very involved with the children and the people living in the dump. The organization is called *Families at the Dump. Winnie Giesbrecht* is the founder and mission director. They have done so much work to help further and better the lives of the people living in the landfills; struggling just to survive.

Some of the amazing programs set up by Families at the dump are feeding 150 children lunch every Monday-Friday. 25-30 children attend day care at no charge, and 30 children attend English and computer classes. They have opened an activity room that is available daily. Two nights a week, 30 children attend a homework club, and 1 night a week 20+ children attend a reading and comprehension class.

In the summer of 2008, "Feed the Children Vallarta" began offering a free summer camp to the "School of Champions". It is intended for students and children in the neighborhood of the dump. It offers them a chance to see places in Puerto Vallarta, places they would otherwise never have a chance to see. The camp includes art, dance, music, English, computers and swimming. More than 130 children attend each year.

The reality of the dump.

This picture is about as real as it gets. It shows one of the children, on a morning hunt for bottles and cans. Can you picture your child, walking barefoot through a dump, trying to survive, trying to find enough cans in the garbage so they could eat that day?

I was blessed to have met with Winnie on a few occasions. There were a couple of times where I did participate and help out with Families. I do want to make it clear, I was there with Bill and Renee, designing and building a school. Through them, I was able to have met with Winnie, and was able to be of service on numerous occasions.

It was an experience that is hard to put into words. I was getting so involved with the church groups. There was the designing of a school for these children, and getting intertwined with the people living in the dump. It opened my eyes to things unseen and softened my heart. To be honest with you, I have tears running down my face as I write this. It brings back not only the memories, but I have a clear picture in my mind. Visually, it is all coming back to me, and I cannot fight the tears.

So my life was amazing, I was working, and helping others in Mexico. I had not had a drink in 11 months, nor had I done any drugs in

6 months. I cannot include the 5 months in hospital as clean time. Remember the morphine drip, but I can include the month in detox where I was drug-free.

While I was in Mexico, I had my first tattoo done in memory of my daughter. It was her name done in Chinese, on the back of my right leg, on the calf. There would eventually be two more tattoos, each one done in a different country. I don't want to stray off the path, and take the journey in another direction with things going so well in my life. As I have mentioned, the story is real and honest. So here we go again, after 5 amazing months, something happened, something that would change everything in Mexico.

One of my best friends from high school, Mike, was battling his own demons and struggled with an addiction to alcohol and drugs. He was having a hard time coping with life, and all it was throwing at him.

He drank a lot and did his share of drugs. In the end, addiction, as it did with Glenn, accomplished its goal. I received a phone call from my mom while I was working out at the dump one afternoon. She informed me that Mike had hung himself, he had ended his life. Another one of my best friends was dead; addiction won out again. It did what it set out to do, killing my friend.

I did not handle this very well. As a matter of fact; things were going to get real bad for the remainder of my stay in Mexico. There is something of grave importance for an addict, or anyone struggling with addiction. After a traumatic event, we need to be able to talk to someone who can relate. I could have talked with the people at the church, but they would not have been able to understand the addict mind. They are what we like to call normies, people who have never had to deal with drugs or alcohol. People who have never dealt with addiction do not have the same mindset as an addict.

There is something imperative that you learn in AA and NA; that is *one addict helping another addict;* it is a huge part of recovery and the recovery process. We need to have people that can relate to our situations, people that have, as you say, been there and done that. *The therapeutic value of one addict helping another addict.* The normal person just can't understand what is going through their mind, or what the addict is thinking.

I was alone, no support group and I had no one in my life that I could reach out to for help. So what does my addict tell me to do? It tells me to get a drink, something to numb the pain, and block out the emotions I am dealing with. I am an addict, and an alcoholic; at this point in my life, I had not learned any other way of handling loss and grief. The only way I knew how to deal with emotions was to bury them. Why does an addict bury the emotions? It is so that we do not have to feel, so we don't have to carry the weight of the world. We drown it out with alcohol and drugs because we have not learned another way to live, it's all we know.

It was at the 5-month mark that I received this information about Mike. For the next month, I drank and did drugs. During my drinking spree, I became close friends with a bartender who worked for one of the cartels in Mexico. This meant cocaine; he dealt coke from the bar he was running.

So while I was deep into my drinking, I was also doing cocaine. I fell from all my service work; I could not function. I could not, and would not show myself while being in the state I was in. The work at the dump came crumbling down, and since we are talking about addiction, and a life crumbling. I was kicked out of my place on the mountain top, forcing me to find another place to live.

Here comes the astonishing part of the story. The place I rented was tucked behind another villa. I had to go through the main part of the house and walk along a path to get to my place. I came home one night and was fairly drunk, and high on cocaine. As I went to go through the entrance, the door was locked. I took a look around, and the only answer I could come up with was to walk along the 40 ft. tin roof above. This lead to my place and my bad decision making, and my addict way of thinking was going to lead to total disaster.

I mustered my way up to the roof, in the dark, and walked along the tin roof. Being sure to step on the cross beams so I would not fall through. I can't say I was very quiet; it was noisy and loud as my feet smashed against the tin making my way home. I made it to the end, and jumped down to the ground, into the villa.

I was so alone and broken. I finished a bottle of tequila that was in the villa. In my cocaine haze, in my drunken state, and in my hopelessness, I grabbed a Bic shaving razor. I began to tear it apart, and with the razor sticking out of the plastic part of the shaver, I began to slash. Frantically slicing, and cutting at my wrists, it was very messy. I just wanted to hurt myself, to cause physical pain. I was not in my right mind, thinking that in some way it would help with the nightmare I was living.

As I sat there in my bedroom, I was paralyzed, and in a state of shock, blood was pouring out everywhere. It was covering the floor below, and my clothes were soaked. There were pieces of skin dangling from my wrists; blood was running down my arms because I was using a broken up bic razor.

Unbeknown to me while all this was going on, the lady living below the tin roof made a phone call to the police. She thought someone was breaking into the complex. I could not believe it; as I looked up, there are four Mexican Federales with machine guns drawn. They are yelling at me to put the razor down. Their guns were pointed at my head, blood is splattered all over the place, and an incredible commotion occurred. I was yelling in English, and they were screaming in Spanish.

I was drunk, and high on cocaine, and I had lost a lot of blood. I don't remember what happened after the commotion; I blacked out. The next thing I knew I was in jail, in a Mexican jail. Once again I did not know how to deal with life; I could not cope with my friend's suicide. It was my bad choices and my addiction that took me back to the pits of hell.

I awoke the next morning in a cell, lying on a dirt floor, in jail, surrounded by three other men, hung over, with my wrists all bandaged up. I had no idea how I arrived at such a place. They wanted to charge me for breaking and entry, even though it was my own place; you have to remember this was Mexico. The bloody spectacle at the villa and the sliced up wrists did not go over well with the authorities. They did not approve of myself destructive behavior or the intoxicated mess I was in.

I was able to make a few calls, so I called a friend of mine who had some connections in P.V, and he helped me out tremendously. He was able to get a hold of one of his friends at the Canadian consulate. Once again, God showed up. The person at the consulate was friends with the police chief at the jail. Through this relationship, and a couple of dollars, the police chief allowed me to leave after a three-day stay.

The only stipulation was that it would be a good idea if I were to leave Puerto Vallarta and make my way back to Canada. The lame attempt at slicing open my wrists did not go over very well. They felt it would be best if I went home, and found some help. The next day

I was driven by my friend to the airport, and I was on a plane back to Canada. Experience is a great teacher because it does not give the lesson till later.

Upon my arrival in Calgary, I was homeless, and I had nowhere to go. I could not stay at my mother's place for another 2½ years. I had been drinking and doing coke for the past month. Something to remember, it only took a month while in my addiction, to crumble everything to the ground.

My mother, being the wise women that she is, suggested that I needed to go back to the detox. So off I went, back to the same one I stayed at before I headed off to Mexico. I had no idea my trip to Puerto Vallarta was going to end the way it did. I went to serve and help others, which I did. But not in my wildest dreams could I have imagined that I was going to end up right back where I started, the Red Deer detox.

I would spend a month there, coming off the booze and coke, getting my bearings straight, and clearing my mind. As I continue to write the rest of the book, you are going to hear more about that *someone*. Throughout my life, He has continually shown up, usually in the worst of times. He is always there, good times, and bad; but when I fall, I always need *someone* to pick me up.

Speaking of God showing up; He would show up again in an amazing way. You remember the 8 x 10 from the nurse. It was the picture of Jesus, that *someone*, holding me, the broken man. I would lie in bed, staring at the picture before I headed off to Mexico. Well, God showed up again; in this same place.

About three weeks into my stay, I saw a poster on the wall. It was not much bigger than the 8 x 10, but this was a poster for Teen Challenge. This would be the second time I felt a nudge from the Lord. He was calling me, but I just needed to open the door and let Him in. This act of obedience would be a very big part of my walk with Christ.

The advertisement also showed a broken man and read Teen Challenge a 1-year Christian recovery program. I have been to at least 15 secular treatment centers, and none worked, so I was intrigued to say the least. It is crazy sometimes how God shows up in our lives. The thing is we need to be listening, and observant; we need to have our eyes, and ears open to the prompting of the Spirit.

So, God had planted a seed in me, and it gave me the overwhelming desire to serve and help others, off to Mexico I went. It was a life changing experience. I spent 5 months working with people in a place most would never imagine going. God used me in a mighty way, whether I knew it or not at the time. God had a purpose for me in Mexico.

Did God want me to start drinking, and doing cocaine, then end up in a Mexican jail? No, we have free will, and we make our own choices. What God did do, was pick me up, dust me off, and put me back on my feet. He brought me back to this place, and at three weeks in, He showed me where I needed to go next.

He had a plan for me. I made some calls to the main office in London, Ontario, and had a few conversations with them. They had centers across Canada, some had beds available, and other centers were full. In the end, there was a center outside Saskatoon, Saskatchewan. A week later, I was back on a plane again, making my 34th move. I was off to Saskatchewan, to get my life back in order, and to try something different this time.

Teen Challenge, a Christian faith-based, 1 yr. recovery program was definitely something new for me. God first planted a seed in me back at the hospital with that 8 x 10 picture of Jesus holding the broken man. So I went to Mexico to be of service, just like Jesus came to do; He came to serve. Once again, after having some clean time, I fell in Mexico. I went through detox in Red Deer, and God watered the seed prompting me to go to the middle of a field, to a center, near a tiny town called Allen, about forty minutes from Saskatoon.

The center is big, and it was new. It had 24 beds, a chapel, a huge cafeteria downstairs, and a state of the art kitchen. There was a huge walk-in freezer, new gas stoves, and a dish washing machine. I mean the center was beautiful, but it was located in the middle of nowhere, but there is a reason for this.

Most recovery centers around Canada and the States are located in cities. So, if I was in a center and I wanted to use drugs or drink, the opportunities are usually right around the corner. With Teen Challenge, as with most of their other centers, they are not situated in the city. Some are, but most are out in the middle of nowhere. This is a good precautionary measure on their part because it takes the chance of anyone just walking out the door to go and use.

This is part of the norm for addicts in recovery, they come, and they go. The ones who really want it will stay to save their lives. Some come in, but they are not ready, so they go out. I have a saying for such actions; I call it *research*. Some make it back; some end up in jail. Some will end up in a hospital bed, and some may die while out there doing more research. Sorry to say, but these are the honest statistics. It usually takes something catastrophic to happen in the life of an addict, until they decide they have done enough research.

When the research is done, and you want to get to know about a Loving God, to learn the bible and get to know, and understand the Gospel of Christ; when you have had enough, and you are broken, and you want to change your life: Then this is the place for you!

It is very structured, and it is a very disciplinary program, meaning there are rules, lots of rules. For most people coming in off the streets from addiction, rules are very important. We are used to doing things our way. As you know from reading the book that does not usually work out very well. So discipline, rules, and structure are important. They definitely provide all of the above. I can go on writing about all the benefits and the wonderful things that the program offers. But that will come in the next chapter, you will see why in a bit.

First I want to briefly tell you a little story about *the founder*, and *previous director of Teen Challenge Saskatchewan*; his name is *Serge LeClerc*. Please let me share a bit about the amazing story and testimony of Serge.

Back in the day, Serge LeClerc was one the most dangerous drug dealers and gang leaders in Canada. At the age of 15, he was heading the gangs in Toronto, running alcohol stills and extortion rackets. He spent 21 years of his life behind bars. In 1984, Serge was busted for running a 40 million dollar drug lab in Quebec. He was the co-leader of Canada's most powerful crime family, pulling in 130 million dollars a year. Serge was Canada's number one importer of hashish, working with the top importers from India. Here comes the conversion, the change that took place in Serge's life. It all happened while he was behind bars in prison.

Remember I told you God will use people, places, and things in our lives. He has many ways of showing Himself, to bring us to Him. As I mentioned earlier, God used an 8 x 10 picture, and then He used a poster, advertising Teen Challenge, to help guide me to Him. In Serge's case, God used a person, a little man who was handing out magazines to the prisoners on his cell block. At first, Serge had hatred towards this little man; he was always smiling, and doing a volunteer job that no one would want to do.

One day, the man was at Serge's cell door, and Serge lashed out at him. The man was startled, but in the end, he just kept smiling; the man was a Christian. They began to talk, and something sparked in Serge's heart. Another day, while at the Chapel, Serge was given a Red Bible. It is a Bible that whenever Jesus speaks, the words are written in Red. The rest of the wording is in traditional black. He began to read the New Testament, and in Serge's words, this is how he equivocated what he had read.

There was this gang leader, this Christ, and he was pretty cool. He had the authorities miffed, and the country was in an uproar. He did all this with 12 guys; they ended up busting him. Then one of the gang members became a stool pigeon and ratted him out.

The other 11 went into hiding. Then they ended up beating and whipping the gang leader, and eventually killing him, hanging him on a cross.

The question was, why did the 11 guys come out of hiding, allowing themselves to be beaten, tortured and killed? Unless what they saw was the **truth***!*

Serge then looked at Christ like he was a big brother. He thought that if this big brother told him what to do, to straighten out his life, how to be happy, to stop the misery, the pain, and rage, what would he say to me?

What Christ told him in the New Testament was, to follow me, to become a disciple and you will know the truth. If you want to walk out of darkness, follow me. I'm the truth the way and the life. Obey my teachings and you will have life, an abundant life.

So Serge LeClerc began the journey, the beginning of his transformation process. He knew Christ, and he knew that what Christ was telling him was *truth*. Christ was telling him of a right way to live, to have peace, happiness, and to get rid of addiction. God told him that all things were possible through Him. I will give you the strength, and I will walk with you. So Serge was given an identity, that he was loved by God. He knew Christ had died for him on a cross, that his sins have been forgiven, and that he was loved by God.

As I mentioned, Serge was the founder of Teen Challenge Saskatchewan, and he became an MLA in Saskatoon. Serge also spoke all across North America about drugs and addiction, and about finding that *someone*. As we now know, that *someone* is Christ. Hearing this story about what Serge had done, where he had been, and where Christ took him, is simply amazing. For all things are possible through Christ who strengthens us, *I truly believe that Change, inner change, comes and begins with a spiritual journey.*

If you are not a believer, and you think that you are too bad, and you have done too many horrible things in your life; where forgiveness is not possible for you, then take a look at Serge's story. I mean, this man was the worst of the worst. Let's be honest, thousands of lives were ruined and destroyed because of all the drugs he was either making in the lab or having shipped in from India.

God forgave Serge, He forgave me, and God can forgive you for anything, and everything you have done in your lives, from the day you were born, up until now. God transformed Serge LeClerc, he took him from the life he was living, and gave him a new life; and God can do the same for you.

> *David had an affair and was a murderer*
> *Noah was a drunk*
> *Abraham was too old*
> *Jacob was a liar*
> *Joseph was abused*
> *Rahab was a prostitute*

God used, transformed, and changed these people. God can, and will use the least of us. So if He can change and transform Serge, then why not you? God was in the process of transforming me, and I must mention He accomplished His goal, it just took a while. Why do you think He cannot transform you, and give you a new life? Maybe you need to take a minute and ask yourself; Why?

If I could get a bit personal, may I suggest that you try something? You may be at a Starbucks right now, or sitting in the park, on a bus, or at home. Say a prayer, have a talk with God, say it to yourself, under your breath, or out loud, talk to Him. There is no specific way to pray, talk like you would with a friend. Give it a try; ask for strength, or guidance, it could be something you may be dealing with right now in your life. Ask Him for help, I mean really, what do you have to lose? Absolutely nothing, trust me, God answers prayers.

I began my spiritual journey at Teen Challenge; it was the beginning of the process for me. I really began to learn, and understand who this God was. About His love, and what the Gospels were telling me. It is a one year program; most will think a year, are you kidding me? My reply is how long have you been out there drinking and drugging?

In my case, it was twenty years of drinking, and up till now, about eight years of hard drugs, so twenty-eight years in addiction. Take the twenty-eight years of chaos, and hell. Then think about taking one year, just one year out of twenty-eight to change your life. Do you see where I am going with this; I hope it becomes a little clearer.

At three months, you are just starting to get healthy, at six months your brain is just beginning to clear. It takes time; give yourself a year to begin the process of change. They say we need to change one thing, and that is everything. Then you can begin to live a new life; Teen Challenge will give you that.

I would be making my way back to another center in 2010. So in the next chapter, as I mentioned, I will get more into the details about Teen Challenge. What their program is, how they operate, and what they do to change your life. I would end up spending six months at the center in Saskatchewan. In that time, I grew in the Lord; I was digging into the bible, learning about what Jesus did, and how He walked His life. I began to pray on a regular basis, read the bible daily, and I became a huge fan of worship music.

Things were actually going really well in my life; I was in the process of changing and learning how to walk with the Lord. I had six months clean. Then I had a day pass to leave the center. To go shopping, have a nice lunch, just get out, and enjoy Saskatoon. Once again something happened in my life, and once again, it was not good.

First I want to let you know what happened. Then after I explain the chain of events, I want to try to bring some understanding as to why I would make the choice I made. My good friend Nino, who was a graduate of the Teen Challenge program, came to the center. He was there to pick me up to leave for a day pass. While making our way to Saskatoon, we made a pit stop at Ninos boss's house. He was doing some house sitting while they were away on a vacation. We went into the house, and Nino was going through some mail, and I asked if I could use the bathroom. He said to go upstairs; it was on the right. So I made my way upstairs to the bathroom.

Now remember, I have been at the center for six months, and this was my first taste of freedom. You never leave the center unless it is to go into Saskatoon for church on Sundays. One other thing I have not previously mentioned that ties into the story. Many years back, when I was working in L.A.; I was not a good boy. If we were on location filming at a person's house, I would, while in my addiction, go to their bathrooms. While I was there, I would open the medicine cabinet to see if there were any Vicodin's, or any other type of opiates.

I want to tell myself that I was a good addict because I would never take the person's whole prescription. I would never take the whole bottle and leave; that would not be very nice. I would just take 5 or 6 pills from the bottle, and go back to filming for the day. I am assuming you are getting the idea here, do you see where I am going with this bit of past information?

Yes, I opened up the medicine cabinet at Nino's boss's house. There before my eyes was a bottle of Hydro Morphine, an opiate painkiller; can you say temptation? There I was, standing there with six months clean, face to face with my D.O.C, my drug of choice. What are the chances, pretty good obviously?

Now, what should have I done? And what did I do? What I should have done, was repent, turned and walked away. I should have gone to Nino, and told him what had happened, that I needed to talk because I was struggling. Sorry to say, this was not the course of action that I took. What happened was the *mental obsession* kicked in. Remember I spoke about this earlier in the book. My addict mind tells me to grab that bottle and take 5 or 6 pills from it. I know what they are; I had taken them in the past many times. So I take one right away and save the rest for later.

The *disease* is always active, while in recovery and while we are staying clean and sober, our disease is doing push-ups. It always stays strong, just waiting for the opportunity to come back. It never gets weaker; it only gets stronger. When the opportunity presents itself, the disease comes back in full force. It begins right where we left off; it is as strong as it was the day we last used.

It could be a week, a month, a year, or five years, your clean time does not matter. The disease is just as strong as our last day when we were out there. This is a problem, and it is why you hear about so many people overdosing after a stretch of clean time. The disease tells me to go out, and do x amount of drugs, or drink x amount of alcohol after being clean for a while. Now the addiction has kicked in, and the disease is ramped. It tells me I can do the same amount that I was using before cleaning up. Then we wake up lying in a hospital bed. Or wake up in a jail cell, or in the end, we don't wake up at all because we have had an overdose in an ally, or a bathroom stall; we end up dying out there.

I take my one pill, and I spent the day pretty buzzed out there running around Saskatoon. When I make it back to the center that night, a few guys tell me my eyes look funny, that my pupils are dilated. I come up with some lame excuse, but the thing is, an addict can always tell when another one is high. We see it, there is no hiding it. It is not brain surgery, we as addicts can tell right away if someone else is high.

The next morning, we go to a church to do outreach, they do them every weekend. I will get into detail about that in the next chapter when I write about them. We head out to do the outreach, but before we leave. I decide it would be a good idea to pop a hydro morphine; this was a bad idea. We get to the church; it is full of people, and the drugs begin to kick in.

There I am sitting in the pews, and I begin to nod out, meaning it looks like you are falling asleep. A little drool is running down my face; my head is bobbing up and down looking like I am ready to slip into a coma. It is called *being on the nod*, which happens when you take too many opiates.

The next day, Monday morning when the staff came in, I get a call to come to the office. Using any form of drugs in Teen Challenge, or in any treatment center, means immediate dismissal, you get kicked out. There is no tolerance for using drugs, or alcohol, while in the treatment facility. I was asked to pack my bags and leave.

Being an addict, I denied the whole thing and was arguing with them, telling them I did not use. I went so far as to tell them to give me a pee test (which I would have failed) to prove my innocence. I mean really, I knew I was busted, I knew I used, and I knew that they were following procedure. But since I was back into my addiction, my old behaviors did not take long to kick in.

After my losing battle, I packed up the minimal belongings I had. Then a few staff members gave me a ride back into Saskatoon, to be dropped off in front of the greyhound station. There I stood with two suitcases, alone, in a city, I had only been to a couple of times. I was homeless, and I had nowhere to go. Once again because of my bad choices, because of addiction, I was alone, lost, and hopeless.

The way this turns out will blow you away. It even blew my mind. To think, I was standing in front of a greyhound bus station, hopeless, lost, and having absolutely nothing in my life. What would happen to me later could only come from the grace of God, and it did happen. Speaking about God, you may wonder where He was in all this. I had just spent six months learning about Him, and reading His word. Where was He? Well, let me explain the second part to all this.

Teen Challenge taught me, showed me, and guided me; they did what their program is set out to do. There was one small problem, and that was *me*, I *believed* everything I was taught, I believed the Bible, what it said, and what it was telling me.

The issue was that it was all *head knowledge*. I had all the head knowledge a person could attain at the time, but I did not know how to apply it. I did not know how to put it into action. I needed to take it from my head and put it in my *heart*. One other thing missing was *Faith,* and the thing about faith is that it is an action. Until I get personal, until I say this is for me, until I accept this Christ, and understand that Christ is all I have. Then it is just head knowledge. I had all the head knowledge, but I was missing the key ingredient, and that was *Faith*.

To begin our journey with Christ, we need to internalize. I needed to accept that this was for me. We must reach a point where we say, I can't do this, I can't do it alone. I am hopeless, helpless, and I can't do it, it must be personal, and it needs to be internalized.

Faith comes to us individually, and the acceptance of Christ is very personal. Faith is an action that we need to take as individuals. We must understand it for ourselves, and not be told; it comes to us as a gift from God. It is not until we understand what Christ has done for us, that we are helpless without Him.

It comes from inner strength, strength from within, and the strength I am speaking of, can only come from God. We must understand that if there is no conversion, it is just conformity, and this was exactly the point I was at. There was no Faith, I had head knowledge, I did not internalize, and I never put it in my heart.

I was not at the point to truly admit that I was helpless and hopeless. I did not know, or I did not understand. I truly believe this is a huge part of the reason why I grabbed that bottle from the medicine cabinet. I had no inner strength; I had not truly accepted that *someone* whom I needed so bad in my life. It was that *someone* who showed up in an 8 x 10 photo. It was that *someone* who planted a seed to go to Mexico and serve. It was that *someone*, who showed me a poster of Teen Challenge, and guided me to their steps.

God was opening doors for me, and I was walking through them, but there was a problem; it was my addiction. I did six months in Mexico, and I fell. I did six months at Teen Challenge and fell. *Someone* kept picking me back up and putting me back on my feet. My addiction kept sabotaging all my effort to get to this Christ. My time would come, and yes; I would open that door and let Him in.

You may be wondering, after reading through my story, how many more signs must I see? How much more devastation do I need in my life, to get to the point, where I let Him in? Let me tell you, it is coming. It would show up in full force, but something else was going to happen. Remember I was standing in front of that greyhound bus station, alone and lost. Well, two weeks later, I would be running again, this time, it would be on a plane, off to Bali, Indonesia.

CHAPTER 12

Bali: Indonesia

I T WAS 2009; I would be making my 35th move at the age of 42, to another country, another continent. Remember, I was kicked out of Teen Challenge because I used drugs, prescription pain pills taken from a medicine cabinet. Once again, I stayed at a hotel in Saskatoon, lost, alone and not knowing where to go. It was my lack of faith and bad decision making that caused me to grab that pill bottle, and it led to my drinking again.

In addiction, once the mind and body get a taste; *The Mental Obsession* kicks in. The pills led to alcohol. I had not drank in 6 months, but my first night in that room, I was drinking. A very good friend of mine named Dianne came by the hotel and stayed with me. I had suicidal thoughts again. I drank all my life and was never suicidal. The last 3 times I drank, I tried to kill myself. Here I was again, wanting to walk out to the main road, and jump in front of a bus. She knew about my past and took my thoughts seriously. So she stayed and prevented me from doing something stupid.

I want to thank Dianne and her daughter for staying with me, and keeping me safe. She and her husband were huge supporters of Teen Challenge. Once a month they would have all 24 guys, plus staff, over to their house for a dinner. To this day, I am still very close to her, and I want to throw in an acknowledgment. She came up with the name of this book, *From Reel To Real*. Not only did they have dinners, but she kept me safe and alive through that dreadful night. She also arranged for me to go to detox for a week while I was still in town.

I did my week, and while I was there, I received a message on Facebook from a friend. Her name is Villa, and I used to hire her back in L.A. to work in the art department with me. She messaged, and said she lived in Bali, Indonesia, and that she had a wedding and event company. We chatted back and forth, beginning the process of rebuilding our friendship. I had not heard from her for over 14 years. I made my way back to the little town of Innisfail, Alberta, where my mother lived.

As you remember, I was banned from her building, so I stayed in a hotel not far from her house. It all happened so quickly. My conversations with Villa over the next week eventually ended up with me going to Bali. I mean really, where else did I have to go? Why not Bali? Within 2 ½ weeks of my leaving Teen Challenge, everything fell into place. The ticket was bought, and my passport was in check. Before you could blink an eye, I was off and running, flying to the other side of the world, to Indonesia.

Twenty-two hours later, with a brief stop in Taipei, I would be touching down in paradise; Villa had her driver meet me at the airport. He met me right at the arrivals gate, whisked me through customs and the security check. No waiting in lines when you know the right people. Driving from the airport to Villas office was breathtaking, seeing the rice fields perfectly lined up, running parallel up the side of the mountains. All the palm trees, everything was green, with thousands of scooters on the tiny roads. There were very few cars, but it was wall to wall scooters.

Hundreds of little makeshift shops and stores scattered along the roadways; the stifling heat took some getting used to. When I arrived, I met with Villa; she was looking amazing as always. The office was very nicely decorated, a huge T.V. mounted on the wall, flower arrangements scattered about, and a loft upstairs for her employees. The name of her company was *Bali Experience* and the main part of what they did was weddings. She had four employees working for her, and they did world class weddings all over the island.

I was blessed to have worked with her for three months. We did some very expensive weddings, some in the price range of a hundred thousand dollars. We would arrange the villas where the guests would stay, airport pick up, car rentals, and excursions for them to go on. The wedding itself entailed the catering, ice sculptures, D.J, and locations. They were usually in huge multi-level villas overlooking the ocean, many with infinity pools surrounded by palm trees.

We would also arrange the entertainment; fire dancers, Balanisian dancers, local musicians. We planned, and organized the weddings from the beginning, up until the time the wedding party was ready to leave the island. Bali is amazingly beautiful; the Indonesian island is known for its forested volcanic mountains, iconic rice paddies, beaches, and coral reefs. No wonder so many European and Australian couples go there to get married.

I had an affair with Villa, which lasted for the first two months, and in the third month, she had to go back to L.A. for business. I took care of keeping things running at her company while she was away. During the time she was in L.A., we did not see eye to eye, and things did not go well between us.

When she arrived back a month later, we ended our relationship. This, of course, ended my employment at Bali Experience. As they say, *nothing happens in God's world by mistake.* There was something else I needed to do. God had instilled something in my heart. After three months it hit me like a ton of bricks. My heart screamed out, and I heard what God wanted. It was to serve, and give back; I would set out to do another job in the mission field.

My life was good. Every morning I would read a daily devotion, and dig into the Bible for an hour. I would then end with Prayer, having a talk with my Father in Heaven. I would always Pray for wisdom, guidance, and to give me understanding in all circumstances. I would ask Christ to give me strength for the day so that I may walk in His light.

I did this every day for the first five months of my stay in Bali; I was clean and sober. My life was complete; I had peace and serenity on a daily basis. I was walking with Christ, and sharing my testimony with people. I would share the good news, telling about that *someone* who could change their lives. Even though I had a slip while in Teen Challenge, God did an amazing thing.

He drew me back; we leave Him in the busyness of sin, but He is always with us. He picked me up, dusted me off, and put me back on my feet. He set me on a new path. I was getting ready to serve others, give back, and I continued to stay clean; and out of trouble. God had a plan, and I was listening. I heard His calling, and I was obedient. It was time to embark on another mission trip, this time, it was in Bali.

I was blessed to meet Natalia, one of the most selfless and serving women I had ever met in my life. She was the founder and director of *Safe Childhoods Foundation*. Their aim is to combat crimes against children in Indonesia and to protect some of the most vulnerable and at-risk. They seek and find abused children, and youth sold into the sex trade. They work with kids who are riddled with anxiety, depression, and aggression. Natalia's organization also sets out to renovating local orphanages and schools for the street kids of Bali.

This is where I came into play; she was getting ready to renovate an orphanage with 143 girls living there. The kids slept on the floor, most with no matts, just a blanket if they were lucky. There were no windows or any form of ventilation in the sleeping areas. Most rooms had 8-10 girls crammed into a tiny space, forced to sleep huddled up in a small spot on the floor.

The kitchen area had no windows, and it was equipped with one huge pot and one propane burner to cook meals for all 143 kids. The outside was dirty, and in the rainy season, there was no overflow, so everything would flood. These children were living in a crumbling, run-down orphanage, all the while going to school on the site. The classrooms all needed work as well. We needed to bring this orphanage back to life, and we needed to help these children.

I put my mind to work, pulling out some tricks of the trade from my years doing set design in L.A. We came up with a plan and a blueprint to change and fix all the problems the orphanage was facing. Natalia had grant money from donations, so we redesigned the entire place. Ceiling fans and windows were installed in the girls sleeping quarters, and matts were purchased for all the kids. The kitchen was enlarged, and more supplies and cooking elements were brought in. The classrooms were all remodeled; the landscaping was improved with plants and flowers, along with some palm trees planted throughout the facility.

Finally, we redid the overflow system, making run off ditches so when it rained the orphanage would not flood. Doing this selfless, serving work brings such satisfaction. It gives an overwhelming sense of what it is like to help others and to give back to people in need. I believe this is what God has us all here on this earth to do. Get out of self, and into service. It does not matter if it is a block from your house, or on another continent. We are to help the less fortunate in any way we can. I was blessed to have helped in Mexico and now here in Bali. I believe God has more work planned for me.

While all this was going on, I was living in a villa owned by two friends whom I grew very close to. Yarri and Toya, two amazing people; Yarri was from L.A., and he is one of the most amazing artists that I have ever met. On the property, there is a huge art studio and gallery where Yarri's artwork is displayed. His artwork is known around the world. Toya is a local Balanisian woman who has her own clothing line.

Life was good; I had been following and walking close with the Lord through all this time. I trusted Him with everything in my life, and God had provided abundantly for me over the time I had been in Bali. Then a small problem occurred, and I don't understand why. For no particular reason, I slowly stopped doing my devotions in the morning, reading my Bible, and my prayer life began to fall apart. I began to fall away from my reliance on the Lord and began to do things my way. There would be consequences for my disobedience.

I was five months into my stay, and I had to take a trip to Singapore. I needed to renew my visa. I booked the short flight from Bali to Singapore; this would not be good. It is an island city in southern Malaysia known for its global commerce, transportation, and financial hub, with the world's 3rd-largest foreign exchange center.

The downtown is lined with high-rises and malls; I called it the city of malls because the entire downtown core is full of them. Everything is connected underground. You could start at one end and work your way down the maze of escalators and elevators that take you from mall to mall. It is quite amazing and beautiful. The main downtown corridor was lined with street performers, restaurants, and theaters. I fell in love with this city, and the people were very friendly and helpful.

Here comes my addict, at five months clean. My mind tells me that some OxyContin would be nice. Here I am in a foreign country, in a city that I have only spent three days in, surrounded by high rise buildings. What do you think the chances are of finding, and getting some opiates?

Well, remember I said that addicts and alcoholics are very intelligent people. When we want something, chances are very good that our creative minds will find a way. We have to change our way of thinking and apply it for good. If we could only use our minds in a positive way, changing our mischievous ways into something positive, like starting a business or running a company. We could perform miracles!

My addict has been doing pushups and working out for five months. It has been getting stronger, and stronger, waiting for me to open the door. Well, the floodgates opened, and my addiction came rushing in like a roaring river.

I found a doctor's office on the 33rd floor in one of the buildings downtown, only to find out there were doctors' offices scattered all over the upper level. I made my way to the receptionist; she said the doctor was booked, and that I should go to the 36th floor to see another doctor.

So off I went, up the elevators, to accomplish my mission. Once I arrived, the wait was not long. Before I knew it, I was sitting with the doctor. Did I lie, and manipulate? You bet I did, there was OxyContin on my mind. I told him I was from Canada and was living in Bali doing mission work. I mentioned my L5, S1, the fractured disc, and that I could not sleep at night. I told him the pain was shooting down my leg, and up to my back. It was unbearable, and at times, I could hardly walk.

I continued with my deceitful lies; I had the play on words embedded in my mind. This was not my first go at manipulating doctors, as you well know. I told him that my prescription had run out and that I was heading back to Canada in a week.

I knew the next play was not to be greedy, so I told him I only needed 10-14 pills, just enough to last the week before heading home. My acting was award winning, and the next thing I knew I was walking out of the office with a prescription for OxyContin. I paid the $80.00 bill and was out the door heading down the street towards the hospital a few blocks away. There was an entrance going into the emergency department, and along the corridor sat a pharmacy. I walked up, handed them my prescription, and a very short time later, I was walking away with a bottle of OxyContin.

Here is the mind-boggling part of it all, from my first thought of getting pills, until the time I had them in my hand was 1 ½ hours. In downtown Singapore, alone, and not knowing the city, it took my addict 1½ hours to accomplish the mission.

I was very high for my flight back to Bali. The next few days I continued to take the pills; taking them orally, not snorting, or shooting them.

There is something about addicts and addiction. When we take that first one, it acts as a springboard, a starting point on our road back to the pits of hell. When an addict gets started, as I did with the pills, the *mental obsession* kicks in, and the *phenomenon of craving* is alive and well.

So I continued, knowing good and well where it is going to take me. We do not think about the consequences or the path of destruction we are going to leave behind. All we want to do is get high, or drunk, nothing else matters. Our driving force becomes seeking, and getting the drug, or finding a place to get your booze, everything else is secondary. Addiction is a nightmare, and it is powerful and deceitful, our minds do not work like a normal person.

In the next few pages, I will explain the insanity of it all. If you do not know the meaning of insanity; *it is doing the same thing over and over again, expecting different results.* I knew the consequences, I had been doing it all my life, and the result was always the same. As they say in A.A. and N.A., *jails, institutions, and death.*

I had been in jail, I had been in hospitals & institutions, and I could not have come closer to dying, especially after diving four stories of a balcony. So what would be different this time? Would this round of *research* be any different? When someone is in recovery, or has clean time, and they untimely make the choice to go out again and use, I call it *research.* Sometimes we feel that one more go at it will be different. No, it never is, it always ends in disaster, hence the insanity of it all.

Everything I am about to tell you started from taking *one pill,* one OxyContin. Now my mind and body have had a taste of a substance that altered my feelings. My way of thinking wanted more. It would not matter what it was; my addict wanted more of anything that would give me the same results. I needed something to numb the emotions, something to make me feel better.

Later that week a friend of mine Zoe, who is a techno D.J. from Holland, and I are on our bikes heading to Kuta, the party district in Bali, to get some magic mushrooms. They are a hallucinogenic and are sold legally for religious ceremonies. I had done them quite a few times while living in L.A.; they are one of my favorite drugs to take. Colors are very vivid, you laugh a lot, it is a visual type of high, and the main thing is that you are in control of your actions.

We arrived at a little shack where the mushrooms are sold with our bottle of fruit juice. They pull out a baking tray with little bags of mushrooms lined from top to bottom. There are about 20 bags on the tray; we each ordered two bags, and then they proceed to pour your drink into a blender, add the two bags, and blend it all together.

We sat out front, had our drink, and watched the party goers running around all dressed to the nine's. Zoe was a D.J. at one of the big nightclubs in Kuta, so we walked right into the massive three level club. There were upwards of a 1000 people dancing, drinking and doing drugs. It was basically Sodom and Gomorrah; with-in a half hour the mushrooms kicked in and all the colors intensified.

To explain it best, it would be like watching a Pixar movie, Finding Nemo, or Monsters Inc., on an HD T.V. Then envision what you are watching, and intensify it by 20. We walked from level to level, listening to the techno music, talking with friends; then we had to leave. Mushrooms are not a club drug, like ecstasy and GHB. Mushrooms are, shall I say, a nature drug; you need to be in the desert, a forest, or in our case, Bali, enjoying the great outdoors.

We were in paradise, high out of our minds on the mushrooms, racing around on our scooters. We drove through the rice fields where bamboo homes on stilts were scattered everywhere. We twisted our way through the canyons looking down at the ocean, having the time of our lives. I am not here to promote, or boast about how great, or how much fun a drug is. During this awesome excursion, as it was with any drug induced time in my life, it always seems to end in disaster; this would be no different.

This fun filled mushroom trip would definitely not end the way I intended it to. We decided to make a stop at a friend's restaurant. It was full of people, eating, drinking, with music playing. There was a fun-filled, festive energy in the air. Since we knew the owner, he set us up with a table away from all the action. Remember, we were tripping on mushrooms, so being on the outskirts of all the action was a good thing. The bad thing was Irac, a local moonshine; every country I have been too has a local drink.

These types of drinks are not sold at liquor stores, they are not legalized, but still, it is very popular with the locals. I had not had a drink in five months, and since I was high, the thought of drinking became a good idea. We did shot after shot of Irac, a white, clear, potent drink that in the end, will mess you up. Well, that is exactly what it did to me. By the time the evening came to a close, I was plastered. Zoe hopped on his scooter; he lived in the opposite direction I lived, so off he went. I got on my scooter and was about to make an attempt to drive home.

This would turn out to be a tragic event with irac and mushrooms flowing through my system. I made my way down the side streets of Bali, weaving my way in and out of traffic. I then made a right turn, heading out towards the rice fields near the villa I was living at. The problem; a brick wall with two scooters parked alongside it. I was high, drunk, and out of my mind. I lost control of the bike and slammed into one of the parked scooters. I was driving so fast the other scooter was demolished as well as mine. The chain reaction caused me to fly off my bike, slamming head first into the brick wall. Do you think I was wearing a helmet?

I laid there unconscious, with carnage all around me bleeding profusely; by the grace of God, a family heard the accident and came running out. They carried me into their little shanty shack and called an ambulance. Everything was spinning out of control, my mind was blurred, my face was smashed up, and I had split my head wide open. Blood covered my face and body, my lower back was a mess, and the pain was ripping down my leg, towards my knee which was split open. I laid on the dirt floor, in the little shanty shack, asking myself, Why? I did not remember much of what had happened. The next thing I knew, I was waking up, or coming too, in a third world country, in the hospital, staring up into the faces of four young doctors examining me.

I was not wearing a helmet, and I should have had a lot more damage done to my face and head, but once again, God had angels surrounding me. I ended up with 14 stitches above my left eye and 18 stitches on my right knee.

What did I mention earlier, jails, institutions, and death? I can guarantee you, that while you are active in your addiction; one of the three will come into play. I have to thank God it was not death. This time, it was an institution, because of my drinking and drugging. I should have died. If you are asking where God was in all this? Well, He was there the whole time, protecting me, while in my drunken state and in the midst of my bad choices; He was there! To this day, I have a scar above my left eye, and on my knee. In a third world country, they do not do the best stitching work. So I have another reminder, it goes along with the other scar I have above my left eye from running into the metal door at the psych ward back in L.A.

The nightmare did not end there. A few days later, I went to a party and met an incredibly beautiful woman. She was so cute with short blonde hair, and an amazing little body. I was introduced to her, and of course, we hit it off and began to see each other. Here I am in Bali, on the other side of the world. There are women from all walks of life, and I end up falling in love with a woman from Canada. Her name is Bonnie, and she had been living in Bali for 12 years. She was a clothing designer and had a store called Kiss, Kiss, Bang Bang. She designed and made her own clothing line. When I met her, she was in the process of moving back to Canada. She was going back to Toronto, where she would continue her designing career.

This is where the drinking started to get out of hand; I moved in with Bonnie after dating for only a week. I began waking up in the mornings and started drinking. Later I would drive my scooter to the local store, and buy beer, lots of beer. For the first week, all we did was drink and have sex, all day and all night.

After the first week, my behaviors and actions began to get way out of control. Do you think the abundance of alcohol flowing through my system played any part in all this? Bonnie was getting sick and tired of the chaos I was continuously causing because of my drinking. Sometimes sleeping till two or three in the afternoon, waking up, and then it would start again. This lasted about three weeks until Bonnie finally said enough, and kicked me out.

My life continued to crumble in Bali; my visa had not been updated because I missed my appointment in Singapore. I was too busy seeking my OxyContin's, so updating the visa became secondary. After Bonnie had kicked me out, I had a friend from South Africa who came and picked me up to stay at his place. That lasted three days; I was getting into the Irac from some locals near his Villa. I drank to oblivion, just a mess. I could hardly walk, falling down the stairs at his place, and causing problems with the locals. I had burned all my bridges; people did not want to be around me. I had run out of places to stay, and Bali would not be the best place for me to be homeless.

The Australian consulate had my passport, so my friend and I went to the consulate and paid a large fee to get it back. I had caused some problems at Bonnies where the police were called, and they had showed up there more than once. They had a record of my incidents, and once again, it was suggested that I take my passport, arrange for a flight back to Canada, and leave Bali.

I was in the depths of addiction, my choices, and my decision making was all out of whack. I made some decisions in Bali that I would never have made if I was sober with a clear mind. I wanted to do it my way. When I do that and take my will back, thinking I have it all together, my life quickly falls apart. I made a choice to stop following Christ, and there were consequences for my actions.

Three days later; I was on a plane flying back to Canada. I was in despair and riddled with grief. It seems Gods plan was to strip everything away. I needed to come to the understanding that all I had was Him. He undid the veil until all I saw was Him. I needed to pursue Him, and I needed to open my eyes.

Calgary airport, once again I was homeless, hopeless and had nowhere to go. I was expecting my mother to pick me up, but this would not be the case. My mother had enough. My actions and my drinking and drugging were killing her; she was an emotional wreck. If you remember, this would be the third pick up at the same airport. When I came back from six months in Teen Challenge, she picked me up. When I came back from six months in Mexico, she picked me up. Now coming back from six months in Bali; she was not going to pick me up. She was done, and I was stranded in Calgary, at the airport.

I felt like Tom Hanks in the movie *Terminal*, where he was also stranded at an airport, but he was not an addict in the movie, and this was real life. I had my suitcases set up next to a row of chairs away from the main traffic areas. I was drinking before I left Bali, on the plane coming back, and while I was living at the airport. It began to get out of control; I had run out of money. So I had to put on a few of my masks, and my academy award acting came into play as I approached people to get money.

I came up with a hundred ideas or reasons for my needing money; I played the stranded guy at the airport routine, I was hungry, or I needed money to catch a cab. My mind was sharp, I had a need, and my addict was going to find a solution. I would, and did find ways to get money to satisfy my insatiable craving to get liquor flowing through my body.

I was pathetic. I look back, and once again my actions make me sick. The things we do while stuck in our addiction are appalling. We do things that we would never do sober; I am not that person. Dwayne, the addict, does sick messed up stuff to get what he wants. Dwayne, the sober and clean guy, would never think about doing the things I did while in my addictive state. Two different people like Jekyll and Hyde; I don't want to be that person. I still have a bit more to share. Remember, Dwayne the addict was in full swing, which means things could only get worse.

On the third day, I could not take it anymore. I was sleeping on the floor, asking for money, and drinking all day and night. The loneliness and being detached from everyone and everything was tearing me apart. There was no way for me to process the agony and suffering. I came up with another brilliant idea, a way to get out of the airport.

Are you ready for this move; my mind tells me to call 911 and tell them I am at the airport, and that I am suicidal. I told them I wanted to kill myself. They take something like this pretty serious, as I was about to find out.

Within ten minutes, there were eight policemen surrounding me; three of the officers had their hands on their guns ready to be drawn. I was thrown to the ground and handcuffed. After the initial chaos, they sat me down, and we talked. They went through all my luggage and searched me from head to toe. They did not know if I had a weapon, or if I was going to harm myself or others. So when an addict calls, saying they are going to kill themselves at an international airport; they do not take it very lightly.

I was fairly drunk, but honestly, in my heart, I was afraid. I felt there was no escape, and darkness was covering my soul. I was not really going to kill myself, but my mind thought it was a good solution. This would lead to another trip, once again, to the psych ward.

I would spend a week; it gave me time to clean up from my drinking spree. While I was there, my thinking was a bit clearer, so I called Pastor Andrew; a good friend of mine who pastors the Alliance church in my mom's town. I explained my situation, but he had already known. I guess my mom had a long talk with him before I arrived back from Bali. He came and picked me up, and brought me back to the same hotel as before, not too far from mom's house, in the little town of Innisfail.

Things would get better, but I had to cause a little more destruction, and chaos before my life would change. It was a quick, but devastating little run. The plan was to drink; the insanity of it all, it does not make sense. The normal person must be mind boggled. How can a person continue to make these bad choices? It's called addiction, and it is pure evil.

My first night at the hotel I was drunk and almost had a fight in the lobby. The police arrived, and I was thrown into jail. The second night I drank and was causing problems. Someone called the police, and they took me back to jail. I am being completely honest with you, the third night came, I drank, and was wrecking the hotel room. The same police arrived, cuffed me, and brought me to jail.

They made it perfectly clear if they got one more complaint about me they would kick me out of town. The fourth night came, and my mom stopped by for a visit. I was drinking again, and we had an argument. I became angry and began acting out, so my mom called the police. They arrested me and kicked me out of the little town of Innisfail. Not only was I banned from my mom's place, but I was banned from entering the town. Oh, the joys of addiction.

Up to this point in my life, I have been deported from The United States, kicked out of Puerto Vallarta, and asked to leave Bali, Indonesia. The fourth mass exodus for me was not to come back to Innisfail until I found some help. If you are struggling with some form of addiction, or someone you know is struggling, get some help, go to detox, and find a Christ-centered facility; you may just save yourself, or someone you love.

Alcohol, drugs, and the addict mind? What makes us tick? Why would I not stop drinking on the second or third night? Why would I keep drinking? I will tell you why, because when we start, there is no stopping us. We go on a run, as we call it, and it usually takes something catastrophic to happen in our lives before we stop. When Satan has you in his grips, it is very hard to stop and find a way out.

The mental obsession and the physical allergy have set in. This is followed by the phenomenon of craving, which is manifested in the allergy, both mentally and physically. We need the drug, or alcohol, just to maintain, to keep feeling normal. Our normal is nothing like the normalcy a person feels who is not dealing with addiction.

It is about the chaos and the adrenaline rush. When things are out of control, when we are running on pure energy to survive and maintain, we feel normal. Anything that differs from that is not normal. So we are comfortable when life is uncomfortable; does that make sense? Our brains do not operate the same as a normal person does. We are let's say, wired differently.

I want to do a quick rundown on the infamous *six months*. As I wrote earlier in the book, it seems to play a major factor in my life.

Most of my relationships were around *six months*; but here are a few of the most recent events.

A four-story dive of a balcony, lead to *six months* in the hospital. After my recovery, I would spend *six months* in Puerto Vallarta. Then, it was back to Canada, and a *six-month* stint in Teen Challenge. Two weeks later, it was off to Bali, Indonesia, yes, for *six months*. There is some insanity here, don't you think? I could not plant roots; every six months my mind tells me to run. What was I running from? And why was I running? I needed to break the six-month cycle. There was something I needed to do different, to stop the insanity in my life, and I would soon get my answer.

Here we are after all the bad drinking and drugging stories. I finally have some good news to share. After I had been kicked out of Innisfail, I went to Red Deer, where I had attended high school and found a hotel to stay at. While I was there, something happened that would change the life I was living. I want to be clear with you; this is real, and it was audible. It was as if God tore the roof off the hotel, and spoke to me while I was standing in my room. He said; *you are going back to Teen Challenge, and you will complete the year.* It was a crystal clear message from God, a first for me, where beyond a shadow of a doubt, He spoke to me.

The first piece of good news; a week later, I was flying to the East Coast of Canada, to the city of Sault Ste Marie, where I would spend a year at Teen Challenge North. The second thing is, and only by the grace of God; I have not touched a drop of alcohol since July 2010. From this very second, as I write this, today it is Aug 20, 2015, I have not had a drink for over five years.

There is an answer, a solution, and it is that *someone*. It is having a relationship with Christ, trusting Him to guide you and to direct your path. It has worked for me, and it can work for you as well. All you have to do is open the door and let Him in.

Teen Challenge North, I would spend the next year living in a house with eleven other men, on the outskirts of Sault Ste Marie, Ontario. This would be a life changing year for me. As I mentioned, it is a year long Christian recovery program, the keyword is Christian. It is all about that *someone* in the 8 x 10 picture; it is about Christ. God has a plan and a purpose for us all, even when we are so low, broken, and have lost all hope. He will pick us up, put us back on our feet, a tell us to take more steps.

We can never have done too many horrible things in our lives, where our loving, and caring Father cannot, or will not forgive us. I was a mess, helpless and hopeless. I did good things in those countries, but my addiction showed up and overpowered me. Why? Because I had no defense, I had no way to fight off the demons of addiction. I had head knowledge about God from the Teen Challenge in Saskatoon, but no Faith. All that would change; a lot would change in my life over the next year. God would use Teen Challenge to bring me to Him, to a new way of living, and put me on the path He intended me to travel.

David Wilkerson, who founded Teen Challenge, was a preacher from rural Pennsylvania and was drawn by Christ to go to New York in 1958. He was awakened by reading an article in *Life Magazine* one evening. It was about seven boys being on trial for a gang murder. He heard a voice that said: *Go to New York and help those boys.* I am certain it was the same voice that said to me, *you are going back to Teen Challenge, and you will complete the year.*

So he left his church and went to New York to help the teen's involved in gangs struggling with drugs and alcohol. He went because God spoke to him; he was obedient to Gods calling. Later in 1958, David founded Teen Challenge; the program began in a small house located in Brooklyn.

When we are listening to God, when we are in sync with Him, He can do amazing things in our lives. Teen Challenge began in a house in Brooklyn; they are now in more than 90 countries, with over 1000 centers worldwide. They are all over North America, Europe, Asia, Africa and Australia.

Why? A pastor from rural Pennsylvania was obedient to Gods calling. He went to New York and started Teen Challenge. They are saving lives and bringing people to Christ because God used a preacher from Pennsylvania to do his work. He can use you and me, we just need to be listening, and seeking Him.

I told you a little story about Serge LeClerc, the founder of Teen Challenge in Saskatchewan. It was a story about his conversion, and what Christ did in his life. I want to share another story. It is about another man, who was as far from Christ as you could imagine.

Nicky Cruz, at the age of 15, was sent by his parents from his home in Puerto Rico to New York to live with his brother. He would have none of that, so he hit the streets and became a member of the notorious street gang, *The Mau-Mau's*. He was said to be one of the most violent gang bangers in New York. He sold drugs, beat and tortured people, and within six months he was proclaimed warlord of the gang.

While David Wilkerson was working the streets, he came in contact with members of the Mau-Mau street gang. It did not go well at first. When he met Nicky, he told him that Jesus loved him and that Christ would never stop loving him. Nicky responded by slapping David's face and then threatened to cut him up into 1000 pieces. David's response to him was, every piece would still say, *I love you*.

Here comes the miracle. Christ has all of our lives so well-orchestrated, and this is where He put His plan into action. David decided to have a rally one evening in a theater, and he included the Mau-Mau's to come to the event. Nicky showed up with alternative motives, but when he arrived, Christ began His work and softened this man's heart. This violent, dangerous warlord had an overwhelming feeling of *guilt* for all the things he had done.

Later in the evening, David asked the Mau-Mau's to take up the collection, or offering from the people in the crowd. Nicky and his gang members did the collection, and after, while in the back, he saw the exit sign. He was going to run off with the money. Something happened to him that night. He did not run. He walked up to David and gave him the money. At the end of the service, there was an altar call. Nicky walked up to David, and they prayed together. After praying, Nicky broke down and asked God to forgive him for all the wrongs in his life.

Nicky Cruz, the toughest gang member in New York back in 1958, turns his life over to Christ. He was sick of living the way he was, and he finally found that *someone*. After his conversion, he went to Bible College and began studying the Word. He became a preacher and returned to the streets of New York to help the teens. He also converted most of the Mau-Mau's to Christianity.

He became the director of Teen Challenge, working under David Wilkerson. Today, he is a Christian evangelist and the founder of the Nicky Cruz outreach ministry. This is an amazing transformation story because a preacher from Pennsylvania was obedient and went to New York. If you would like the whole story, you can either watch the movie or read the book called *The Cross and the Switchblade*. It is based on David Wilkerson's story, Nicky Cruz, and the beginning of Teen Challenge.

I committed myself, and I would complete the task at hand. I knew in my heart that I would finish out the year. I spent many years in addiction and knew this was my chance to do things differently. This was my second go, and I was familiar with the program. This time, I needed to take it from my head and put it in my heart. I needed Christ to be the center of my life. God would take my hardened heart, and soften it; He would mold me as a potter molds his clay.

The program is called Teen Challenge, but today, it is by no means a program just for teens. I was in my forties. There are guys ranging from their twenties, and thirties up to fifty. When I was in the program, we only had one or two guys in their teens. In the beginning, back in New York, David started the program for teens. Over the years, it has expanded and is now a program for anyone struggling with addiction. The minimum age requirement is 18 to enter into a Teen Challenge facility.

The day starts with a wake-up call at 6:15 am, every morning, except weekends. Guys who come in the houses can't believe they need to be up so early and ask why? Well in the real world, if you had a job, and were living a normal life, you would be up at this time to go to work. Guys come in with having had no structure or discipline in their lives.

This is part of the change I mentioned; everything has to change. Guys need to learn what it is like to be a productive member of society. So by doing this, it begins to institute some structure in their lives, and it prepares a person for the future. At 6:45 each morning, you have 45 minutes of devotion time, reading your Bible, praying, and meditating on the Lord. What a great way to begin your day, spending time with the Lord; it gets you in sync, aligned with Him, and prepares you for the rest of your day.

Next was breakfast, followed by a trip across the parking lot, to the huge garage/chapel, located beside the main center. There was a stage set up, with drums, guitars, and amps, along with rows of seating for up to fifty people. We would do a worship time, singing 3-4 songs with the band playing.

After the worship, guys would go up to the podium with a devotion to share. Something prepared from the Bible, a piece of scripture, or something from the heart. I thrived on this and put a lot of effort into my devotions. My friend Sue, who has been working there for an eternity, said my devotions were always something she looked forward to; thank you, Sue. I was committed, and I gave a hundred and ten percent into why I was there. I went to change my life; I had enough, and I wanted something different. When I did my devotions at the podium, I would share about things pertaining to our lives, some topic I covered were redemption, forgiveness, and salvation.

When we finished, it would be back to the house where we would begin the morning classes. They would vary from Spiritual formation, Bible study, coaching, and scripture memorization. Yes, we had to memorize scripture for Tuesdays and Thursdays; this was a blessing. The verses would always change; they were from various parts of the Bible, Old, and New Testament. In the end, it helped me with remembering scripture whenever the time arose where I may have needed to apply it.

There was a break for lunch, then after we would head out to the back of the property for our afternoon work detail. Every Teen Challenge has some form of a work program. In the real world, you get up and go to work. You learn to be responsible and complete the task at hand for the day. At our facility, we sold cords of wood. There would be 8-10 of us out in the back, all with individual jobs to do. The logs were stacked beside the garage; having been trucked in.

The first thing we did and the most entertaining was dropping the logs. One guy would use a huge metal clamp, and pull one of the lower logs out. Then the stack of logs would come crashing down. It was awesome at times, with the roaring sound of huge logs, tumbling to the ground.

Once the logs settled, one guy would have a stick already cut to the appropriate length; about two feet long. He would walk down the length of the logs, marking them every two feet. After that, the chainsaw guy would cut the logs on the marks, leaving about 8-10, two-foot pieces. They would then be picked up by two other guys, and carried over to the splitter. Two guys would split the pieces into smaller pieces and then load them into a truck. In the end, we would stack one or two cords of wood onto the truck, which would then be delivered, and sold.

This was very good for a lot of the guys to learn work ethics. It prepared them to go out into the world, find a job, and hold a job. This is an important part of the program because the skills they learned at Teen Challenge prepared them for a future and a hope. Money had to be raised to support the center because it is a Christian facility. Our government hears the word God, and runs! How sad it is, but it is the truth. Teen Challenge centers must raise their own funds through churches and donations. There is also a sponsorship program, where you can sponsor a student going through the program on a monthly basis.

One way all centers raise money is through the outreach program, which was one of the best experiences for me. Every weekend there would be six to eight of us. We would travel around Ontario, to various churches, youth groups and functions. We began the service singing a couple of songs, and I want to let you know that God did not bless me with singing. I was horrible, but the other guys sang louder than me, so it worked out O.K.

After the singing, our Team leader Bryon, a wonderful God fearing man, would read scripture, and share about Teen Challenge. He would explain the program, and how God was changing lives every day. When he finished speaking, there would be two or three of us who would go up to the podium, and give an 8-12 minute testimony. We would share what it was like and the changes that were happening in our lives through a relationship with the Lord. I was always one of the three. So for about 9 months, every Sunday, I would give my testimony, and this is where the idea for the book began.

This was when God planted another seed. It was 2010, and into 2011 when God would use people, yes, many people to do His work. After we finished each service, all the guys would stand around a table. It was set up with brochures, sponsorship packages, and information about Teen Challenge. We would have a meet and greet, talking, and interacting with the people attending the service.

Not a word of a lie, there was always two to three people, who for 9 months, every weekend, at every service, would come up to me after I gave my testimony, and say, *when is the book coming out, or when is the movie coming out*? At the time, I kind of blew it off, laughed at the thought of such an endeavor, and said thank you. I was polite, but I never put too much thought into it. The thing was, God had a plan, and at the time, I did not know, or understand what He was doing. He was planting a seed for something that was to come a little later in my life.

The point is God paints on a canvas far greater than we can see. This is a perfect *example* of just how God works. He knew I would write this book; He knew to plant the seed every weekend, for almost a year. We have to remember everything is His timing. It would take another four years until God began to water that seed.

At the time, I did not know Gods plan, but four years later, when I was in Africa, God whispered to me; "*when you get back to Canada, you are going to write a book.*" The book will be a story. It will cover the world of addiction, your journey through life, and in the end, finding that *someone*. I will explain a bit more in the next few chapters about my trip to Africa. I spent six months serving at an orphanage in Malawi. Ha, ha, you have to laugh, the crazy six months, again.

While I was giving my testimony every weekend, and having people continuously asking when is the book coming out, I could only see a small portion of the canvas. As the years went by, God allowed me to see more. I step back now and see how four years ago He was using people to accomplish his mission.

Waiting on the Lord requires faith; just because we can't see what He is doing, does not mean that He is inactive. Our heavenly Father works outside of our visible realm, arranging and orchestrating events to bring about His plan for our lives. This is why we need to trust Him with all our hearts, and the Lord's ordained outcome will become evident, and He will direct our path.

We had a great group of guys in the house; there were 12 of us. The center in Saskatoon has 24 guys, and the one in London has 50. I was more comfortable with fewer guys; this meant less gossip and less chaos in the house. I was there over the winter, and this would be my first real winter in Canada. Snow, I mean lots of it, and cold, yes it gets cold in Canada. We had fun, we laughed a lot, and I must say it was one of the best years of my life. I had so much destruction and loss; now I had peace, friends, and was surrounded by people who genuinely cared.

There was a hill behind the house, so we decided it would be a good idea to build a luge track. It ran from the top of the hill, with a few curves and bumps along the way down to the bottom. Our adrenaline filled addict minds decided it would be a good idea to build a huge jump. We worked hard, cutting it out, flattening it, and constructing the jump. So at the end, when you hit it, you would be assured to get air time.

We would dress up in silly costumes, and do videotaped interviews with the guys for Luge feast 2000. This was the title we came up with for our festive event; we put together a little T.V. show. My main man Jeff did all the editing and put music to it. Jeff came up with a name for his production company; it is called *Grand Design Studios*. You can check out some fun videos we made while at the center.

It was hilarious, watching guys wipe out, and see their bodies hit, and bounce off the snow filled landing area. As I mentioned, the program is amazing at Teen Challenge. Christ-centered and very structured. In the end, we laughed and cried, we worshiped and prayed; we bonded, and grew in community together.

Teen Challenge is a strict and disciplined program. There are rules, lots of rules that you must follow. When they are broken, there are disciplinary actions. They called it D-board, where each week you go before the staff. You talk about your infractions, and then they decide what the punishment will be. This is common ground for all treatment centers, Christian or Secular; if you break the rules, there are consequences.

It varies from no seconds at meals, to no coffee, or they take your phone privileges away. Sometimes you will have to write out scripture, or memorize a scripture or two, all pertaining to your infraction. The reason for the strictness is because we as addicts don't like to be told what to do. We want to be in control, and we think our way is best. Well, that is not the case, and this way of thinking and living must be changed. When you come into treatment at Teen Challenge, they offer a way to change and show you a new way to live.

I began to put things in perspective about what was really important, to see the world through a different lens. My behaviors were slowly changing as well because the Holy Spirit was working in me. When you come to Christ, when you are born again, Jesus said he will leave you an advocate, a helper. He said He would leave us a gift that will live in you, guiding you, and giving you discernment. That gift is the Holy Spirit. As I continued my walk with Christ, He began helping me. Changing the way I spoke, my foul language was one of the first things to go. We come into the program with a suitcase full of defects; anger, impatience, selfishness, lust, intolerance, the list goes on and on.

In recovery, we need to unpack the suitcase, to get rid of resentments, and self-defeating behaviors. The world tells us we can do it on our own. Let me tell you how that works. Look at my past. I have tried to do it on my own, and there I was, in another treatment facility. I want to impose upon you that what the world is telling you, is *wrong*; we need help to change. I have tried it over and over on my own; it does not work. I know hundreds of men who have tried on their own, always getting the same result, *failure*. There is help, and a way to change, that help comes from the Holy Spirit. Let me make this very clear for you, *Only God can change you from the inside out, and give you a renewing of the mind.*

Christian based training is the aim of Teen Challenge. The program helps us deal with our defects of character. We all have issues in our life that we need to change. The program teaches us the spiritual aspects of life; responsibility, accountability, and dependability. It also helps with many other aspects of living an effective, and satisfying Christian life. If we want to change, I truly believe it begins with a relationship with God.

The Bible clearly states, God will change us from the inside out, and that we will have a renewing of the mind. Teen Challenge had opened my eyes to the Lord. I began to walk with Christ, I was willing, and I surrender my all to Him. During my stay, I was baptized. A public declaration that I was a Christian, my old life had passed, and a new life had begun.

I was done doing it my way, things began to change in my life, some right away; some things took a little more time. As addicts, we want everything right away; well that is not how life works. We need to learn to be patient and wait upon the Lord. His timing is not ours, He works on His schedule, and God paints on a canvas far greater than what we can see. So we need to trust Him with our lives, completely.

If you think you can change yourself because this seems to be our new world way of thinking, you are wrong. If you think your counselor, friends, or pastor can change you, then you are wrong. They can help, but in the end, only God can change you, only God can get inside a person's heart and cause them to change. It is a process of being transformed by Christ. We need to seek Him, and follow Him, and He will do the sanctifying work for us, to redeem us, and to reconcile us to Him.

I would like to end the chapter with a few key and interesting breakthroughs. The first major accomplishment was finally breaking *the six-month cycle.* Over the past two years, I had moved or bounced to another country or continent four times. Yes, I did it; I actually stayed in one place longer than a year.

Second, I stayed and completed the program. What a major hurdle it was, not to run, but to stay, and finish the race. I committed and completed the year-long program. These were two major successes in my life. I stayed on solid ground for over six months; I was clean and sober and was ready to move forward with the Lord.

Faith, hope, and love, I learned about all three while at Teen Challenge. The most important of all is love. We can go out and serve, or do mission work. We can evangelize, but without love, we are like a clanging cymbal. In my life, I did not know what love was, or what love felt like, until I came to Christ. He showed me what real love was; He cared for me, protected me, and carried me. All through my life He loved me. He was just waiting patiently for me to open the door and let Him in.

I stopped doing things my way; I let Him take me by the hand, to guide me, and to direct my path. During my year at Teen Challenge, God had finally accomplished his task, to bring me to Him. He had to strip me of all I had, to drop me to my knees; I surrendered my entire life to Him. I had no one else to turn to, and nothing left to go to, except God. I opened the door and let Him in. The lyrics, from one of the songs I learned while I was in the program really touched my heart: *Into the darkness you shine, and out of the ashes we rise.*

CHAPTER 13

Hope for Freedom

WHERE WAS I going to go? I completed a year at Teen Challenge, but there was a small problem. I had no real relationships, no home, nothing stable, and no place to go. I have been living a nomadic lifestyle, and these are some of the consequences of such a life. During the last month in the program, I began trying to figure out where I would go. I was going to move in with my friend Dianne and her husband, but that did not work out. A friend, whom I went to Teen Challenge with back in Saskatoon, called about three weeks before I completed the program. His name is Chris, and he had an apartment. At the time, I felt the call was a blessing, but in the end, it would turn into an unimaginable nightmare. It seemed like the right thing to do, I mean two of the answers to my dilemma had Saskatoon in the picture. So it was move number 37, I was 44 years old, and I would once again be on a plane. This time, it was back to Saskatoon, to begin a new life, so I thought.

Chris had a one bedroom apartment, so I ended up sleeping on the couch; this meant I did not have my own room; problem number one. Number two, Chris had a girlfriend, and he worked all the time, so he was never home. This would not be good because I was always by myself, isolating in a lonely desolate place.

I was living a Christ-centered life, and I had begun the process of building an incredible relationship with God. I started each day reading the Bible, doing daily devotions, and spending time in prayer.

There was peace in my life, and a time of contentment. I was seeking God, and walking with the Him for the first six months.

Does this ring a bell? Remember Mexico and Bali. Both places the same thing occurred at the five- six-month mark, and it was about to happen again. I stopped seeking and walking with the Lord. Why did it happen again? Why, after a year at Teen Challenge, and being so on fire for God, would I stop seeking and walking with Him? Why did I slowly begin to fall away from God? I had a year and a half clean, I had completed the program, and I learned so much about Christ. I felt I had all the knowledge, but did I truly have it in my heart? Was it still head knowledge? Was I able to move everything I was taught, and what I had learned, and put it in my heart?

Once again, I would take my will back, and I would pay for my disobedience to God. It is not His plan for us to walk away. He wants a relationship, and no matter what we do, or what decisions we make, He loves us. Satan does not want us to have a good life, serving others, to have relationships, or to be clean and sober. He wants to take us to the pits of hell; he wants to pull us away from God. As I mentioned earlier, Satan's number one tool to destroy us is addiction. Do you want to know what another one of His most powerful tools is? It is the one he uses on all addicts, that incredibly powerful tool is, *Loneliness*.

I was alone; had no friends, no support group, and no other addicts to talk to, there was no one who could relate to my pain. My biggest downfall was not allowing people into my life or having a close friend. I have moved so much that I did not, or would not, allow myself to get close to anyone. What I wanted at that moment was companionship, support, and comfort so that my emotional pain would go away.

I was disconnected from God, from life, and from people. The problem was, I would not ask God for help; I would not ask anyone. I needed to reach out to others. Loneliness is one of life's most painful experiences. Without people in our lives, we become detached. In turn, we begin to fall into the trap of social isolation. God created us as relational beings; the absence of companionship can be very discouraging. He did not create us to be alone, and for the addict, this is a very dangerous place to be.

I was clean for the first six months while I was living in Saskatoon; plus the year at Teen Challenge. So I was 1 ½ yrs. clean. The biggest issue I was dealing with was loneliness. I was depressed, hurt, and I isolated myself. The days were long, and the nights were mine alone. At times, I would ask myself if I was sure that I had enough of this life. But I needed to hang on; I would not let myself go. Everybody hurts, and everybody cries, there is pain and suffering in this world. We all go through the lonely nights and the long days, we all hurt. I had too much of this life of solitude, and for the addict, there was only one answer; to get high. I could not take the emotional pain anymore; I did not want to shed any more tears. In addiction, we choose *dysfunction over loneliness*.

Once again it all started with one pill, a hydro morph, the same type of opiate pain killer I took out of that medicine cabinet. This one pill would turn into a yearlong run. I would once again be hooked on opiates. In addiction, we want to bury our feelings because we are hurt, scared and angry. We become vulnerable, so *we don't talk*, *we don't trust*, and *we don't feel*.

If I had not fallen from God, if I had leaned on him while I was going through the storm, things would have turned out much different. The problem was I shut Him out. I had fallen on my face, and I could not see the one who paid the price. I took my will back, and I tried to do it on my own. We cannot do it alone; we all need *someone* to lean on. I should have chosen Christ and not the pill.

I moved out of Chris's apartment and found a basement suite; this is suicide for the addict. A place with small windows and no light, it has to be the worst place an addict should live. Where there is no light, there is darkness. It was bad; I had no furniture, a matt to sleep on, and an empty fridge. Any addict reading this will laugh, and relate to the normalcy of this situation. The messed up part is that I had a full-time job working for Connect signs, and being so deep in my addiction, I still collected welfare while I was working. This was not enough money to support my habit.

I am not a winter guy, and here I was in minus 25-degree weather, in a bucket truck, hanging huge signs on the sides of buildings. I would be hanging signs for The Gap, Banana Republic, Tim Hortons, you get the idea. I would be twenty, thirty feet up, mounting letters and signs at factory outlet stores. The wind blowing and the cold would freeze my fingers to the point where I was close to getting frostbite. It was not always that bad, but I still hated the cold and working outside in the middle of winter.

I needed to begin my morning at 6:00 am with a shot, a whack of down as we say; *down* another street name for opiates. I cooked up my pill, had my morning fix, and by noon my body would be screaming for another; but I had it down to a science. I would go to the bathroom at the location where we would be installing signs, fix my rig, and do my shot within 5 minutes.

I would then head back out, hop into the bucket and swing my way back up, installing signs all day. When I arrived home to my lonely empty apartment, I would need to do another fix. Opiates are very bad, and unlike most other drugs, you need it every day, a couple of times a day. If you don't, you get dope sick. When you get to that point, there is no way to function until you get more of the drug in you.

Sometimes I would fix in the bathroom at work before we headed out for a job. One morning I was careless and left a syringe lying by the side of my desk. I was always careful and clean, but this day I was sloppy, and it was found by the owner. She was incredibly kind and showed more care and concern for me than anger. They let me go, but she said to go get help, check into treatment, and my job would be waiting for me.

It seems like God always has a plan, even though I was heavily into my addiction. I look back, and I can see how He was orchestrating my way back to Him. He did not want me to make the choices I made. I spent a year changing my life, walking with Him, giving my testimony, sharing how He can get inside a person, and change us from the inside out. In my loneliness, I had lost all hope. There was something missing? Why with me, always at the six-month mark, did my life crumble? I always seem to run, from what I am not sure, but I do, and in turn, I abandon it all for drugs.

I had no job, no friends, and no money; I was living in a basement apartment with no furniture and an empty fridge. This brings me to a conversation I had with a friend. We were watching a National Geographic special about Russian prisons in Siberia. Men, living in these tiny little cells for 23 hours a day, pacing back and forth, some sentenced to life. We thought how horrible it would be to be stuck in one. Then, another thought occurred to the both of us. While in addiction, in my basement apartment, there was not much difference.

My *self-worth* while in addiction dictates that I deserved nothing better, so I sentence myself to imprisonment; to my basement or a bug infested hotel room in Vancouver's downtown eastside. I was alone with my thoughts, isolated, hopeless, having no family or friends. As with the convict choosing to commit the crime, in the addict's case, we make the conscious decision to pick up the drug. So we sentence ourselves, we are the prisoner and our own guard. We are comfortable when we are uncomfortable. The end result is that we are alone, and locked up, just like solitary confinement; we resign ourselves to that existence. So really, what's the difference?

Once again, God would use a person in my life to help me. He used an old friend named Clinton. I went to Teen Challenge with him back in 2009. While I was living in my little Russian prison cell, we had a few conversations together, and he noticed something was off. He could tell by my speech that I was high and using drugs. Remember, I mentioned addicts can tell if someone else is high, instinctively it is ingrained in us. He told me about a program he attended in Port Coquitlam B.C., a suburb of Vancouver. He said it was a Christian, twelve-step recovery program, and that he had been through it. Clinton was coming up on three years clean.

I was at another bottom and had fallen again. I had run out of options, but the idea of going to another Christian program was very intriguing, and this one included the twelve steps. Out of the goodness of his heart, he paid for a ticket to get me out to Vancouver. He assured me that there was a bed waiting at the facility when I arrived.

Does God get angry when we fall? Is He mad at us? Let me give you my analogy, and an answer to this question:

If I have my one-year-old daughter Alyssa in my hands, and she is getting ready to walk, I would patiently set her on her feet. She may take a step and then fall. Do I get angry and yell at her? Or do I pick her up, give her a hug, tell her how much I love her, and how proud I am that she took a step.

I would then put her back on her feet, and this time, she may take two or three steps, and fall. Again, would I get angry, and yell at her because she only took two or three steps? Or would I again, pick her up, tell her I love her and put her back on her feet.

This is exactly how God responds when we fall; eventually, we will take four or five steps, and maybe fall. In the end, we will be walking. The falls will get shorter, and the walk gets longer and eventually we will be jogging. Along our walks, God is guiding and loving us all the way. Soon we will be

running, and with Christ at the center of our lives, we will eventually stop
falling. No, He does not get angry!

God picked me up, dusted me off, and put me back on my feet.
He wanted me to keep walking, to take more steps. I had fallen from
Him; I decided that I wanted to control my life again. I took my own
will back and put Him in the back seat. Well, we know how that works.
I had taken steps in my life and fallen in Mexico, Bali, and now after
a year at Teen Challenge. Why did I continue to fall from God and
always around the five or six-month mark? The end result was always
the same. As I have said before; jails, institutions and death, complete
chaos, and total destruction. My life was going to change. God loves
me, and He set me back on my feet. This time, I was on a plane off to
Vancouver; move number 38.

I arrived, and of course, I was coming off opiates. I needed to go to
detox; it was the beginning of a lengthy nightmare. As the saying goes,
you need to go through hell before you get to Heaven. I was about to
go through hell coming off the drugs. I was at Creekside detox out in
Surrey, B.C. for 7 days; they had me on a methadone taper to help ease
the withdrawals. I had not slept for the last 3 nights I was there, and
this was going to continue for quite some time. After a week, my friend
Clinton picked me up, we stopped for a coffee and then drove to the
office and main house of **The Hope for Freedom Society**.

Before I get into the program and the lifesaving services H.F.F.S.
provides, I would like to share a bit about how it was started; the
beginning of a society that has expanded tenfold since the start. It
began with a man who would have a mighty impact on a lot of people,
his name was Fred Milne. He was a drug addict who had committed a
few crimes in his day and spent time behind bars. While in his forties,
something told him to get some help. So he checked into a facility in
Victoria, B.C., and began the grueling nightmarish detox of heroin.

Something amazing, let's say a miracle was about to take place
in his life. It was something that could only be of God. While he was
going through the pain and agony coming off the heroin, a group of
Christians showed up at the center. The group began talking with him
and asked if they could pray for him. He was accepting of the offer,
and they began to pray for healing, and for God to help him through
the hell he was going through.

Here comes the miracle. After they had prayed, something happened; a sense of peace and calm overtook him, and the withdrawals stopped! God had once again planted a seed. This was a turning point for Fred, and God had a plan for him. Like the others I have spoken about, he was obedient to Gods calling, and many lives were going to change.

Fred moved to Coquitlam, B.C. and attended a treatment center called Intervisions. During his stay, there was a retired police officer and his wife who would stop by the center. They would load up 6-8 guys and bring them to the Christian Missionary Alliance Church in Coquitlam. To shorten it I will use (C.A.C.) for the remainder of the chapter. Once again, God was planting seeds. Fred would meet a few men at the church who would have a major impact on his walk with Christ.

It was 1996; Fred had completed his stay at Intervision's and was renting an apartment. He was working at a plastic plant, and in the meantime, he would have junkies and addicts crashing at his place. He would sometimes go to the DTES and find people who needed help and bring them back to his place. He realized the apartment was not cutting it, so he rented a house on Grant St. in Port Coquitlam, B.C. This was the beginning of the society; he wanted to start a Christian, 12 step recovery program. He called it *Resurrection House*.

The house began to fill up with men seeking help and freedom from addiction. He knew it had to expand, so he found another house a few blocks away on Prairie Ave. Eventually, the society expanded, and became Hope for Freedom Society, H.F.F.S. They now have five houses, each housing up to 8-10 men. There is also the Glory House, for women suffering in addiction. On an average day there are 40-50 men in the houses, and 14 women in the Glory house.

Since one man who was an addict and a criminal found God, because of his obedience to Gods calling, and he listened; countless lives are being changed. People are breaking the chains of addiction because one man listened. God can, and will, use the least of us to have a major impact on society. We just need to be in sync with Him and be obedient when He calls.

Hope for Freedom Society began in 1996, and has been running for 19 years; I cannot go on unless I mention a few of the key people involved. Who, in the beginning, jumped on board with Freddy and turned what was one house into what we have today, a place of spiritual growth and restoration.

I would like to begin with Neil; he was also an addict, drug dealer, and someone who was very familiar with the correctional institutions of B.C. Let's say, he was not a very productive member of society back in his day. This was all about to change. In 1996, he had been clean for a couple of years, and he met Freddy at an Area meeting in New Westminster. He was going to college at the time, and Fred asked if he could fill in for him for a week. He was obedient and worked the week filling in for Fred. This one week would turn into something amazing, something God was calling Neil to do. He would eventually team up with Freddy, and ever since, he has been changing men's lives. Neil is the Executive Director of the H.F.F.S., and if we do the math, he has been there 18½ years and has been clean 21 years.

Dennis, another amazing man whom God had called to save lives; he was an addict and an alcoholic. I would like to share a little bit about him; in the past, he was not a very good person. One day he decided he would rob a gas station; the problem was he also worked there. He would spend his 19th birthday in prison. He ended up doing a year and a half behind bars. In 1997, he was bartending and was bored with his job, and he was not sure what to do. I swear, God intervened and orchestrated the next chain of events. He was at Bailey's restaurant, where they held A.A. meetings back in the day, and he ran into an acquaintance that was monitoring at H.F.F.S. The friend asked him if he would like to volunteer at the facility; he said yes. This would turn into the answer he was seeking. Dennis is the Administrating Director at H.F.F.S. and has been there for 17 years. He has been clean for 18 years.

The third man who was also involved in addiction is Pastor Paul; he was a hardcore alcoholic back in his day. It was November 1981 when Paul would turn his life over to the Lord. A few weeks later he was prompted by the Holy Spirit to pour all the booze in his house down the toilet, and said, enough. He continued his walk, and in 1997 God had a message for him; it would change the direction of his life. He was on his way back from Seattle, after attending a Promise Keepers meeting when God spoke to him. The voice he heard said: *There will be no bullets, I want you to go.*

God wanted Paul to get involved with helping people struggling in the world of addiction, and he was obedient to Gods calling. As was David Wilkerson, Serge LeClerc, Nicky Cruz, and Fred Milne. The list goes on in this book about people hearing from God and hearing a specific voice with a message. Every man in this book heard, and responded; look at the miracles God did in each of these men's lives. It is not only about the work God has done in their lives, but the transformation of so many other lives because they listened, and followed Gods calling.

Paul was involved at C.A.C. church, the same church Freddy had been attending. All the interactions which occurred at C.A.C. took place because a retired police officer and his wife were Christians, and their heart strings were pulled. That *someone* said to go help people struggling with addiction and bring them to church. This is where Freddy met Paul; tell me God does not orchestrate everything in all our lives to eventually bring about good! It was the fall of 1997, and they started to build a friendship, which in turn would lead Paul to run the morning Proverbs classes at Resurrection House. When they met, there was only the one house on Grant Street; so Paul was involved pretty much from the very start.

Paul has been saving lives ever since. He taught Bible classes twice a week on Tuesdays and Thursdays, as well as doing steps with guys on a continuous basis. He is an amazing man, ordained by God to bring people to Him. He has been working with guys coming in from prison, the streets, and from the pits of hell; most of the guys wanting nothing to do with God. In turn, he would soften hearts and lead somewhere around 25-30 guys a year to Christ. Once again, let's do the math; he has been used by God to bring an approximate number of 600 men who were battling their demons in addiction to Christ. He has been with H.F.F.S. for 18 years and has been sober for 33 years.

The last member of the team is Rob. He is a man of God and was raised in a strong Christian family. Personally, he has never been addicted to drugs or alcohol. So what brought him into a world filled with alcoholics and drug addicts seeking help and recovery? Let's get back to God, and how He is so good at orchestrating our lives. He would touch Rob, and change his life forever through another man.

Who do you think God used? Here is a hint; Rob was a member of the C.A.C. church in Coquitlam, the same church Pastor Paul attended, and yes, the same church Fred was attending. Addiction fell close to home for Rob; his daughter's husband admitted he was addicted to heroin. Not knowing much about addiction, the family believed that if they took him to detox for a week, that this would be the answer. Well, as we know, detoxing is just the beginning; it is only the first stage of recovery.

Rob retired in 2000, and he was going to pursue some other endeavors for selfish reasons; God was going to have none of it. At C.A.C. Fred kept asking him to get involved with the program, but he continued to decline until he felt a prompting by The Holy Spirit. He began seeking out and doing some research at various treatment facilities, three secular and three Christian. Something began to resonate in his heart about Fred's persistence for him to get involved with H.F.F.S.

It was a Monday, three days after Rob retired that he walked through the doors of Hope for Freedom; he arrived that morning to sit in with the guys while they did the morning Proverbs. The first week he attended only three times; the following week he was there every morning. Does this ring a bell, God used the morning Proverbs to get Paul involved, and He was going to do it again. There were three new men in the house who were not believers, who had never prayed, and who knew nothing about God.

In Proverbs, you begin with each man saying a prayer out loud, and then you read the Proverb for that day. In the end, each man shares about something that touched him in the reading. The three men, in turn, began to pray out loud for their first time. Rob was astonished as he heard each of the men crying out from their souls. He heard the emotions of these addicts, crying out for help, these broken men reaching out for the first time. As he was sitting there something happened as he heard the cries of these men; he knew he was being called by God to do something.

He began to hang around more and more, talking with the guys, mentoring, and doing some work in the office. He joined the board of directors, who at the time were all members of C.A.C. The church was a big supporter of H.F.F.S., and they continue to support the program to this day. Rob eventually became Chairman of the Board, and he continues to manage H.F.F.S. helping people struggling with addiction. Rob has been with H.F.F.S. for 16 years, and he has always been clean and sober.

God needed a sign to let these men know He was there; He had placed lines that were being crossed over the atmosphere. These lines drew four men together, to have a common bond with one man. This man was Fred; back in 1996 he had a vision, and God provided an incredible team of men to forward His Kingdom. They have helped countless people battling their demons and struggling with addiction.

They never gave up, and never needed a reason for the way things had to be. They each knew in their hearts; God had a plan for each of their lives. These men have been around since the beginning, which is unheard of. I have been to treatment all over North America and nowhere has there been staff dating back 16-18 years.

These men were committed to what God had ordained for them, and they are all still at the same facility, changing lives and giving people hope. There is 70 years of sobriety, wisdom, and knowledge helping others recover from addiction. All three men are clean and sober today, what does that tell you? Be of service, give back, and follow your heart, like these men did. They are walking examples of what recovery, and what Christ can do in an addict's life.

I came into the houses after spending a year doing opiates. Coming off them was one of the most horrific experiences I have ever had to endure. The most devastating part about detoxing is there is no sleep; our bodies produce melatonin, which helps us sleep. After your body gets used to the opiates, it stops producing melatonin. It takes time for the level to come back and for the opiate to work its way out of your system.

The first month I was at H.F.F.S, I had a total of 18 hours sleep. Alright, let me expand on the topic. There are 30 days in a month times 7 hours sleep a night = 210 hours. This would be what an average month's sleep looks like. I cannot explain in words what sleep deprivation was like. Somehow you still function through the day, at times you begin to hallucinate, and the anxiety sets in. The excitation and emotions weigh so heavy on the soul; your heart is broken as the shame and guilt ridden feelings overtake you.

I almost jumped out the two story window at the house three times because the lack of sleep. It was by far the worst month of my life, but I made it through, only by the grace of God. I never gave up; I did not run and go score drugs to ease the pain. I was done, and I knew in my heart that I needed to get through it.

Hope for Freedom has five houses. Upon arrival, you begin your journey in House one. Guys are coming in from jail, the streets, and from broken homes. Each man is filled with an abundance of suffering and brokenness. Every morning you begin at 8:00 am with Proverbs, which last 45 minutes. At 9:30 there is a group, always dealing with recovery or addiction. The classes are taught by an incredibly wise man named Thomas, from Sri Lanka; he has been teaching there for 14 years. Twice a week there is a Bible class to help men begin their spiritual journey. In the afternoons at 1:00 there is another group taught by Thomas, which runs until 3:00. It is very structured, and as with all centers, there are rules and guidelines.

As you get back on your feet and begin to do your steps and continue completing the assigned programs, you slowly begin to move through the houses. As you get to house two and three, it is more stable, guys are committed. There becomes an amazing bond and a strong feeling of community in the higher houses.

In the evenings, there are always mandatory meetings you must attend. Mon-Fri nights there are N.A. or A.A., and in-house meetings, along with Bible studies. Saturday evenings is God Rock at a local church. Christian rock bands perform, followed by a message. The energy is high, and people really get into the music. This, in turn, helps guys feel more comfortable since many have never attended church. On Sundays, everyone goes to The Port, a sister church associated with C.A.C. All these meetings and church are mandatory.

Once you progress and are moving forward, H.F.F.S. has three main courses which are mandatory for all clients; each course is ten weeks. The first two are *Relapse prevention* and *Anger Management*. Tell me anyone who is coming out of addiction that does not need to apply and incorporate them into their lives.

The third course is much more in depth, and takes commitment and willingness, with a desire to change. It is a ten-week course called *Stand Firm*, a life skills course taught by three amazing people. They give their time freely to help men coming out of addiction, men who are seeking change in their lives. Rebecca, P.K, and Dave each teaches various modules the course provides.

Stand firm consists of five modules; Spiritual, and Physical, Emotional and Mental are combined, Relational, and Functional. The modules are an introduction to wellness in life, and they all relate to spiritual wellness. The relapse and anger classes show you what went wrong in your life, and how to work on past mistakes.

Stand Firm is about moving forward in life. It shows how to live your life with a different perspective, bringing you to a place of acceptance for your past, and a purpose for your future. God changes us with *integrity*, not success. Faithfulness is a success, obedience is a success, and completing and graduating Stand firm is a success. We all need a little success in our lives and a lot of *integrity*.

Another imperative part of the H.F.F.S. curriculum is the twelve step program, a set of spiritual and guiding principles. It outlines a course of action to attack problems such as drug addiction and alcoholism. It is a *spiritual program of recovery*; allow me to explain. Back in the day, The Oxford put together basic ideas for the steps. Bill and Bob took those ideas and added to them, coming up with the original steps we have today. The steps are based on biblical principles, which were taken from the Bible.

If you count the twelve steps, six directly apply to God; the other steps are about personal inventory and amends to others. For me, without having that *someone*, without Christ being at the center of my life, and involving Him in the program that I am working, my chances of success lessen. One last fact, did you know that the program of Alcoholics Anonymous brings more people to Christ each year than any Church, denomination or organization?

Every person in addiction must do the 12 steps if they want any hope of recovery. The first step, and I would say one of the most important is; *we must admit that we are powerless over our addiction and that our lives have become unmanageable*. Once a person comes to the conclusion that they have a problem, they will have overcome the first hurdle. Secondly, we admit the wreckage and the devastating path of destruction that we have left behind, which in turn has made our lives unmanageable. Now we are ready to begin recovery.

The other step that people have hesitation about doing, and some have a real fear of tackling, is step four. First, I want to say that F.E.A.R. means *False Evidence Appearing Real*, a little analogy for fear. Step four, as they say, is a monster because you need to open the floodgates of Heaven. You need to get honest with yourself. You must dig deep into the recesses of your heart and soul, pulling out all the wreckage from your past. If you do the step properly, people usually end up with 40–80 pages of material. *Step four is making a searching and fearless moral inventory of ourselves.*

There are two main parts to the step, defects and assets, the good and the bad. You need to take a good hard look at yourself. The one problem addicts have in doing this is that they focus more on the defects, as oppose to the assets. They fill themselves with guilt, shame, and remorse. One must remember to take into consideration all the good qualities we possess.

The step is about willingness, to get brutally honest with ourselves; it is about getting to know who we are. Then we can begin the work to make the appropriate changes each individual needs in their lives. I believe anyone can do a set of steps. You don't have to be in addiction to take a good hard look back at your life. The *truth* shall set you free.

I want to be very clear right now; it is of vital importance for anyone doing step four. You must get the skeletons out of the closet. The deep dark secrets, things you have never told another soul. We ignore the roots of sin. As with a weed, they go deep, and it is of little use to chop the heads off while their roots remain in the ground.

You must attack the root, and not just the heads. If you're simply managing behaviors, but not removing them, the weeds will simply sprout up in another place. You need to dig deep and grab hold and pull it all out; it is a heart changer because the heart is where behavior comes from. Wherever our heart is, that is where our actions will follow. You must be seeking a heart change, not just conformity.

I spent the first four months at H.F.F.S. doing all the core programs; I had finished the twelve steps and completed Stand Firm. I was at a point as to what I should do next, what would my next move be? I had always wanted to go to Africa, to serve and give back. There was something pulling me towards doing mission work in another foreign land. I have been all over the world, but Africa was not one of the places I could cross off my bucket list. My thirst and reverence for the Lord was amazing. I became so on fire for God, and in my heart, I wanted more wisdom and knowledge.

One of my mentors and an amazing friend to this day is Doug; one day he had a brilliant idea? He asked me, "Why don't you commit to a year of Bible College?" It did not take long before the Holy Spirit gave me discernment. It became very clear to the decision I needed to make. I had been attending all the evening Bible classes at H.F.F.S, working at the church on Saturdays doing the food bank, and I was preaching to everyone. I knew God was calling, and I knew to be obedient. I had a hunger to learn more, so in the fall of 2014, at the ripe age of 47, I was off to Pacific Life Bible College.

P.L.B.C. is located in Surrey, another suburb of Vancouver, and I was living in Port Coquitlam. This meant a two-hour commute for me to get out to the college; it was two buses, the sky train, and another bus. Then I would have 4 hours of class and a two-hour commute home. This meant by the time I arrived back; I had put in an 8 hour day. I stayed locked in with H.F.F.S. for the entire time I was attending College. I was living in house three. I continued to work with other guys, went to Bible studies and continued going to N.A. and A.A. meetings in the evenings.

Remember, I was older, and had not been to school since I graduated High School way back in 1984. My first day at college was a bit overwhelming. I did not know what a Syllabus was, and I never knew what citing meant. Another major problem, I did not know how to operate Office Word. I was blown away when I saw the Syllabus for my first class; I went into a state of shock. Just kidding, but when I saw all the projects, exams, and writing, I did not know if I could do it.

The semesters are around 4 months long. I took two semesters, which meant 8 months. So when I say a year of Bible College, it was eight months, but two semesters would technically be a year. I did not go to get a degree, a diploma, or to become a pastor. I only committed and went to attain more knowledge and wisdom. I believe wisdom comes from the Bible. I also believe that *Wisdom is the application of knowledge*. If I got to know the Word and began to understand what it was telling and teaching me. Then, in turn, I went and shared that knowledge with others; this becomes *wisdom*.

I picked the classes I thought would help me in my walk with the Lord. The first semester I took four courses; Old Testament Survey, Spiritual Formation, English Comp and Survey of Christian belief. The second semester, I took 3 courses to ease up on the workload, because Africa was calling. The three classes were Evangelism, Science and the Bible, and an Apologetics course.

There is something to be learned from this. I was out there in Saskatoon getting high every day for a year. I only had four months in recovery and then jumped into Bible College. There was a massive workload, but it was possible. I also know that I can do all things through *Christ* who strengthens me. This means it is not by Dwayne's strength that I could do a year of College, get good grades, and finish the race. It was through Christ, who took my hand, and walked with me through my journey. Never limit yourself, or cut yourself short. If you are walking with Christ, *anything* is possible.

Once again, the canvas, the one God paints. The one we only see a little bit of, until He reveals more, in His time. On my first day of College, when I saw the Syllabus and saw the workload, I asked myself; how am I going to write all these essays, reports, and assignments? I had to learn how to operate and use office windows to do the work.

I hooked up with a friend named Tom. He is a pastor, and also taught at the Bible College. He is an amazing man, with an incredible story. He miraculously, within a day, taught me and guided me through the learning process to work Office so I could complete all the work that lay ahead of me.

O.K. here come the canvas, and God at work three years prior to P.L.B.C. God planted seeds in me; a heads up that I would be writing a book in the years to come. He used all those people, after giving my testimony and asking me when the book was coming out. Part of the reason to learn office was for Bible College. I truly believe in my heart, God was prepping me for the book. In His infinite Wisdom, He was preparing me for the future, for a project years later. I would need to use Office to write a book. I look back at the canvas, Gods painting, and I can now see Him at work.

I have mentioned Africa and a calling to go serve. The Bible says if I trust the Lord with all my heart, he will direct my path; well, He certainly did. I was attending Northside Church where a lady named Shannon was pastoring, yes a female pastor! We became good friends, and in conversation one day, she mentioned that her mom Pam lived in Africa with her husband. She also mentioned they ran an orphanage with 130 children in Malawi, Africa. This began a few months of back and forth conversations with Will, Pam's husband. He would grill me and ask me a lot of questions in his e-mails. It was very trying at times, but he just wanted to get to know me and to see if I was prepared to go and serve at their orphanage.

Here I was living in the houses of H.F.F.S, working with others, going to meetings, and I had finished the first semester of Bible College. I was on fire for the Lord, sharing the good news with others, and doing some service work. I was preparing to go to Africa when I finished College; my life was good. I had 10 months clean, I had not done any hard drugs, and I had not touched a drop of alcohol since 2010.

Sometimes we should not ask *Why*, but *What*, when situations or bad things happen in our lives; it is always, why? After a traumatic event like the one I am going to share with you, I needed to ask myself three questions. I needed to ask the Lord, *what* do I need to learn? *What* is God showing me? And how do I *react* differently next time it happens?

Something very bad was going to happen, the day was a Friday, Jan 24th; I called it *Black Friday*. I have only shared this with a few people, even to this day. I wrote about this incredibly horrific event, three days after it happened. Here it is, in its original, raw, unedited form. I want to share my Black Friday with you.

BLACK FRIDAY
Dwayne Higgins
Waves Coffee Shop
27/01/2014

This event took place on Friday, Jan 24/2014. How do I start? I start with Prayer, and then I let the Holy Spirit guide me through my story. I have been clean for Ten months, going to Bible College and evangelizing with people all over PoCo. I think my walk with Christ is strong, my thoughts take me to thinking that I please God with all my good works (these are my thoughts). Christian's do not have to do all these good works to please God, He loves us either way, with a book full of good deeds or a ½ a page of stuff, He loves us.

Yet, I walk around having days where I think about jumping in front of a bus flying by, I picture getting hit and smashing into the windshield, then, flying through the air and slamming into the ground. Do I have hidden sin in my life; am I doing some shady things that I have not surrendered? The answer is Yes, I have to change a lot of things in my life and stop talking about death and dying. This is a story and a wake-up call, or God hitting me in the head with a board to wake me up. The answer again is Yes He did wake me up. On black Friday, I literally arose from the dead and was brought back, by the Grace and love of God.

I was sitting at Bible College, in a Spiritual formation class, thinking about Mission fest, and working the Booth that Hope for Freedom had set up there. I left College in good spirits and was on my way downtown on the sky train. Does Satan dig his claws into me and fill my addictive mind with thoughts of getting a pill, a dilauted or hydro-morph? Right at Main st and stadium exits the enemy attacks, but the Holy Spirit tells me No.

I continue on and into mission feast, hundreds of people, a youth rally at one end with hundreds of kids. Josh McDowell speaking in another auditorium and I am at the booth talking with people for a while. Then, what do you think happens? The enemy comes back in full force, oh yeah, the pills, yes go get a pill and slam it, forget all the people and the energy surrounding Canada Place. Forget Josh McDowell is speaking. So I leave and take the sky train to stadium exit, and walk past the Lotus Hotel, old home away from home. I make my way to Main and Hasting to score; am I out of my mind? Where was God in my decision making? Where were the Angels surrounding me? The answer is they were there, but they would show Gods Glory a little later.

Here I am in Satan's playground, demonic forces surround everything, and I am trying to score some pills. I have no fear, zero fear of anyone or anything. There are no pills to be found, so after a while, a guy comes by who was also looking for pills earlier. I asked if he scored, he said no, but a guy in front of in-site has good Heroin. This would turn out to become a very, very bad situation.

My addict, which is now in full control tells me that there are no pills, so why not a little Heroin; sounds like a good idea. I walk in front of in-site and the guy pushing the Heroin for this lady was in the houses 3 weeks ago, and we recognized each other. In the pits of hell, I know the guy selling the heroin, how messed up is that? So I get 2- $10.00 bags of heroin. Before I go into in-site, I ask, should I do one or both of these? His answer, do only one and then try to other.

Walking into the safe injection site, a place I have been many, many times before, but it has been a long time, I go to the front and give my code, it works, and the code is still in the system. The problem is that 12 people are in front of me, and it will be a 20-30 min wait. Street people all over and my thoughts take me to getting all the supplies at the front counter and heading up to McDonalds and doing it there. In-site has all the rigs and ties at the front counter so you can load up and go home and do your drugs', I walked up and was looking down at the supplies and ready to grab *everything and head out. The Holy Spirit Showed, and said to me, what does the Bible say about patience, to wait and be still. This is the exact thought that went through my mind, and I acted on it, and said to myself, I will just wait and do it in the shooting gallery; it is safe, clean, lots of room, so I decided to be Patient and wait, **this decision would later save my life.***

Ally 143 are you here, I jump up, yes I am, that is my code, and it is still in the system. Think of a place in North America that Satan could make as close to hell as possible. Well walking into the shooting gallery at Hastings and Main would be one of the closest places to hell that one could imagine. Full of lost and struggling souls, Gods children in there tweaking out and slamming needles and drugs into their temples. Satan's stronghold controls this place; I tell them I am doing heroin, because when you go in, they need to know what drug each person is shooting in case of an overdose. I grab my supplies and head to booth 12. I sit down, lay everything out and open the first bindle and pour it into the spoon. It does not look like much, I ignore my friend's advice, and my addict and the powers of Satan tell me to pour the other bindle into the spoon, so I do. I get it ready and draw up Satan's poison into the syringe. With the poison in hand, I find a well-used vein and put the tip of the needle into it, slowly injecting the needle, I draw back being sure I see the blood drawing into the syringe. Then I plunge the liquid heroin into my vein and throughout Gods Temple.

I sit up in my chair and feel nothing for about 10 seconds; then I start to feel something coming on. I think that it is starting to work; well, it was working because I blacked out. The next part is told to me by staff and paramedics, I Overdose, I am dead, it is 8:20 pm on Friday night and I lay dead in Satan's playground.

My face and head smash down into the top of the counter. They pull me up, and my whole body was blue, it had shut down; my heart stopped, and I was dead. In-site staff grabbed the Narcan and flipped me while in the chair, back onto the ground. They took the Narcan and slammed it into my paralyzed body; I lay there dead for about 5–6 minutes. The problem with this amount of time is that there is no oxygen going to the brain which can cause brain damage." God will never leave you nor forsake you."

I start to slowly come to, my vision is blurred, but little by little my sight comes back, and I see the paramedics standing over me. During this time, there were no visions! No vision of Heaven or Hell, it was just black. A few things to remember, it reminds me of Job and how God says to Satan, you can have him, but you cannot kill him. I have had 3 suicide attempts in the past, but this by no means was a suicide attempt. God took me from death and said No, not now. This is not Dwayne's time, I am God, and you are Satan, you have no control, this is my child, and I am taking him back. I have plans, a purpose, and a future for this faithful servant of mine.

Another very important decision made earlier saved my life; if I had gone to McDonalds and done the heroin, I would be dead right now. The Holy Spirit intervened, even in Satan's pit; God had His Angels surrounding me. Patience was the word. The decision to have patience saved my life. I stayed, and I am alive because of the guiding of the Spirit, there would have been no staff, no Narcan, just me Overdosing in a stall at McDonalds. One word, one decision; patience saved my life; the other decision would have led me to McDonalds, and killed me. Two decisions, one killing me and the other saving me.

A kernel of wheat falls to the ground and dies; it remains alone, but its death will produce a plentiful harvest of new lives. I feel I had to die first before I could produce good fruit.

God's grace saved me; His grace is sufficient. *Grace*, something we don't deserve, but He gives it to us anyway. I had a 2nd, 3rd and now He has given me a 4th chance. God did not make us perfect, and God doesn't require us to have perfect lives in order to finish strong. I lay dead on a floor for 5-6 minutes, and you say, where was this loving God?

Let me tell you, He was there. If He wasn't, you would not be sitting here reading this book! He has walked with me, and carried me my whole life, to bring me to this point. Through incredible mountain tops highs, and very deep dark valley experiences; woven, and intertwined throughout my journey. He is real; mercy found me upon a broken road and lifted me beyond my failings.

O.K, how do I transition, and get back on track after Black Friday, and my mini monolog? I have to admit, I did not tell a soul about this incident until after a week or so. I needed help to deal with the emotions that were tearing me apart inside. I wrote what you just read, and shared it with 4 people; in turn, these people reached out to me and guided me through the healing process.

Before I close the chapter, I need to tell you about another place that helped change my life over the year. Let's go big, let's go positive, let's go to **C.L.A. Recovery Church** out in Langley, B.C. Where do I begin with this incredible spirit filled gathering? I have been to churches, youth groups and conventions all over the world, and let me clearly state, nothing compares to Recovery Church, C.L.A. (Christian Life Assembly).

Every Sunday, since coming back from Africa, and the year prior, I have never missed Recovery Church; I would not miss it for anything. Pastor Larry, an incredibly selfless man, drives from Langley to Port Coquitlam every Sunday and picks up all the guys at H.F.F.S. When the service is finished he drives them back to PoCo. A 40-minute drive, times two, is a lot of time he commits to each week. He has been doing this for seven years, and has walked with, and helped countless men in addiction to find hope and salvation from their past lives. As my good friend, Bart says, Recovery Church *is the best way to end your week, and the best way to begin your week.*

Recovery Church is an instrument used by God to change lives; I have seen it over and over. People from recovery houses scattered across the lower mainland, coming in with broken and shattered lives. There are men and woman, coming out of the dark life of addiction and seeing the light. The Holy Spirit fills this huge sanctuary every Sunday night, and His transforming power is unlike anything I have ever experienced. I always say, when Recovery Church ends, I float out of there, being so energized, and filled with the Spirit of God.

The worship at the beginning is an experience unto itself. Tanya, one of the main singers, has the voice of an angel. The band is out of this world, all the lyrics for the songs are shown on two huge screens; everyone is on their feet, singing as loud as they can. I can't sing, but at CLA, I am singing my heart out, (because no one can hear me), it is all good. No one judges anyone; you can be yourself at Recovery Church. People have their hands in the air, heads held high, and just giving God their worship. I have such a hard time explaining how amazing it is.

I will round up guys from the houses, some who don't know Christ and bring them to Recovery Church. It changes their lives, and they then continue to go every Sunday. All I can say is that if you are in Vancouver, go check out Recovery Church on Sunday evening. I promise it will grab you in such a way that your life will begin to change. God is so at work in this church, helping and guiding people to a better way of life through a relationship with Him.

I have shared stories throughout the book about people who were lost and broken. Some were struggling with addiction; some did very bad things, yet they had their lives transformed. They are now serving and helping others, opening treatment centers, and starting their own ministries. I pray that through their stories, and mine, that your heart will soften, your eyes will be opened, and you will give this God a chance. He is waiting for you, all you have to do is open the door and let Him in.

I have one more person whose transformation story I would like to share with you. He is the lead pastor at Recovery Church, Pastor Jason. Let me begin with the fact that he was an addict; he experimented with every drug, thinking he would find an answer to his pain and misery. He was not living; he just existed, living a selfish, meaningless life. The Good news is that God had a plan for this amazing man, and as with my story, it would take a little time.

Jason grew up in a reputable family, his dad was a doctor, and his mom was a teacher and a follower of Christ. Something happened with his family that would take him to the pits of hell. His parents divorced, his father left them, and the relationship ended. This left him alienated, hurt, and angry. Most kids believe it is their fault when their parents separate, which is wrong. It causes confusion as they try to figure out what they did wrong. He was troubled, and his answer to ease the pain was drugs. At the age of 13, in the 9th grade, he began a ten-year run, starting with an addiction to Crystal meth.

His parents tried everything they could to help get their son back on track. He spent his high school years at a posh boarding school on Vancouver Island. When this failed they sent him to various institutions and universities, his addiction followed. He had turned his back on God and wanted nothing to do with Him.

He continued to use drugs as he traveled around Europe, hitchhiking from country to country, doing drugs, selling drugs, and living a life of debauchery. This would continue until he was 23, at which time he was introduced to Satan's ultimate poison, heroin. He moved back to British Columbia, Canada, and was living in White Rock, in a desolate apartment, alone, and broken.

Once heroin entered the picture, his life crumbled as he isolated in his apartment. He could not function; he was mentally unwell, and he became housebound. Thinking back, does this not remind you of the Russian Prison analogy? Satan had a strong hold on him; he had no self-worth, and in his addiction, he sentenced himself to imprisonment. Alone with his thoughts, isolated, and hopeless, he thought his only way out was to die.

Now it's time for God to intervene; He had a future planned for this young servant. He would use this broken soul to save many lives, and to have a powerful impact on people struggling with addiction. Alone in his apartment, he prayed for three months for two things, one was for help; the other was for God to kill him. The answer to prayer came, and once again, God would use a person to pull this lost soul out of his addiction.

Jason's mother arrived one day; the thing is that she never went to the apartment. Only by the guiding of The Holy Spirit, did she go to this hellish place. She found her son laying on the floor, strung out on heroin, sleeping. She was dismayed, but never gave up; she woke him, and her only comment was to go get help, go to Wagner Hills. She said enough of this, as she gazed upon her hopeless son, living in a ransacked apartment; get your life back in order. He had nowhere to go, and he was on death's doorstep. He was accepting, and he committed to go to the Farm and change his life.

At the age of 24, Jason checked into *Warner Hills Farm*, a faith-based recovery center for men struggling with addiction. It is along the same lines as Teen Challenge, biblically structured, to bring men into a relationship with God. He spent four months at the Farm. Back then, it was the length of time for your stay, today it is a year long program.

It was the worship that took hold of his heart; he did a crossover, but not for another drug; he replaced heroin with God. He began seeking God the same way he would have sought heroin. He dug in deep; he began to structure his life, and he had a hunger for the Word. He was willing, and he surrendered his life to the Lord. The transformation began; he opened the door and let Christ into his life.

Jason was attending services at C.L.A., and one day he had a talk with Pastor Brent. He shared his story, and he began to work with men in addiction at the church. He had attended Trinity University and Summit Bible College. The next thing you know, he is in Hong Kong, working with an amazing lady named Jackie. He came back to Canada, to C.L.A., and started to learn some Russian. He would soon be off to Russia for two years, working with addicts attending a Bible College there. He taught awareness about drugs and alcohol; he was bringing these lost souls out of the dark and into the light.

Jason came back to Canada, teamed up with his wife Nicole, and they were off, back to Russia. They spent two more years there serving, helping, and giving back. They both were ministering in a different culture, bringing men and women to Christ, and out of the depths of addiction. They would return back to Canada, back to C.L.A., where a beginning was to occur, the beginning of Recovery Church. He wrote a 16-week program called U-Turn, a 12 step, biblically based freedom session.

The beginning of Recovery church started in a small room at the church, thinking they would only have 40-50 people; this was a low guess. People began to flock to the church. One night someone shared about suicide, it was real and personal; the church plateaued. They moved to the gym, but that was not going to work because Recovery Church caught on in all the recovery houses. Men and women were seeking an answer, a way out of addiction, and Recovery Church would guide them to the answer, to that *someone*. It was about worship, high energy, spirit-filled worship, and a message to touch the hearts and souls of people struggling with addiction.

Recovery Church now has an average of 250-300 people every Sunday night. Why? It is because of one man who was lost, hopeless and stuck in the world of addiction. What happened? God took hold of this man, lifted him out of the pits of hell, put him on his feet, and said take more steps. He took steps, and changed his life; he turned it over to the Lord, and God said; "let me show you what I can do with you."

Over the years, Jason went to China and served. He also organized a team of people and funds from Canada to build a recovery center in Russia. Another accomplishment in his life was that he started Recovery Church at C.L.A. If that is not enough, years back, he was asked to be on the board at Wagner Farms; he graciously accepted. He is now the Executive Director of Wagner Hills Farm and the lead Pastor at Recovery Church. If God can accomplish this much through one man, I am positive He can use you. All you have to do is trust Him; He can accomplish infinitely more than we might ask, or imagine.

Individually, you need to come to an understanding that God loves you, just as much as you love your own child and more. He has our lives orchestrated, and He wants to use us all, the lost, broken and sick.

Through God's grace and mercy, He will help you, guide you, and take you from where you are, and put you back on your feet. He will bless you with an abundant life.

If you are not a believer, I pray that by now, after hearing the stories of these many men and their conversion, that it will touch you in some way. It is about God, and how He has blessed all these men and given them a new life.

Not only has God transformed Jason, and all the other men. It is about the lives transformed by these men. It is a countless number of people, touched and changed because all these men listened, and were obedient when God called. There is an answer, and that *someone* is waiting to change your life. He is calling you to a better life, so open the door, and let Him in. Let's be honest, what do you have to lose?

It was the end of April 2014; I completed my one-year commitment and finished Bible College. I also completed, almost to the day, one year in H.F.F.S. I know you are sitting there saying, what happened to the six-month mark? Everywhere I went, and everything I did in the past was six months long. Here I am completing two huge parts of my life, and committing longer than six months.

We all need to break patterns in our lives, to change and move forward. My faith strengthened immensely. My walk with the Lord was strong, and God was going to use me, in a place far away. Come on, you know my story by now. I can't stay still longer than six months or a year. I was 47 years old, and keeping count, this was my 39th move; once again I was on a plane; this time, it was off to serve, in Malawi, Africa.

CHAPTER 14

Malawi: Africa

THIS WILL BE my last trip in the book. Twenty-two hours after leaving Vancouver, with a stop in London and Johannesburg, I would arrive at my final destination, Blantyre, Malawi. My only glitch happened at the very beginning of the trip, at the airport in Vancouver. I had a dream, something that has always been on my heart was to go to Africa and set up a soccer field; with nets, balls, and jerseys. Marisa at Coquitlam Ford soccer club was the answer to my dream. I had three suitcases, and one was dedicated to soccer. It was filled with 12 deflated soccer balls, two full-size nets, 13 purple, 13 green, and 2 goalie jerseys. Along with a bunch of miscellaneous t-shirts and toys, all donated through their support.

At the check- in for the bags, we found out that the soccer suitcase was overweight by 18lbs; this was going to cost me $80.00. I spent every dime I had to get to Africa; I was broke. As I was unpacking, some-how trying to lose 18lbs of weight, a supervisor came by to check my passport. She asked what I was doing, and I explained that I was going to an orphanage in Malawi, and the suitcase was overweight. She stared down at me, and gave me a smile that could only have come from an angel, and said; pack everything back up, and go help the kids in Africa.

I arrived in Malawi, and as soon as I walked off the plane the heat hit me, it was sweltering. I made my way into the customs area and pulled a total Dwayne move. I had a dozen baseball hats with Canadian flags on them, donated by my friend Zorn. I decided to hand out a couple to the customs officials. All of a sudden, they are all rushing at me asking for hats. I turned the customs area into a fun filled party scene; they did not even look through any of my bags. They were giving me hugs and saying thank you, waving and smiling at me as I left customs.

A little bit of info for you about Malawi; it is a landlocked country in southeast Africa. It is bordered by Zambia to the northwest, Tanzania to the northeast, and Mozambique on the east. Malawi is among the world's least-developed countries, with around 85% of the population living in rural areas. It is a poor and underdeveloped country, and the effects of this can be seen everywhere.

Malawi has a low life expectancy and a high infant mortality rate. There is a high prevalence of HIV/AIDS, and it is having a devastating effect on the country. Its influence permeates every aspect of life. Approximately 250 new people are infected each day, and at least 70% of Malawi's hospital beds are occupied by HIV/AIDS patients. In 2006, Madonna was there to adopt a child. When she saw the devastation, she founded *Raising Malawi*. It is dedicated to helping with the extreme poverty, and the hardships endured by its one million orphans.

When I arrived, Will and Pam, the founders of Tiyamike Mulungu Center, were there to pick me up. TMC is a three-hour drive from Blantyre, which is the center of finance and commerce; it is the second largest city in Malawi. Will and Pam have a house in Blantyre because every month there is a trip from the orphanage in Bangula, up to Blantyre, to pick up food and supplies. We stayed a week in the house, running around town every day, going to various shops and businesses. During the week, after driving all over the city, I was beginning to get a real feel for Africa, the people, and the culture.

At the end of the week, with a loaded open back five-ton truck filled with supplies and a huge water tank, I began my trip deep into the heart of Africa. It was a three-hour drive, heading through a massive canyon, winding our way down into a low-lying valley. We went through various checkpoints along the way. At the bottom, there was a huge river. Once we crossed over the bridge, I started to see the gritty reality, the realism, and the evident truth of Africa. While cruising along in the back of the truck with my new Malawian friend Alfred; Africa became real!

The adversity these people face day in and day out. They live in such poverty, seeing the ram shackled huts in the villages was very emotional for me. While driving through the deteriorating towns that were in disrepair, my heart was broken, and a deep sadness overtook my soul. There were hundreds of people walking along the two-lane road. I saw children going to school, others carrying jugs of water to the local boreholes so they could provide for their family. My eyes were opened after the long drive. I had seen it on T.V., but you cannot even begin to comprehend what it is like.

This is what it looked like when we passed through various towns along the way to the orphanage in Bangula. No buildings, no grass, and no glass.

The small villages I saw off in the distance had tiny little huts scattered about. The huts were all pieced together with mortar and brick. The roofs were pieced together with a combination of bamboo and straw. The floor was dirt, and if the family was lucky, there might be a bamboo mat on the ground to sleep on, with a slim possibility of owning a few blankets. No fridge, no stove, no electricity, no running water; and we think we have it rough. They have a little metal rack to place a pot on; then they use wood or coal to heat whatever the family may cook up for their meal. All the signs along the highway and in the city are filled with holes, as though someone went at them with a shotgun. The reason is because if there are no holes the people would steal the signs to make pots and pans. The staple food in Malawi is nsima, which is thick maize (corn) porridge. The porridge is molded into patties and served with beans, or vegetables in a tomato and onion sauce.

This is a typical hut in any given village in Malawi.

After our long 3 hour journey, we arrived at the center. In Malawi they do not call the children orphans, nor did Will& Pam call the facility an orphanage, but a center. We drove up a long dirt runway that runs along the length of Tiyamike, then through the gates of the complex. As soon as we pulled in, kids were streaming out from every corner of the center, smiling, yelling, and running alongside the truck until we stopped. The kids ranged from 4-18, boys and girls so happy to see Papa Will and Aimi Pam. The kids are taught to call Will, Papa their father, and Pam, Ami, their mother; myself and other visitors would go by uncle or aunt. So I immediately became Uncle Dwayne to 130 kids.

Tiyamike Mulungu Center is located in the very tiny town of Bangula, in southern Malawi. Bangula lines the main road between Blantyre, the largest commercial center, and the town of Nsanje, right down in the southern tip of the country. As Bangula is situated in a low-lying valley, the climate can be quite challenging. In the hot season, the temperature soars up to 50+°C; and along with the stifling heat comes the mosquitoes.

Will & Pam definitely have their hands full, because according to the Department of Social Welfare, there are over 40,000 orphaned or vulnerable children in Nsanje. That is just one of the twenty-eight districts' in Malawi. The shocking thing is there are only 250,000 people living in the district of Nsanje where the orphanage is located.

Will and Pam started Tiyamike Mulungu Center, which means 'let us give thanks to God,' back in 2003. They had both felt a calling from the Lord to serve and to help the orphans in Africa. Leaving their family of seven children, and now fourteen grandchildren must have taken a huge amount of commitment and dedication. They came in their early 50's. Their heart and home is here in Malawi, and it was their obedience to the Lord that brought them there.

In June of 2003 they moved to Bangula, and in the beginning, they lived in Red Cross tents on the current TMC site. No electricity, hence no fans with temperatures of 50+°C at times. This was the beginning of what has now become Tiyamike Mulungu Center. It was not long after the tents were up that a report from the Public Health Officer arrived. It mentioned that they had sent their people out, and they found over 158 orphans in the area. Some of them were living with relatives, but some were found in very difficult circumstances.

The Tiyamike family is one that cannot help but continue to grow. This is due to the ongoing needs of orphaned babies in the area. Mothers die from AIDS, opportunistic diseases, lowered immune systems, HIV, malaria, birth complications, dysentery, cholera, and a host of other afflictions.

All because Will and Pam were obedient to Gods calling, because they listened, and followed the Will of God, kids are being saved, given love, a home, and food. TMC also has six large classrooms on their site. While I was there, they had purchased a house not too far from the center and turned it into a school. So along with everything they are doing, the kids are all provided with books, teachers, a place to learn and get an education. When we listen and follow Gods calling, many lives can be affected, as they are by two truly amazing people, Papa Will, and Ami Pam.

When I first arrived, I began to get to know all the children, to build trust and relationship. I worked with the older boys, helping them to read and understand the Bible. Then I had to check off another box on my bucket list, to build a soccer field. On one of our trips up to Blantyre, I purchased all the metal to build two frames for the soccer nets. There was a welder working at the center, so we got busy and welded together the frames. I attached the nets to them, dressed the kids with the soccer jerseys, pumped up the balls, and out to the runway in front of the center we went. The runway is only used a couple of times a year, so we etched out the field and put bamboo posts to line out the four corners. There I was, in Africa, two teams, two full-size nets, playing soccer with all the kids. God is good!

Another huge project I took on was painting the entire complex. The colors were brown, and I wanted to brighten it up for the kids. So with Will's approval, I went with yellow and blues. To describe the complex, I will start at the front gate where you enter. Along the left side is a workshop, and then four buildings which are classrooms. At the far end are the boy's bathrooms and showers. Making our way around the back corner are the rooms for the younger boys, and next to that is a medical room.

Running along the back is the nursery for the infants, the babies of Tiyamike, then Will and Pam's house. Attached to their house is a library, with a kitchen, and Wills office. The room I lived in was also part of the library. Moving up the right side is Mary's little house, she has been there for 10 plus years. A servant of the Lord for sure, Mary is from England. She sews cooks, teaches, and mentors the kids. The older girl's rooms run along up to the front, and finishing at the end of the complex are the rooms for the young girls. Located in the middle is a huge dining hall and kitchen for feeding all the staff and kids. The Sunday church service is held in the dining hall as well, so yes, there was a lot to paint. It took months to finish the massive project, but in the end, the children loved the vibrant colors of their home.

There were many trips or adventures out to the surrounding villages, to help injured people, or to pick up kids who were orphaned because the parents had died. I have so many stories I could share with you, but I will narrow it down to two specific events that shook me to the inner core. The first story is about a one-month-old baby named Chisomo, we called him baby Grace.

Chisomo was born May 7, 2014. His father died of HIV/Aids September 2013, and within a year of the father's death, the mother died of HIV/Aids on May 27, 2014; twenty days after the birth of Chisomo. The aunts and uncles were not equipped to care for the baby. Chisomo was brought to Tiyamike by the Grandmother on May 29, 2014. This type of event often happens, as Tiyamike is the only place people can bring orphaned children left without parents due to the various diseases spreading throughout Malawi.

It was June 5th, and Chisomo was not doing well. The loss of weight due to sickness and diarrhea was staggering. The baby was watched and cared for by the staff and Pam. She was involved in the caregiving and the feeding program set up for Chisomo. The baby continued to lose weight, and the sickness turned into sepsis and pneumonia.

The decision came at 9:30 pm on June 12th that we would make the three-hour trip up through the canyons to Blantyre, and take Chisomo to the hospital. The truck was loaded with supplies, accompanied by a caretaker and Pam. With me at the wheel, we headed out into the darkness of the African night. We would make the nighttime journey to save this small innocent little babies life.

We made the trip safely, without any problems along the way. Things can happen in the dark of night while traveling through Africa. It was 1:30 am when we arrived at the hospital. We brought the frail, tiny baby into the nursing station. I remember sitting next to the nurse as she tried over and over again to put an IV into Chisomo's arm. His arm was so tiny that there was no way to get an IV into it. They admitted the baby, and being completely exhausted Pam and I headed back to the house in Blantyre for some sleep. The caretaker stayed with the baby.

Saturday morning came quick, and at 8:00 am we were back at the hospital; things were only getting worse. Chisomo was, as they say, on his death bed, fading fast. Pam stayed for the day; she was not going to give up on this child. I came back later to take her for something to eat. But as we were out, her heart was pulling her back to the hospital.

I dropped Pam off, and she stayed the night with Chisomo. Sunday morning came, and when I arrived at the hospital; Pam was grieving, with tears welling up in her eyes. She told me that Baby Chisomo died at 3:00 am from sepsis and pneumonia. It was devastating news, we all tried so hard to save this baby's life, but God had plans to take little Chisomo home. Here is a picture of Chisomo at the hospital the evening before he died.

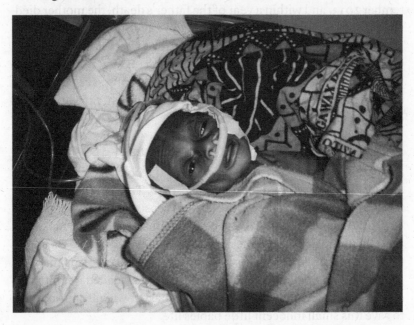

Baby Chisomo that evening in the Hospital

The story continues. For some reason we needed to take the baby with us, the hospital could not keep Chisomo after passing. We ended up driving around the city for three hours with Baby Chisomo wrapped in a shawl, lying on Pams lap. They made a coffin back at the center and sent it up to us on one of the minibusses that commute from Bangula to Blantyre. I mean, can you imagine driving around where you live, with a one-month-old baby, dead, wrapped in a shawl on your lap? Pam has to be one of the strongest and most compassionate women I have ever met. God created this woman for service. This was not Pams first time in this type of situation, but it was my first time.

Here comes another heartbreaker; after driving around, we went and met the minibus at a little dirt bus stop. I walk to the minibus and retrieve the suitcase sent up from Tiyamike. I walk over to our 4x4 Toyota where Pam was holding baby Chisomo, and open the suitcase.

There before my eyes was a tiny wooden coffin that was built hours before at the center. This rocked my world. I pulled out the tiny little coffin and opened it, and then Pam, with tears streaming down her face set Chisomo, wrapped in a shawl, into the coffin. We put the lid on, and now it was time for a journey deep into the heart of Africa, to the village of Chisomo's family.

It is a three-hour drive back to the center on the two-lane paved road that runs from Blantyre to Bangula, and at the half way mark, we made a right turn. It was onto a small dirt path that led us as deep as you could go into the African plains. It was getting late into the afternoon as we made the 14 km drive along the path, going through village after village. This is by no means a road; it is bumpy, going through dried up river beds, winding past huge Boa trees. I mean we were deep; we were in the middle of nowhere when we arrived at the village.

I got out of the truck and made my way to the back, and pulled out the suitcase with the coffin in it. We were surrounded by 30-40 locals and elders, all crying, and wailing over the death of baby Chisomo. I turn it over to Pam; she was much more familiar with the culture and the people. So I stood back as Pam pulled the coffin out of the suitcase and handed it to the Grandmother and immediate family.

Now comes the burial. It is getting dark, every day at 5:00 pm, it is dark in Malawi. We take a 45-minute walk through trails and paths, leading to their local cemetery. There was no light; we were strolling along in the pitch black dark of Africa; I mean if you held your hand in front of your face, you could not see it. We were using our cell phones for whatever small glow of light we could get from it; we then made it to the cemetery. There are no headstones, just mounds of dirt showing past burials. The area was very eerie, with a sense of calm. We walked up to a large circle of villagers surrounding a hole in the ground dug out about three feet deep, with a pile of dirt next to it. They place the tiny coffin holding baby Chisomo into the ground and shovel the dirt over it, covering the coffin. In the end, there was a mound of dirt, prayer, crying and people falling to their knees.

We made the long walk back to the village in the heat and darkness of the night. When we arrived, Pam and I went into the elder's hut. It was made from brick and straw, with a dirt floor. We sat in a circle on the ground with them. Pam prayed, and I prayed. I was very emotional, and a bit shook up. We were in the middle of Africa, in a hut, praying for Baby Chisomo with his Grandparents and family. We walked back to the truck and made the 1½ hour drive through the pitch black night on the dirt paths, finally making it to the paved road. Then the 1½ hour drive back to Tiyamike, arriving late into the morning. Here are a few pictures to show you as best I can what it was like.

Family at Chisomo's grave   *Grandmother's hut we prayed in*

The second story I would like to share with you I call *The Bubba Saga*. I was at the market one day in Blantyre; the town Tiyamike is located in. It was a Saturday afternoon; people were selling bags of rice and beans. Chickens were being decapitated; the ground was cover with blood. Goats were being butchered, hanging from hooks attached to bamboo frames; it was by no means a Safeway or Costco. As I was walking, I saw Bubba, a tiny 10-year-old boy. He had no shoes and was wearing filthy torn clothes, trying to scrounge up money for food. As I took a closer look, I saw he was covered in scabies, and puss was flowing out from his wounds on his arms and legs.

I had Alfred with me, my Malawian friend who translated for me. I immediately knew what to do; he needed medical attention. We decided to take him to the local medical clinic; his sister was with him, so the four of us made the journey. We arrived, and a local doctor was working. Bubba stripped down, and the doctor covered him with calamine lotion to begin the healing process; he also prescribed some antibiotics.

My mind began to think that the parasites and the infections Bubba picked up from bathing in the local river would also mean their hut must be infested as well. We walked to the village where Bubba lived, and I went into their hut. I will attach a picture because it is so hard to put into words. The grandma was living in this tiny little hut with Bubba and his sister. It was filthy, pots and pans strewn about, worn blankets and old clothes piled up.

I knew we needed to clean the place out, to throw all the clothing and worn blankets away, to start fresh. I walked back to the market and bought two bamboo mats for the floor, and three blankets for them. They also needed food, so I bought a huge bag of rice, a bag of beans, and some vegetables. We walked back to the hut, and with rubber gloves in hand, we cleaned everything out. After the hut was cleared, we laid down the mats and blankets, put the bags of food in the corner. Thinking the mission was accomplished, something else happened.

The Grandmother was complaining about having a lot of pain in her leg. I took a closer look at it, and after trying to move her, she screamed out from the top of her lungs. We knew the leg was broken. I later found out that in a fight over some money, Bubba took a wooden stool and smashed it onto her shin, breaking her leg. Part two of the mission; I walked back to Tiyamike and one of the boys named John, whom I had grown very close to, had an idea. He said we should get two long pieces of bamboo and nail three planks of wood to them, to make a stretcher. He is a genius, we quickly began constructing our stretcher, and off we went for the long hike to Bubbas hut to rescue the grandmother.

We arrived at the hut, and I had to figure out a way to get her from inside the hut, and out onto the homemade stretcher. I thought we should lay out one of the blankets, and then the four of us take her by the arms and legs and raise her up onto the blanket. She was screaming out in pain as we lifted her. Once we had her on the blanket, each of us took a corner and walked her out of the hut and onto the stretcher. Once she was stable, the four of us grabbed hold and walked through the brush to a medical center. She was eventually transported to the hospital in Nsanje, where a cast was applied to her broken leg.

I continued to stay in contact with the family; we had the local church get involved in the care of the grandmother. She could not get up to go the bathroom, so pampers were supplied, and a cleaning station was erected next to the hut made of bamboo. I would stop by every so often with food and money for the family. People always say, look at the multitude of suffering in Africa, what good can anyone do? I can start with this one family and begin to branch out in the village, helping others. You can't save them all, but it is about the ones you are saving that count.

I have attached a few photos, to let you see the reality of Bubba's saga, words can only go so far, but a picture has a thousand words.

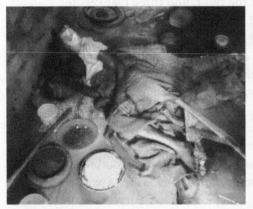

First impressions of the hut

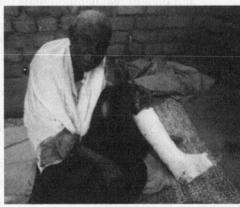

Grandma after triage

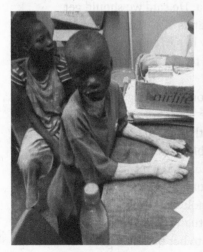

Bubba at the clinic

Off to the medical clinic

I have so many adventures from Africa that I could share with you, but as with the L.A. stories, it would take another book. Since I am on the topic of books, something happened near the end of my stay. I was working at Tiyamike, and it was late one afternoon when I heard an audible voice; the message clearly said, *When you get back to Canada, you will write the book.* I began thinking about Teen Challenge and all the people asking me when the book was coming out. I knew Gods plan for me; He wanted me to share my journey through life, my struggles in addiction, and my transformation process coming to Him. I would be obedient to His calling.

Africa was an amazing life changing experience. I grew in the Lord, and I really knew what it was like to be of service and to help others in need. I truly believe that is our purpose in life. Our purpose is to give back what we have, be it your time or money, it is as simple as that. It could be traveling and spreading the Word to bring others to Christ, so they too can know what love is, and then freely give it back to society. It could be on your own city block, at a shelter, a feeding program, or working with abused and single mothers. You could get on a plane and fly to a third world country, and really see the condition of the world we live in. The rest of the world is not North America, we are a blessed culture, and we have all we need here at home. So why not take all you have been blessed with, and go help? Save lives, and shower people with nothing but love.

I know I have not previously mentioned it, but I am sure it won't come as a shock to you; my stay in Africa was, yes, six months. I spent six months serving, doing missionary work, and helping people who were so desperately in need. I have been all over the world, but Africa was like no other place I have ever experienced.

They are the nicest people you will ever meet, and most believe in God. When Sunday church services start, the places are packed. Everyone puts on the best of whatever clothes they own, to show respect, and to worship the Lord. Here at home, we have an hour service, and God forbid it goes over an hour. They worship and have service for hours, not just one hour like back home.

It was at the end of November 2014 that I boarded the plane in Blantyre, I was leaving the Dark Continent. It would take two days of travel to arrive back home, back in Vancouver Canada. This would be my last move, number 40. I really needed to stay somewhere and plant some roots.

At the time, I did not know, and I was not able to comprehend, what was about to happen. I had seen things in Africa that were very disturbing, things that were not right, things that touched and affected me deeply. I was incapable of handling my emotions; I was not in my right mind, and I was questioning God about Africa, I needed help, but I would not reach out.

When I arrived back, I stayed with a good friend named Brian. He is a longshoreman and works at the docks in downtown Vancouver. His house was only about six blocks from the houses of The Hope for Freedom Society. I knew hundreds of people, all the staff at H.F.F.S, and I also had many friends who pastored at churches around town. I would have none of it; I would not pick up the phone. I was socially disconnected from the world.

I came back from Africa and hit an emotional wall. I was mentally, physically and spiritually broken. I sat around Brian's house for two weeks. I was a hollow shell of a man. I did not want to talk to anyone, and I did not want to have anything to do with anyone. I felt that I needed to adjust back to our culture; to paved roads, sidewalks, stores full to the brim with food; 10-20 choices of cereal.

This was not normal after six months in Africa, seeing homes and buildings with glass windows, everything structured perfectly. None of this was in Africa. I was struggling and mentally, I could not cope. I could not snap out of the pressure to get back to North American normalcy. What is normal here is by no means normal in Africa. In my heart and soul, I was deeply affected by some of my traumatic experiences there, and it was tearing me apart inside. I fell out of sync with God and was transformed by grief.

I am an addict, and I had been clean for a year and a half, but I was hurt, and I was alone with my thoughts. Depression and anxiety riddled through my body. I was in the middle of a breakdown, and I would not, or could not reach out for help. Satan had me in that house, stuck with my memories of the travesties I had witnessed in Africa. I needed out, I needed to get out of my head, out of my feelings; I did not want to hurt anymore. I was broken inside, and after two weeks, my addict told me that it knew a way out.

In my desperation, in my weakness, I buckled under the tremendous weight of the world; I was not equipped for this. The next thing I knew, I was on the 160 bus heading to the downtown Eastside of Vancouver, the pits of hell. I would pay a visit to my old stomping grounds. I needed out, I needed help, and my addict told me the answer lay in the D.T.E.S. I would go and score some pills, some opiates; it was my addict solution. The weight of the backpack I was carrying around full of fear, guilt and pain would be lifted. The problem is that I used the wrong substance to lift the burdens of life. Once again, I chose the pill, and not that *someone*. I should have sought Christ, not the pill.

I mentioned earlier about us falling and that God will pick us up, dust us off, and put us back on our feet. After I attended Teen Challenge North and went to Saskatoon, my fall lasted a year. My falls while in Mexico and Indonesia were only for two months. My fall when I arrived back from Africa only lasted three weeks. In my life, my falls have shortened, and my walks continue to get longer.

I needed to stay close to God, to seek Him, and trust Him with all my heart. I had some issues with God after Africa; I was lost while locked up in my Russian prison cell. Did I reach out to God? Did I pray, and ask Him for help? Was I relying on that *someone*, or myself? The answer is that I tried to do it on my own. I did not ask for help; I did not seek God. When an addict tries to do it own their own; they *Fall*.

I spent that Christmas isolated in a room, withdrawn and hopeless. No phone calls, no friends, and no family. Just me; broken and lost in my addiction. It was the worst Christmas of my life. I came back from serving in Africa for six months, and for what, to end up back on opiates, destroying my life? After three weeks of using, God said enough, this is not part of the plan. My head cleared just after Christmas. I needed to move forward; I needed to stop the drugs and get back on track. I did not want just to survive; I wanted to live. I could not change or heal anything unless I acknowledged it.

I could not take it anymore. I would not let my addict win, and I would not allow Satan's stronghold control me anymore. By the grace of God, I would once again break the chains of addiction. I was free, and it was time to do Gods will, not Dwayne's. The first thing I needed was to clean up, and detox of the drugs I had been pumping into my system.

I reached out to my old friend Craig; he used to be my roommate while I was going to Bible College. He is now staff at H.F.F.S, but I could not pick up the phone while dealing with my fallen and crumbled life. I was carrying around too much shame and guilt, so I began reaching out with a few texts.

I also spoke with another staff member at H.F.F.S, a very good friend named Mark; he has also been transformed by Christ. Mark was a very violent man, involved with crime and drugs. He would break into houses, accompanied by his brother. He would beat people, and then rob them blind, leaving with a smile on his face. This was his old life; a new life has begun. Mark has turned his life over to the Lord, and he is now four years clean.

I ended up having a few conversations with Craig and Mark while in my addiction. They both encouraged me to come back for a refresher, to get back on my feet, and that there was a bed waiting for me. What touched me the most was that they both told me they loved me and cared for me; these were the words a broken and hopeless man needed to hear. I called Creekside detox out in Surrey and spoke with Russ, my Christian friend who works there. It was a three-week wait to get in, but once again God intervened, and Russ was able to get me in the next day. I spent a week at Creekside, beginning my opiate detox again. After seven days it was back to H.F.F.S.

The detox was not as bad as it was during my first round at H.F.F.S, but the sleepless nights went on for about a month. I bounced back and was on my feet again. I spent two months doing a few core programs. After completing everything, I made the move to a house on Oxford St. in Port Coquitlam. My mind had cleared, and I did another set of steps, the 12 steps of N.A. After completing everything, the time had come to do Gods work; it was time to begin my journey. It was time to start writing the book. I told myself, from the beginning, before I typed the first word; *This was and is a journey ordained by God for God.*

I have said over and over again, this book is real, and it is honest. When I began to write, I was only two months clean. I have not touched alcohol for six years, but I had only been off the opiates for two months prior to organizing the layout, chapters, and all the material for the book. So, to be honest, I was not clean for years before taking on this challenge. God wanted me tender, and raw; He wanted me at a point where my emotions would flow. I was definitely ripe and real while taking on this enormous project God had set before me.

My point being is that as addicts we can accomplish infinitely more than we can do, or imagine. This is a promise from the Lord. Do not put restraints on yourselves, or time limits. I went to Bible College with four months clean, and I began to write a book at two months clean. If I can do it, I truly believe, anyone can do anything that is set before them.

Walking with the Lord is oh so very important; allow me to give you an example. I had completed the year at Teen Challenge in Sault Ste Marie, and six months after; I was a year and a half clean. I walked away from God, and *I fell* within two weeks. I had another year and a half clean while in H.F.F.S. and Africa. I walked away from God, and within two weeks *I fell*. If it were not for the three-week relapse after coming back from Africa; I would now have two and a half years clean. Do you see a pattern here? When I devoted my time, and life to the Lord, when I seek Him and ask for guidance and help, my life is good, and I stayed clean. When I take Dwayne's will back, when I walk away from God; *I fall*. I am coming up on a year clean. I guess the moral of the story is to walk humbly with the Lord, love mercy and act Just. If I continue to do that, in my heart, I know I will stay clean.

Writing this book has been an emotional rollercoaster, it was kind of like doing a 270-page step four. I had days and weeks where I hated everyone. I did not want anything to do with a single soul, anger overtook me. I had times when I cried and was feeling the pain and grief as I wrote about my mother and daughter Alyssa. This has been so therapeutic and healing for me. It has guided me closer to the Lord and strengthened my relationship with Him.

The first issue is that for you the reader, to have come to some conclusion, some understanding about addiction. What it does, what it wants, and how it is cunning, baffling and powerful. How purely evil addiction is. In my story, it gives a crystal clear cut reminder about addiction, and how it will take your life and crumble everything to the ground. I believe it is Satan's number one tool in society today, to shatter your inner core. When you have lost all hope, in the end, addiction wants you dead. I hope that through the deep dark valleys and the mountain top highs in the book, you have found an answer, a solution, that *someone*.

The second and more important issue is that you have gained some wisdom and knowledge about God. How He can transform anyone's life. I have shared about real people, living lives that were out of control, and being saved. They made a decision, and they came to the conclusion that they had enough, and it was time for a change in their lives. God will work in you as he has in me, and all the people whom I have shared stories about. We have all found the answer, and the shalom shaped hole in our hearts has been filled by that *someone*. We can all be transformed by Christ. You can never be too bad, or have done enough evil in your life where Christ will not forgive you for all you have done. He is waiting at the door for you, all you have to do is let Him in.

I don't want to preach to you here at the end, but my heart tells me the point of this book is to let you know about salvation, and that you can be saved. You can live a better life, and spend eternity at home with God. It is a book about Hope. Through my journey, I lost hope many times, but through the amazing grace of God, he showed me love, and He gave me hope.

I am now walking in sync with God, and if you have made it this far, and the word *God* has not made you throw the book in the garbage, I am honored. To resist is to persist; there is *someone* touching you. I know you want to fill that Shalom shaped hole in your Heart.

After all you have read, after all the transformation stories, and after reading my transformation story, are you still thinking to yourself; there is no God? Do you still doubt this God thing? If you think He is not real, and the Bible is just a bunch of stories, then I need to ask you one question?

In your finite earthly wisdom, How do you know?

I feel that this is just the beginning of another journey for me. Amen.

Acknowledgements

Page Two Strategies—Jessie, thank you for the amazing work you and your team accomplished. I am also grateful for you helping me and guiding me through the maze of behind the scene projects we needed to finish in order to get the book out into the world.

Connie Faulkner—The Graphic designer. Connie the cover layout is amazing. Thank you for freely giving your time to help forward The Kingdom of God.

Doug & Rebecca Friesen—Thanks for getting me through the hard times while I was writing the Fall. The encouragement for me to keep pushing forward through this journey.

Douglas Ladron—A.K.A. The Wick—Thank you for painting the amazing book cover Douglas. Thanks for putting up with my daily rant—*"Wick, where is my book cover?"*

Greg Higgins—Thanks little brother for the structural editing, and being a part of the book.

Michael Rosset—Thank you for the computer help and answering all my questions.

Financial help—Lindsey Gauthier, Fraser Valley Roofing, Todd Hiebert, Jerry & Pat, Dr. Ron. Elloway, Larry Stevenson, Trish Otter, Bart Phillips, Terry, Diane Arbinski, Jeff Gelineau, Ron Sturm, Clivee Burgees,

Kevin McArthur—Thanks for pushing me to keep going and to finish the race. P.S: Thanks for showing up on short notice to take the Picture for the back cover.

Sue Murtonen—Thanks Sue for the guidance while writing about Teen Challenge. Also for reading and helping with the TCN Edit.

Lorenso Watson—Thanks for designing the web-page, could not have done it without you.